DOGMATIC THEOLOGY

II

THE DIVINE TRINITY

A DOGMATIC TREATISE

BY

THE RT. REV. MSGR. JOSEPH POHLE, PH.D., D.D.

ADAPTED AND EDITED

BY

ARTHUR PREUSS

SIXTH REVISED EDITION

WIPF & STOCK · Eugene, Oregon

Wipf and Stock Publishers
199 W 8th Ave, Suite 3
Eugene, OR 97401

The Divine Trinity
A Dogmatic Treatise
By Pohle, Joseph and Preuss, Arthur
ISBN 13: 978-1-60899-775-6
Publication date 7/20/2010
Previously published by B. Herder Book Co., 1911

TABLE OF CONTENTS

TABLE OF CONTENTS

THE DIVINE TRINITY

INTRODUCTORY REMARKS

1. It belongs to the first treatise of Dogmatic Theology (*De Deo Uno*) to show that God is one and personal. The pantheistic fiction of an impersonal God is sufficiently exploded by the Almighty's own solemn declaration (Gen. III, 14): "I am Who am."[1]

Whether the infinite personality of God must be conceived as simple or multiplex, is a matter which human reason cannot determine unaided. On the strength of the inductive axiom, "*Quot sunt naturae, tot sunt personae,*" we should rather be tempted to attribute but one personality to the one Divine Nature. Positive Revelation tells us, however, that there are in God three really distinct persons: Father, Son, and Holy Ghost. This fundamental dogma, which essentially differentiates the Christian conception of God from that of the Pagans, the Jews, and the Mohammedans, is designated in the technical Latin of the Church as "*Trinitas,*" a term first used, so far as we know, by Theophilus of Antioch[2] and Tertullian,[3] and which later became cur-

1 Cfr. Pohle-Preuss: *God: His Knowability, Essence, and Attributes.*

2 *Ad Autolyc.*, II, 15: "Τριάδος τοῦ θεοῦ καὶ λόγου καὶ τῆς σοφίας αὐτοῦ." (On the three books *Ad Autolycum,* see Bardenhewer-Shahan, *Patrology,* pp. 66 sq., Freiburg and St. Louis 1908. On the word τριάς, cfr. Newman, *Athanasius,* II, 473 sq., 9th ed., London 1903.)

3 *De Pudicitia,* c. 21: "*Trinitas*

rent in ecclesiastical usage and was embodied in the Creeds.[4] In the private symbolum of St. Gregory Thaumaturgus mention is made of a "perfect Triad" (τριὰς τελεία). Didymus the Blind, Cyril of Alexandria, Hilary, Ambrose, and Augustine have written separate treatises "On the Trinity."

2. Unity, simplicity, and unicity are as essential to the mystery of the Blessed Trinity as the concept of triunity itself. Hence it is not surprising that all these momenta were equally emphasized by the early Fathers.

Thus we read in the Athanasian Creed:[5] "*Ita ut per omnia . . . et unitas in Trinitate, et Trinitas in unitate veneranda sit* — So that in all things . . . the Unity in Trinity, and the Trinity in Unity is to be worshipped." The first canon of the Lateran Council held under Pope Martin the First[6] reads thus: "*Si quis secundum sanctos Patres non confitetur proprie et veraciter Patrem, et Filium, et Spiritum Sanctum, Trinitatem in unitate et unitatem in Trinitate . . . condemnatus sit* — If any one does not with the Holy Fathers profess properly and truly the Father, and the Son, and the Holy Ghost, Trinity in Unity and Unity in Trinity, let him be anathema."[7] If we pay special regard to the note of threeness, the Trinity presents itself mainly as a threefold personality in one Divine Nature. If, on the other hand, we accentuate the note of unity, the Trinity presents itself as Triunity (*triuni-*

unius divinitatis, Pater et Filius et Spiritus Sanctus."

4 Denzinger-Bannwart, *Enchiridion Symbolorum*, ed. 10, nn. 213, 232, Friburgi Brisgoviae 1908.

5 Quoted by Denzinger-Bannwart, *l. c.*, n. 39.

6 A. D. 649.

7 Quoted by Denzinger-Bannwart, n. 254.

tas),[8] a term which expresses the numeric unity of the Godhead common to all three Divine Hypostases. Both points of view are not only legitimate in themselves, but demanded by the nature of the mystery and the heretical distortions to which it has been subjected. As against those Antitrinitarians who (like the Monarchians, the Sabellians, and the Subordinationists) exaggerate the notion of unity so as to deny a true and immanent Trinity in the Godhead, Dogmatic Theology has to prove the existence of three really distinct Persons. In refuting the opposite heresy of Tritheism, which exaggerates the notion of threeness and postulates three separate divine natures, substances, or essences, it is necessary to show that the Divine Trinity is a Triunity.

3. Antitrinitarianism in both of its antithetical forms is by no means a thing of the past, but under various guises still has numerous adherents.

Whilst the few remaining partisans of Günther's theological system continue to teach a sort of veiled Tritheism, present-day Socinians, Unitarians, and Rationalists move entirely within the circle of the heretical notions of Sabellius. Kantian Rationalism debases the mystery of the Most Holy Trinity by treating it as a mere symbol indicative of the power, wisdom, and love of God. The school of Hegel pantheistically explains the Father as "*das Ansichsein des Absoluten,*" the Son as "*das Anderssein des Absoluten in der Welt,*" and the Holy Ghost as "*die Rückkehr des Absoluten zu sich selber im menschlichen Selbstbewusstsein*"— for the meaning of which obscure phrases we must refer the

8 Cfr. Isidor. Hispal., *Etymol.*, VII, 4.

reader to Dr. J. Hessen, *Hegel's Trinitätslehre* (Freiburg 1922). Schleiermacher does not deny the Trinity, but regards it as such an unessential "mode of existence of the Divine Being" that he has acted wisely in relegating it to the appendix of his *Glaubenslehre*. The position of liberal Protestant theology at the present day is well stated by Adolph Harnack when he says:[9] "Already in the second century Christ's [natural] birth into this world assumed the rank of a supernatural, and later on that of an eternal generation, and the fact of being begotten, or passive generation itself, became the characteristic note of the second Person [in the Blessed Trinity]. Similarly, in the fourth century the promised [temporal] 'mission' of the Holy Ghost assumed the character of an 'eternal mission' and became the discriminating badge of the third Person within the Holy Triad. Nowhere have we a more characteristic example of what the imagination is capable of doing when it undertakes to evolve ideas." With the exception of the relatively few champions of Lutheran orthodoxy, whose number is, moreover, constantly dwindling, modern Protestantism no longer holds the Christian idea of the Blessed Trinity. Liberal theology is everywhere triumphing over orthodoxy. The demand, which is constantly growing louder and more widespread, even in this country, that no specific creed be imposed upon the members of any denomination, ultimately strikes at the dogma of the Holy Trinity and that of the Divinity of Christ. Among German divines Krüger confesses this quite openly.[10] Catholic theology, which alone upholds the banner of true Christian belief, in asserting and defending the dogma of the Trinity finds it necessary above

9 *Dogmengeschichte*, 3rd ed., Vol. II, p. 281, Freiburg 1894.

10 In his book, *Dreifaltigkeit und Gottmenschheit*, Leipzig 1905.

all to demonstrate by the modern scientific method that this dogma is truly and clearly revealed by God, that it is solidly founded in Christian Tradition, and that it does not, as unbelievers allege, involve a contradiction.

4. Since theistic philosophy is unable to establish this dogma on the basis of unaided human reason, the Catholic theologian is compelled to adhere closely to the teaching of the Church. He must first *believe;* then he may *inquire.*

The most perfect and complete Trinitarian formula that has come down to us from Patristic times is that composed by the Eleventh Council of Toledo, A. D. 675.[11] We prefer to base our exposition on the briefer and more perspicuous formula contained in the Athanasian Creed, which has the additional advantage of being vested with the primary authority due to an ancient Christian symbol. The dogma of the Most Holy Trinity is there set forth in the following terms:[12] "*Fides catholica haec est, ut unum Deum in Trinitate, et Trinitatem in unitate veneremur; neque confundentes personas, neque substantiam separantes; alia est enim persona Patris, alia Filii, alia (et) Spiritus Sancti; sed Patris et Filii et Spiritus Sancti una est divinitas, aequalis gloria, coaeterna maiestas. . . . Pater a nullo est factus nec creatus nec genitus. Filius a Patre solo est, non*

11 Denzinger-Bannwart, *Enchiridion*, nn. 275 sqq. This symbol first treats of the Three Divine Persons in succession; then, in three further sections, it develops and sets forth the general doctrine, *viz.:* (1) the true unity of substance; (2) the real Trinity of the Persons; (3) the inseparable union of the Three Divine Persons, demanded by their very distinction. In later times the dogma received a more distinct formulation only in two points, both directed against most subtle forms of separation and division in God. Cfr. Wilhelm-Scannell, *A Manual of Catholic Theology Based on Scheeben's "Dogmatik,"* Vol. I, p. 262, London 1899.

12 Denzinger-Bannwart, n. 40.

factus nec creatus, sed genitus. Spiritus Sanctus a Patre et Filio, non factus nec creatus nec genitus, sed procedens—The Catholic faith is this, that we worship one God in Trinity and Trinity in Unity, neither confounding the Persons, nor dividing the Substance. For there is one Person of the Father, another of the Son, and another of the Holy Ghost. But the Godhead of the Father, of the Son, and of the Holy Ghost is all one, the glory equal, the majesty co-eternal. . . . The Father is made of none, neither created, nor begotten. The Son is of the Father alone; not made, nor created, but begotten. The Holy Ghost is of the Father and of the Son: neither made, nor created, nor begotten, but proceeding." [13]

The chief points of our dogma may therefore be summarized thus: In essence, substance, and nature there is but one God. However, the Divine Nature does not subsist in one single Person or Hypostasis, but in three distinct Persons, *i. e.*, Father, Son, and Holy Ghost. The Three do not coalesce after the manner of mere logical momenta, but are really distinct from one another, so much so that the one is not the other. They are not distinct in virtue of their nature, which is numerically the same in all three, but solely in virtue of the relative opposition by which the Son is begotten by the Father, while the Holy Ghost proceeds alike from the Father and the Son. The mystery peculiar to this sublime dogma arises from the mutual relations of the two principal concepts—"Nature" and "Person." Within the domain of human experience every

13 The Athanasian Creed was probably the work of St. Fulgentius (468–533); see J. Stiglmayer, S. J., in the Innsbruck *Zeitschrift für kath. Theologie*, 1925, 3 Heft; cfr. Vol. II of the *Catholic Encyclopedia*, *s. v.*—Cfr. Pohle-Preuss, *God: His Knowability, Essence, and Attributes*, p. 318, note 6; F. J. Hall, *The Trinity*, pp. 18 sqq., New York 1910.

complete nature is at the same time a separate hypostasis; in other words, every rational nature is *eo ipso* a distinct person. Hence the axiom, "*Tot sunt hypostases, quot sunt naturae.*" But this axiom has no metaphysical value, and cannot be applied to God, since Revelation expressly teaches that "Nature" and "Person" do not coincide either in reality or in conception. As we acknowledge three Persons in the one Divine Nature, so conversely we believe that there are in Christ two complete natures, the one divine, the other human, both subsisting in one and the same person, *i. e.*, the Divine Person of the Logos-Son. This revealed truth compels Catholic philosophy to draw a sharp distinction between "Nature" and "Person," as we shall show more fully further down.

Since the essence of the mystery consists in this that "we worship one God in Trinity, and Trinity in Unity," we may consider the Blessed Trinity first as Trinity in Unity (*Trinitas in Unitate*), or threefold personality; and, secondly, as Unity in Trinity (*Unitas in Trinitate*) or Triunity. We shall accordingly divide the subject-matter of this treatise into two parts.

GENERAL READINGS: — Above all St. Aug., *De Trinit.* ll. XV (translated into English by A. W. Haddan in Dods's *Works of Aurelius Augustine,* Vol. VII, Edinburgh 1873); and, by way of commentary, Th. Gangauf, *Des hl. Augustinus spekulative Lehre von Gott dem Dreieinigen,* 2nd ed., Ratisbon 1883.— The *Monologium S. Anselmi* and Petr. Lomb., *Sent.,* 1, dist. 1 sqq.— Rich. a S. Victore, *De Trinitate* ll. VI, takes a rather independent attitude.— St. Bonaventure, *Comment. in Libros Sent.,* I; St. Thomas, *S. Theol.,* 1a, qu. 27–43, *Contr. Gent.,* IV, 1–26, together with the commentaries.—*Ruiz, *De Trinit.*, Lugd. 1625... Greg. de Valentia, *De Trinit.* ll. V.—Ysambert, *De Mysterio Trinitatis.*—Wilhelm-Scannell, *A Manual of Catholic Theology Based on Scheeben's "Dogmatik,"* Vol. I, pp. 257–354, 2nd ed., London 1899.—S. J. Hunter, S. J., *Outlines of Dogmatic Theology,* Vol. II, pp. 145–215, 2nd ed.—F. J. Hall (Anglican), *The Trinity,* New York 1910.

The teaching of the Fathers can be studied in the copious quotations extracted from their works by Petavius, *Dogm.*, t. II, and Thomassin, *Dogm.*, t. III.

In addition to the various manuals of special dogmatic theology, consult particularly *Kuhn, *Christliche Lehre von der göttlichen Dreieinigkeit,* Tüb. 1857; Franzelin, *De Deo Trino,* ed. 3, Romae 1883; Régnon, *Études sur la Ste Trinité,* 4 vols., Paris 1872–1898; L. Janssens, *De Deo Trino,* Friburgi 1900; J. Van der Meersch, *Tract. de De Uno et Trino,* ed. altera, Bruges 1928; Stentrup, *De SS. Trinitatis Mysterio,* Oeniponte 1898; Lépicier, *De SS. Trinitate,* Parisiis 1902; Souben, *Théologie Dogmatique,* II: "Les Personnes Divines," Paris 1903; Newman, *Select Treatises of St. Athanasius,* Vol. II, pp. 315 sqq. For the history of the dogma, see Newman, "Causes of the Rise and Successes of Arianism" (*Tracts Theological and Ecclesiastical,* new ed., London 1895, pp. 139–299); Adrian Fortescue, *The Orthodox Eastern Church,* pp. 110, 135 sqq., London 1907; Idem, *The Greek Fathers, passim,* London 1908.—Bardenhewer-Shahan, *Patrology,* pp. 65, 66, 185, 210, 259, 281, 291, 308.—*J. Lebreton, S. J., *Les Origines du Dogme de la Trinité,* Paris 1910 (6th ed., 3 vols., 1928); J. Tixeront, *History of Dogmas* (English tr.), 3 vols., St. Louis 1910 sqq.; Idem, *Apologetical Studies,* St. Louis 1917, pp. 9–38; J. de Concilio, *Catholicity and Pantheism,* New York 1874; L. G. Mylne, *A Study of the Self-Revelation of God,* London 1916.

* The asterisk before an author's name indicates that his exposition of the subject is especially clear and thorough. As St. Thomas is invariably the best guide, the omission of the asterisk before his name never means that we consider his work in any way inferior to that of others. There are vast stretches of dogmatic theology which he scarcely touched.

PART I

THE HOLY TRINITY IN UNITY, OR THE THREEFOLD PERSONALITY OF GOD[1]

Both the fact *that* (ὅτι ἔστιν), and the intrinsic reason *why* (διότι ἔστιν) there are Three Persons in God, is positively revealed to us in the doctrine of the inner-divine processions (Filiation and Spiration). They form part of the immediate deposit of the faith, and constitute the dogma of the Divine Trinity. We have first to prove the fact of the threefold personality of God from Sacred Scripture (Chapter I) and Tradition (Chapter II); then (Chapter III) we shall enter into a dogmatic consideration of the cause of this fact, *viz.:* the mysterious vital processes immanent in the Godhead which are called "Filiation" and "Spiration." In a concluding Chapter (IV) we shall discuss the speculative theological development of the dogma.

1 Cfr. Newman, *Select Treatises of St. Athanasius*, Vol. II (Being an Appendix of Illustrations), "The Holy Trinity in Unity," pp. 315–325, 9th ed., London 1903.

CHAPTER I

GOD'S THREEFOLD PERSONALITY PROVED FROM SACRED SCRIPTURE

There are traces of the dogma in the Old Testament, but they are rather indefinite and obscure unless viewed in the light of the New Testament. It is upon the latter, therefore, that the Scriptural argument is almost exclusively based. After briefly rehearsing the Old Testament intimations (§1), we will marshal the Trinitarian texts contained in the New Testament in a double series, first citing those which treat of all three Divine Persons together (§2), and secondly those which refer to only one of the three Divine Persons without mentioning the other two (§3). The dogma of the Holy Trinity is immutably grounded in the Unity of the Divine Essence. Accordingly, throughout the triple argument upon which we are about to enter for the purpose of tracing out the hypostatic differences of the Three Divine Persons, it will be important not to lose sight of the monotheistic foundation on which alone this dogma can be built up.

SECTION 1

THE THREEFOLD PERSONALITY OF GOD FORESHADOWED IN THE OLD TESTAMENT

1. PRIMITIVE INTIMATIONS OF THE DOGMA.— Some theologians take the plural form of several of the names attributed to Jehovah [2] in the Old Testament as an obscure intimation of the dogma of the Trinity.

We are not inclined to press this argument. Neither do we attach much importance to the theory of Clement of Alexandria, Origen, and Augustine, who point to the expression בְּרֵאשִׁית in Gen. I, 1 as a proof for the Logos, explaining "*in principio*" to mean "*in Verbo, i. e., Filio.*" Upon close scrutiny this more than doubtful interpretation turns out to be of later origin and exegetically unsupported.[3] In Gen. I, 26 sq., however, we come upon what appears to be a definite allusion to the mystery of the Divine Trinity: "*Faciamus hominem ad imaginem et similitudinem nostram. . . . Et creavit Deus hominem ad imaginem suam*—Let us make man to our image and likeness. . . . And God created man to his own image." The hortatory subjunctive plural which heads verse 26, and is followed by an indicative verb in the singular in verse 27, cannot be

2 Cfr. Pohle-Preuss, *God: His Knowability, Essence, and Attributes*, pp. 134 sqq.

3 Cfr. Patrizi, *De Interpret. Script. Sacrae*, l. II, qu. 2.

taken as a *pluralis maiestaticus,* nor yet as addressed to the angels; for man was not created to the image of the angels, but to that of God Himself.

There is a similar passage in Gen. XI, 7 sq.: "Come ye, therefore, let us go down, and there confound their tongue. . . . And so the Lord scattered them."[4] Many theologians in this connection recall the liturgical blessing of the priests, Num. VI, 24 sqq., which they regard as a parallel to the Christian formula, "In the name of the Father, and of the Son, and of the Holy Ghost." This Old Testament benediction, dictated by Yahweh Himself to Moses, is as follows: "The Lord bless thee and keep thee. The Lord show his face to thee, and have mercy on thee. The Lord turn his countenance to thee and give thee peace."

The clearest allusion to the mystery of the Blessed Trinity in the Old Testament is probably the so-called *Trisagion* of Isaias (VI, 3): "Holy, holy, holy, the Lord God of Hosts, all the earth is full of his glory," which is rightly made much of by many Fathers and not a few theologians. This triple "Holy" refers to an ecstatic vision of the Godhead, by which Isaias was solemnly called and consecrated as the Prophet of the Incarnate Word, an office which won for him the title of the "Evangelist" among the four major prophets.[5]

2. THE ANGEL OF JEHOVAH IN THE THEOPHANIES.—The various apparitions commonly known as theophanies, in which Yahweh figures both as sender and messenger, mark the grad-

4 For the Patristic interpretation of this passage consult Petavius, *De Trinitate,* II, 7.

5 Cfr. John XII, 41.

ual breaking of the dawn in the history of our dogma.

The God who is sent is called מַלְאַךְ יְהוָה, *i. e.*, messenger, *Angelus Domini,* the word *angelus* being here employed in its literal sense of ἄγγελος, from ἀγγέλλειν, *to send.* Since the "Angel of Jehovah" is described as יְהֹוָה, *i. e.*, true God, we have in these theophanies two distinct persons, both of them Yahweh, the one "sending" and the other "sent." An apparition of this character was the angel who spoke words of comfort to Hagar shortly before the birth of her son Ismael[6] in the desert. According to Gen. XVIII, 1 sqq., "the Lord [יְהֹוָה] appeared to [Abraham] in the vale of Mambre," in order to announce to him the destruction of Sodom and Gomorrha.[7]

Probably the most familiar of the Old Testament theophanies is the apparition of the Angel of Jehovah in the Burning Bush. Exod. III, 2: "*Apparuit ei* יְהוָֹה מַלְאַךְ *in flamma ignis de medio rubi*—And the Lord appeared to him [Moses] in a flame of fire out of the midst of a bush." It is to be noted that the Lord who appears to Moses is Jehovah Himself. Exod., III, 14: "God said to Moses: I AM WHO AM." Viewing this apparition in the light of the New Testament Revelation, the appearing God can be none other than the Logos, or Son of God, because the Father cannot be "sent." True, the Holy Ghost may also be "sent;" but He cannot have appeared in the bush to Moses because the prophets expressly identify the "Angel of Jehovah" with the future Messias (*i. e.*, Christ). Cfr. Is. IX, 6

6 Gen. XVI, 7 sqq.

7 On this passage, cfr. Newman, *Select Treatises of St. Athanasius*, II, 267 sq.; on the theophanies in general, H. P. Liddon, *The Divinity of Our Lord and Saviour Jesus Christ*, pp. 78 sqq., London 1867.

(in the version of the Septuagint): "Μεγάλης βουλῆς ἄγγελος, *Magni consilii angelus;*" Mal. III, 1: "*Angelus testamenti.*" The interpretation here adopted is common to all the Fathers. Thus St. Hilary teaches: "*Deus igitur est, qui et angelus est, quia qui et angelus Dei est, Deus est ex Deo natus. Dei autem angelus ob id dictus, quia magni consilii est angelus. Deus autem idem postea demonstratus est, ne qui Deus est esse angelus [creatus] crederetur.*" [8]

It is quite another question whether in these theophanies the Logos directly appeared as God in visible form, or through the intermediate agency of an angel. In the latter case the apparitions might with equal propriety be styled "angelophanies." St. Augustine took this view, without, however, denying the theophanic character of such angelophanies. He held that a created angel visibly appeared as the representative of God in such a manner that the words he spoke must be understood as coming not from the actual speaker but from Jehovah himself. This opinion was shared by Athanasius, Basil, Cyril of Alexandria, Eusebius, Chrysostom, Jerome, Gregory the Great, and others.[9] The great majority of the Schoolmen espoused it mainly for the reason that the Second Person of the Most Holy Trinity had never appeared visibly upon earth prior to His Incarnation.[10] The first immediate theophany of the Logos, they argued, coincided with the Incarnation; therefore in the Old Testament theophanies He must have employed angels as His representatives.

8 *De Trinit.*, IV, n. 24.— Cfr. Newman, "Causes of the Rise and Successes of Arianism," in *Tracts Theol. and Ecclesiastical*, pp. 212 sq., new ed., London 1895.

9 Cfr. Chr. Pesch, *Praelect. Dogmat.*, t. II, third ed., p. 262, Friburgi 1906; — Newman, *l. c.;* Liddon, *op. cit.*, 85 sq.

10 Cfr. Hebr. I, 1 sqq.; II, 1 sqq., *et passim.*

3. THE FUTURE MESSIAS AS TRUE GOD.—The Messianic prophecies of the Old Testament were primarily designed to emphasize the Divinity of the future Messias. Hence Christ Himself and His Apostles justly appealed to them to prove not only the divine mission but likewise the Divinity of the Saviour and the fact that He was truly the Son of God.

Among the prophets Isaias speaks most clearly and emphatically. Not only does he refer to the Messias as "the Wonderful, the Counsellor, the Prince of Peace," but also as "God the Mighty, the Father of the world to come."[11] He styles Him "Emmanuel," *i. e.*, God with us.[12] It is expressly said of Him that "God himself will come and will save you."[13] And again: "Prepare ye the way of the Lord. . . . Behold, the Lord God shall come with strength."[14] "His name shall be called God."[15] In Zach. XII, 10, God prophesies His own crucifixion: "*Et adspicient ad me, quem confixerunt et plangent eum*—And they shall look upon me, whom they have pierced; and they shall grieve over him."[16]

The Messianic Psalms complete the picture outlined by the prophets; nay, they go far beyond the latter both in emphasizing the difference of persons by a contra-position of the pronouns "I" and "thou," and also by indicating that the relation existing between the First and the Second Person of the Blessed Trinity is a relation of Father to Son, based upon Filiation. At the same time they do not omit to accentuate the

11 Is. IX, 6; cfr. Luke I, 32.

12 Is. VII, 14; cfr. Matth. I, 23.

13 Is. XXXV, 4; cfr. Matth. XI, 5.

14 Is. XL, 3, 10; cfr. Mark I, 3.

15 Is. IX, 6.

16 Cfr. John XIX, 37.

undivided nature of both Divine Persons, which they express by the word יְהוָה. Thus especially Ps. II, 7: "*Dominus* [יְהוָה] *dixit ad me: Filius meus es tu, ego hodie genui te*—The Lord hath said to me: Thou art my son, this day I have begotten thee."[17] Similarly Ps. CIX, 1–3: "*Dixit Dominus Domino meo* [יְהוָה לַאדֹנִי]: *sede a dexteris meis; . . . ex utero ante luciferum genui te*—The Lord said to my Lord: Sit thou at my right hand . . . from the womb before the day star I begot thee."[18] If the future Messias is the "Son of God," and at the same time Jehovah, it is obvious that there must also be a "Father" who is Jehovah. Consequently, there must be two Divine Persons in one Divine Nature. This notion was so familiar to the Jews that Jesus, in order to prove His Divinity, had merely to advert to the fact that He was the Son of God to provoke them to anger and blasphemy.[19] They well knew that to admit His Divine Sonship was tantamount to recognizing His Divinity.[20]

4. THE TEACHING OF THE SAPIENTIAL BOOKS.—A great step towards the complete unfolding of the mystery is made by the Sapiential Books.[21] There we find the notion of Hypostatic Wisdom closely blended with that of Filiation, and are given to understand that the Filiation which takes place within the Godhead is a purely spiritual process, and that He Who is "begotten by

17 Cfr. Hebr. I, 5.

18 Cfr. Math. XXII, 42 sqq.

19 Cfr. John V, 18; X, 33.

20 Cfr. John I, 32 sqq.; I, 49; IX, 35 sqq.; Luke I, 35 sqq., *et passim*. For further information on this point, see *infra*, § 3.

21 Prov. VIII; Wisd. VII sqq.; Ecclus. XXIV.

God" must be essentially conceived as "Begotten Wisdom" (*Logos*).

The Sapiential Books speak of Uncreated, Divine Wisdom in a manner which leaves no doubt that they mean more than a personified attribute. The following texts read like parallel passages to certain verses of St. John's Gospel. Prov. VIII, 24 sqq. "*Nondum erant abyssi et ego* [*i. e., sapientia*] *iam concepta eram: . . . ante colles* [*i. e., ab aeterno*] *ego parturiebar. . . . Cum eo* [*scil. Deo*] *eram, cuncta componens et delectabar per singulos dies, ludens coram eo omni tempore, ludens in orbe terrarum, et deliciae meae esse cum filiis hominum*—The depths were not as yet, and I [Wisdom] was already conceived . . . before the hills I was brought forth. . . . I was with him [God] forming all: and was delighted every day, playing before him at all times: and my delights [were] to be with the children of men." The subject of this passage is obviously not a divine attribute, but a Divine Person, who is called "Conceived Wisdom." The expression, "I was with him,"[22] has a parallel in John I, 1: "The Word was with God" (*Verbum erat apud Deum; πρὸς τὸν Θεόν*). The Book of Wisdom,[23] in designating Divine Wisdom as "a vapor of the power of God" (*vapor virtutis Dei*), "a certain pure emanation of glory" (*emanatio claritatis*), "the brightness of eternal light" (*candor lucis*), "the unspotted mirror of God's majesty" (*speculum maiestatis*), "the image of his goodness" (*imago bonitatis*), reminds one of the manner in which St. Paul characterizes Christ's relationship to God the Father,[24] *i. e.*, as

22 "*Cum eo eram*"; the Septuagint has: ἤμην παρ' αὐτῷ; the Hebrew: אצלו.

23 Wisd. VII, 25 sqq.

24 Hebr. I, 3.

"the brightness of his glory, and the figure of his substance" (*splendor gloriae et figura substantiae eius*). The following sentence,[25] "And thy wisdom with thee, which knoweth thy works, which then also was present when thou madest the world—*Et tecum* (*μετά σου*) *sapientia tua, quae novit opera tua, quae et affuit tunc, quum orbem terrarum faceres* (*πάρουσα ὅτε ἐποίεις τὸν κόσμον*)," is again distinctly Johannine in style and sentiment. The same impression is conveyed by Ecclus. XXIV, 5: "I came out of the mouth of the most High [as the Word], the firstborn before all creatures."[26]

In view of this striking concordance between the Sapiential Books of the Old Testament and the Gospel of St. John, it is not astonishing that certain learned Jewish rabbis at a later period elaborated an independent theory of the "Word of God," called Memrah,[27] by which they endeavored to explain the Old Testament teaching regarding Wisdom without any reference to Christ.[28] It is easy to see, too, why the Fathers of the Nicene epoch appealed to the Sapiential Books of the Old Testament to prove the Consubstantiality and consequent Divinity of Christ. The Arians, on their part, quoted the Sapiential Books in support of their heretical tenet that the Logos was a creature.[29]

5. THE HOLY GHOST.—The Old Testament references to the Third Person of the Blessed Trinity are neither as plain nor as definite as

25 Wisd. IX, 9.

26 "*Ego ex ore altissimi prodivi [ut Verbum], primogenita ante omnem creaturam.*"

27 A Chaldaic word for Wisdom. Cfr. J. Lebreton, *Les Origines du Dogme de la Trinité*, pp. 145 sqq.

28 This theory is incorporated chiefly in the writings of the Targumim and Onkelos. Cfr. *The Jewish Encyclopedia*.

29 Cfr. Newman, *The Arians of the Fourth Century*, pp. 202 sqq.; IDEM, *Select Treatises of St. Athanasius*, II, 337 sqq. Cfr. also Chapter II, § 2, Art. 3, *infra*.

the texts relating to the Son. "It is natural to expect more references to the Son than to the Holy Ghost in the Old Testament, because it prepares and announces the coming and manifestation of the Son in the Incarnation."[30] The Old Testament references to the Holy Ghost can nearly all of them be explained as personifications. *"Spiritus Dei"* may merely mean a breath of the Divine Omnipotence,[31] or the supernatural effects of the spirit of God, which, according to Ps. CIII, 30, "renews the face of the earth." The Fathers in their exegetical works quote a number of Old Testament texts in which they profess to find references to the Holy Spirit as a Person.[32] But their interpretation of these and similar passages is inspired by, and owes its impressiveness to the light derived from, the New Testament. It is in this light, too, that we must regard Wisd. IX, 1 sqq., the only Old Testament passage in which the Three Divine Persons are mentioned together: *"Deus patrum meorum, . . . qui fecisti omnia Verbo tuo, . . . da mihi sedium tuarum assistricem sapientiam. . . . Sensum autem tuum quis sciet, nisi tu dederis sapientiam et miseris Spiritum Sanctum tuum de altissimis?* — God of my fathers, . . . who hast made all things with thy

30 Wilhelm-Scannell, *Manual*, Vol. I, p. 283.

31 Cfr. Gen. I, 2.

32 Joel II, 28; Job XXXIII, 4; Wisd. I, 7; Is. LXI, 1, etc.

word, . . . give me wisdom, that sitteth by thy throne . . . Who shall know thy thought, except thou give wisdom, and send thy Holy Spirit from above?"

It cannot therefore be seriously maintained that the mystery of the Divine Trinity was clearly revealed in the Old Testament. Aside from certain specially enlightened individuals, such as Abraham, Moses, Isaias, and David, the Jews could not, from the more or less enigmatic hints scattered through their sacred books, have obtained a sufficiently distinct knowledge of the Blessed Trinity to make it appear as an article of faith.

Nevertheless it remains true that the Trinity was not announced in the New Testament suddenly and without preparation. On the contrary, the great mystery of the Godhead was foreshadowed from the very beginning of the Jewish Covenant and assumed more definite and luminous proportions during and after the time of David, until at last it stood fully revealed in the mystery of the Incarnation,[33] and the mission of the Holy Ghost on Pentecost Day.

Readings: — Drach, *De l'Harmonie entre l'Église et la Synagogue,* Paris 1844. (Drach's conclusions are restated and brought into stronger relief by the addition of new matter in F. McGloin, *The Mystery of the Holy Trinity in Oldest Judaism,* Philadelphia 1916).—P. Scholz, *Theologie des A. B.,* Vol. I, §§ 29 sqq., Ratisbon 1861.— Scheeben, *Dogmatik,* Vol. I, § 110, Freiburg 1875 (Wilhelm-Scannell's *Manual,* I, pp. 283 sqq.).

33 Matth. I, 18 sqq.; Luke I, 35,etc.

—*Heinrich, *Dogmat. Theologie,* 2nd ed., Vol. III, §§ 214–218, Mainz 1883.— Franzelin, *De Deo Trino,* thes. 6 and 7, Romae 1881.

On the "Angel of Jehovah," cfr. A. Rohling in the *Tübinger Quartalschrift,* 1866, pp. 415 sqq., 527 sqq.; *L. Reinke, *Beiträge zur Erklärung des A. T.,* Vol. IV, pp. 355 sqq.; J. Lebreton, *Les Origines du Dogme de la Trinité,* pp. 89 sqq., Paris 1910; F. McGloin, *The Mystery of the Holy Trinity in Oldest Judaism,* Philadelphia 1916, pp. 154 sqq., F. J. Hall (Anglican), *The Trinity,* London 1910, pp. 107 sqq.

On the Messias, cfr. *König, *Theologie der Psalmen,* Freiburg 1857; L. Reinke, *Messianische Psalmen,* 2 vols., Giessen 1857–1858; H. Zschokke, *Theologie der Propheten,* Freiburg 1877; H. P. Liddon, *The Divinity of Our Lord and Saviour Jesus Christ,* London 1867; A. J. Maas, S. J., *Christ in Type and Prophecy,* 2 vols., New York 1893–5.— P. Boylan, "Messianic Expectation in the Old Testament," in *The Incarnation,* Cambridge Summer School Lectures for 1925, edited by C. Lattey, S. J., Cambridge 1926, pp. 1–18.

On the Sapiential Books of the Old Testament cfr. *Fr. Klasen, *Die alttestamentliche Weisheit und der Logos der jüdisch-alexandrinischen Philosophie,* 1878; also J. Réville, *Le Logos d'après Philon d'Alexandrie,* Paris 1877; Zschokke, *Der dogmatisch-ethische Lehrgehalt der alttestamentlichen Weisheitsbücher,* Wien 1889; E. Krebs, *Der Logos als Heiland im ersten Jahrhundert,* Freiburg 1910; J. Lebreton, *Les Origines du Dogme de la Trinité,* 89 sqq., 441 sqq., Paris 1910.

SECTION 2

THE THREEFOLD PERSONALITY OF GOD AS TAUGHT IN THE NEW TESTAMENT—TEXTS TREATING OF THE THREE DIVINE PERSONS TOGETHER

Though the exact terms in which the Church has formally defined the dogma of the Blessed Trinity (τριάς = *trinitas,* οὐσία = *substantia,* ὑπόστασις = *persona,*[1] ὁμοούσιος = *consubstantialis*) are not in the Bible, and may, therefore, in a sense be called unscriptural; yet materially, that is in substance, they correctly express the teaching of the New Testament, which, like the Church, explicitly acknowledges three real Persons in one Divine Nature, in which precisely the dogma of the "Trinity in Unity" consists.

As we are here dealing with a fundamental dogma of Christianity, the material correspondence of the New Testament doctrine with the formally defined teaching of the Church must be carefully and stringently demonstrated. We therefore proceed to a minute critical investigation of the various texts that are apt to throw light on the subject. Let us begin with those in which

1 Cfr. Hebr. I, 3, where ὑπόστασις is used as synonymous with *substantia.*

the threefold personality of God is distinctly and formally enunciated.

1. THE GOSPELS.—Four such texts occur in the Gospels. Though their combined effect is sufficiently compelling, they are not all of equal weight. The most convincing is the passage embodying the form of Baptism.

a) The first brief intimation of the functioning of Three Divine Persons is given in the Annunciation: "*Spiritus Sanctus superveniet in te, et virtus Altissimi obumbrabit tibi; ideoque et quod nascetur ex te sanctum, vocabitur Filius Dei* — The Holy Ghost shall come upon thee, and the power of the most High shall overshadow thee. And therefore also the Holy which shall be born of thee shall be called the Son of God."[2] Here all three Divine Persons are distinctly mentioned: first, the Son who is to be born, second, the Holy Ghost, and third, the "Most High," who stands in the relation of a Father to Him of whom it is said a few verses farther up:[3] "*Hic erit magnus et Filius Altissimi vocabitur* — He shall be great, and shall be called the Son of the most High." Where there is a Son of God, there must also be a Divine Father. The relative opposition between the terms Father and Son forbids the welding of both persons into one. This is sufficient evidence that we have here not merely three different names for one Divinc Person, but three really distinct Hypostases, of which one is not the other. Nor can it have been the intention of the sacred writer merely to personify certain absolute attributes of the Deity. The Son of God, who is to be made flesh (Christ), manifestly represents a real Person.

2 Luke I, 35.

3 Luke I, 32.

Moreover, the strict monotheism of the Bible necessitates the assumption that the three Divine Persons mentioned in the text must be consubstantial, *i. e.*, absolutely identical in essence.

b) The most glorious external manifestation of the Blessed Trinity occurred in connection with the Baptism of Christ.[4] Christ, the Son of God, is standing in the Jordan; the Holy Ghost descends upon Him in the form of a dove, and the voice of the Father calls from Heaven: "This is my beloved Son in whom I am well pleased." Here, too, the hypostatic difference between the three Persons, and the impossibility of blending them into one, is quite apparent. The "beloved Son" and the Father expressing His pleasure are clearly differentiated, while the Person of the Holy Ghost is emblemed by the dove, a symbolic figure which would be unsuited to any absolute attribute of the Godhead.[5] Though the identity of Nature of the three Divine Persons is not expressly enunciated in the above-quoted passages, it may, as a matter of course, be presumed.

c) In His famous farewell discourse delivered after the last Supper,[6] Christ announced that He was "going to the Father" and would ask Him to send the Paraclete. The distinction here made between the three Divine Persons is as obvious as it is real. No one can be father and son under the same aspect, nor can any one send himself. When Christ says, for instance: "*Ego rogabo Patrem, et alium Paraclitum dabit vobis, ut maneat vobiscum in aeternum, Spiritum veritatis* — I will ask the Father, and He will give you another Paraclete, that he may abide with you forever, the Spirit of truth,"[7]

4 Matth. III, 13 sqq.; Mark I, 9 sqq.; Luke III, 21 sqq.; cfr. Job I, 32.

5 Cfr. T. J. Gerrard, *The Wayfarer's Vision*, pp. 200 sqq.

6 John XIV–XVI.

7 John XIV, 16 sq.

He distinguishes between His own Person, that of the Father, and that of the "other Paraclete" and clearly identifies the latter with the "Spirit of truth."[8]

The threefold personality of the Godhead appears still more distinctly from John XV, 26: "*Quum autem venerit Paraclitus, quem ego mittam vobis a Patre, Spiritum veritatis, qui a Patre procedit, ille testimonium perhibebit de me* — But when the Paraclete cometh, whom I will send you from the Father, the Spirit of truth, who proceedeth from the Father, he shall give testimony of me." The absolute consubstantiality of Father and Son is taught in John XVI, 15: "*Omnia, quaecumque habet Pater, mea sunt* — All things whatsoever the Father hath, are mine," and it is no less true of the Holy Ghost.

d) The baptismal form, "In the name of the Father, and of the Son, and of the Holy Ghost," enunciates all the essential elements of the Holy Trinity.[9] "*Euntes ergo docete omnes gentes, baptizantes eos in nomine Patris et Filii et Spiritus Sancti* (βαπτίζοντες αὐτοὺς εἰς τὸ ὄνομα τοῦ πατρὸς καὶ τοῦ υἱοῦ καὶ τοῦ ἁγίου πνεύματος)." The hypostatic difference between Father and Son is brought out by the relative opposition, in virtue of which they exclude each other as begetting and begotten. For no one can be his own father or his own son. To admit such an absurdity would be to deny the principle of contradiction and thereby to subvert right reason. Hence there is a real difference between the

8 *Paraclitus = Spiritus Sanctus.*

9 Cfr. Matth. XXVIII, 19.

Father and the Son. As to the Holy Ghost, the co-ordination involved in the use of *et—et* (καί—καί) forbids us to confound Him with either of the other two Persons. Consequently He must be an independent third Person, coequal and consubstantial with the other two. It should be noted that the Johannine text does not say: "In the name of the Father, *or* the Son, *or* the Holy Ghost," but "In the name of the Father, *and* of the Son, *and* of the Holy Ghost (τοῦ πατρὸς καὶ τοῦ υἱοῦ καὶ τοῦ ἁγίου πνεύματος)." The particle καί with the definite article marks off the three Divine Persons very sharply from one another, despite the unity implied between them. For this reason "Holy Ghost" can not be taken as an attribute determining the concept "Son."

In attempting to answer the question, "What kind of unity is it by which the Father, the Son, and the Holy Ghost are one?" we must pay special attention to the words "In the name." It makes no difference whether we follow the text of the Latin Vulgate, *"In nomine,"* or the Greek text with its εἰς ὄνομα. Both εἰς ὄνομα and ἐν ὀνόματι, as well as ἐπὶ τῷ ὀνόματι[10] occur in the original Greek text, and for our present purpose they are equally conclusive. For man to be baptized in the name of the Most Holy Trinity can have no other meaning than that through

10 Acts II, 38.

baptism he obtains forgiveness of his sins in virtue and by the authority of the three Divine Persons; while to baptize εἰς ὄνομα of the Blessed Trinity signifies the devotion with which the person baptized is expected to consecrate himself to and to seek his last end and aim in the "Deity."[11] In either case Father, Son, and Holy Ghost are certainly identical with the Deity itself, because no one can expect forgiveness of his sins from, or seek his final end in, a mere creature, without making himself guilty of idolatry. If the three Persons mentioned are identical with the Godhead, they cannot be three Gods, but must be the One God taught by both Testaments.[12]

The essential identity of the three Divine Persons follows further from the singular form "*in nomine,*" because throughout the Bible "*nomen Domini*" signifies God's power, majesty, and essence.[13] As the Three have but one name, so They have but one essence, one nature, one substance. St. Augustine beautifully observes: "*Iste unus Deus, quia non in nominibus Patris et Filii et Spiritus Sancti, sed in nomine Patris et Filii et Spiritus Sancti. Ubi unum nomen audis, unus est Deus* — This is one God, for it is not in the names of the Father, and of the Son, and of the Holy Ghost, but in the name of the

11 Cfr. Rom. VI, 3 sqq.; 1 Cor. I, 12 sqq.; III, 4 sqq.; Gal. III, 27.

12 Cfr. Pohle-Preuss, *God: His Knowability, Essence, and Attributes*, pp. 212 sqq.

13 "*Nomen est numen.*"

Father, and of the Son, and of the Holy Ghost. Where thou hearest one name, there is one God." [14]

2. THE EPISTLES.—The Apostolic Epistles contain four texts in which the three Divine Persons are mentioned together. Most prominent among them is the much-discussed *Comma Ioanneum* (1 John V, 7).

a) The prologue to the first Epistle of St. Peter reads: "*Petrus . . . electis . . . secundum praescientiam Dei Patris, in sanctificationem Spiritus, in obedientiam et aspersionem sanguinis Iesu Christi: gratia vobis et pax multiplicetur*—Peter . . . to the . . . elect, according to the foreknowledge of God the Father, unto the sanctification of the Spirit, unto obedience and sprinkling of the blood of Jesus Christ: Grace unto you and peace be multiplied." Here we have a Trinitarian form of benediction in which the omniscient Father, the sanctifying Spirit, and Jesus Christ, our Redeemer by the "sprinkling of blood," appear on a par. Consequently the Three are one true God. Though this isolated text is not sufficient to establish a real distinction between the three Divine Persons (for the sanctifying Spirit might possibly be conceived as a mere attribute of the Father or of Jesus Christ), the teaching of the New Testament in many other places makes it quite certain that Jesus Christ is the "Son of God" who differs hypostatically from the Father, as the Holy Ghost differs hypostatically from both the Father and the Son.

14 August., *Tract. in Ioa.*, VI, n. 9. Browne's translation in the *Library of the Fathers*, Vol. I of the *Homilies on the Gospel according to St. John*, p. 87, Oxford 1848.

b) The epilogue of St. Paul's second Epistle to the Corinthians contains a similar form of blessing: "*Gratia Domini nostri Iesu Christi et charitas Dei* [*scil. Patris*] *et communicatio Sancti Spiritus sit cum omnibus vobis* — The grace of our Lord Jesus Christ, and the charity of God [the Father], and the communication of the Holy Ghost be with you all."[15] As grace and charity are supernatural gifts which only the Godhead can dispense, there can be no question that here again the Three Dispensers are One God. But does the text oblige us to postulate three really distinct Persons? We think it does; for the Greek original[16] puts the "grace of our Lord Jesus Christ" on a par with the "charity of God" and the "communication" (κοινωνία) of the Holy Ghost." It is improbable that the "God of charity" should be personally identical either with our Lord Jesus Christ or the Holy Ghost.

c) St. Paul's teaching on the spiritual gifts and the charismata[17] is rightly held to have a special bearing on the doctrine of the Most Holy Trinity. Exegetes deduce from the threefold nature of the effect (χαρίσματα, διακονίαι, ενεργήματα) the existence of a threefold hypostatic principle (πνεῦμα, κύριος, θεός). But, since a little further down in St. Paul's text[18] all these gifts are appropriated to "the same Spirit," that which was at first divided returns to its original unity, and consequently Spirit, Lord, and God are not three gods, but one God. The somewhat involved passage is as follows: "*Divisiones vero gratiarum* (χαρισμάτων) *sunt, idem autem*

15 2 Cor. XIII, 13.

16 The Greek text has: ἡ χάρις τοῦ κυρίου Ἰησοῦ Χριστοῦ, καὶ ἡ ἀγάπη τοῦ Θεοῦ καὶ ἡ κοινωνία τοῦ ἁγίου πνεύματος, which Brandscheid (*Novum Testamentum*, p. 361, Friburgi 1901) correctly translates: "*Gratia . . . et charitas.*"

17 1 Cor. XII, 4 sqq.

18 1 Cor. XII, 11.

Spiritus (πνεῦμα); [cfr. verse 3: ἐν πνεύματι ἁγίῳ]; *et divisiones ministrationum sunt* (διακονιῶν = ministries, ecclesiastical offices), *idem autem Dominus* (ὁ κύριος = Christ); *et divisiones operationum sunt* (ἐνεργημάτων = miracles), *idem vero Deus* (ὁ αὐτὸς Θεός), *qui operatur omnia in omnibus* — Now there are diversities of graces, but the same Spirit; and there are diversities of ministries, but the same Lord; and there are diversities of operations, but the same God, who worketh in all."[19] It is plain from the context that, on the basis of three supernatural operations, St. Paul here means to distinguish three separate Divine Persons: *Spiritus, Dominus,* and *Deus.* That he does not mean to assert the existence of three Gods appears from verse 11: "*Haec autem omnia operatur unus atque idem Spiritus* (τὸ ἓν καὶ τὸ αὐτὸ πνεῦμα), *dividens singulis, prout vult* — But all these things one and the same spirit worketh, dividing to every one according as he will."

A similar change of subject, by which the same external operation is ascribed now to this Divine Person and now to that, occurs in many other places in Holy Scripture, *e. g.*, in the vision of Isaias.[20] The authorship of this vision is in the original Hebrew referred to the Divinity in general (אֲדֹנָי), in John XII, 40, to Christ, and in Acts XXVIII, 25 sqq., to the Holy Ghost. Except on the assumption of a numerical oneness of nature and essence these expressions are absolutely unintelligible.[21]

d) The Comma Ioanneum.—If its textual authenticity could be established, the famous

19 1 Cor. XII, 4 sqq.

20 Is. VI, 9 sq.

21 Cfr. Al. Schäfer, *Erklärung der beiden Briefe an die Korinther*, pp. 244 sqq., Münster 1903.

Comma Ioanneum (1 John V, 7), or text of the three heavenly Witnesses, would be of equal dogmatic value with the form of Baptism. As it stands, it is a pregnant and clear *textus per se dogmaticus,* outweighing, *e. g.,* St. Paul's entire Epistle to Philemon, and enforcing the dogma of the Divine Trinity more perfectly than any other passage in the Bible.

It would, however, be a mistake to suppose that, should it ever become necessary to sacrifice the *Comma Ioanneum,* the Biblical argument for the dogma of the Blessed Trinity would suffer essential impairment. The whole of our present chapter goes to show the contrary. Yet no one will blame the Catholic theologian for utilizing, in spite of certain critical misgivings, a text which has been received into the liturgy of the Church, and for many centuries [22] formed part and parcel of the Latin Vulgate. Aside from questions of textual criticism, it is plain that the dogmatic authenticity of 1 John V, 7, cannot be questioned without endorsing the heretical view that a proposition received into the Sacred Text under the vigilant eye of the Church may contain dogmatic errors. In this *purely dogmatic* sense, therefore, the *Comma Ioanneum* is undoubtedly authentic and may be used as an argument, even though, so long as its textual authenticity has not been securely established, the demonstration based upon it cannot claim to be a strictly Biblical proof.

In perfect conformity with the well-known views of St. John the Evangelist, the *Comma Ioanneum* enumerates the three Witnesses "who give testimony in

22 Presumably since about the year 800.

heaven," as "the Father, the Word, and the Holy Ghost," and expressly declares that "these three are one."[23] Since the three Witnesses of whom the Apostle speaks are "in heaven," they seem to be the three Divine Persons, and they must be really distinct from one another, because they are expressly referred to as οἱ τρεῖς. Inasmuch as they are "one" (ἕν, *unum*), there must exist between them a communication of nature, that is to say, their unity is not merely "*unitas in testificando,*" but clearly also "*identitas in essendo.*" It is true St. John in the following verse also says of the three other witnesses who "give testimony on earth," *viz.:* "the spirit, and the water, and the blood," that "*et hi tres unum sunt.*" But he does not say: ἕν εἰσιν, but εἰς τὸ ἕν εἰσιν = *in unum sunt,* that is, they are one only in so far as they testify, not identical in substance.[24]

3. The Authenticity of the Comma Ioanneum.—On January 13, 1897, the Sacred Congregation of the Holy Office, with the approbation of His Holiness Pope Leo XIII, published the subjoined doctrinal decision:[25] "*Ad propositionem, utrum tuto negari an in dubium vocari possit, esse authenticum textum 1 Ioa. V, 7. . . . Eminentissimi Cardinales respondendum mandarunt: Negative*—The doubt was proposed: 'Can it be safely denied, or at least doubted, that the text of 1 John V, 7 . . . is authentic?' . . .

23 1 John V, 7: "Ὅτι τρεῖς εἰσιν οἱ μαρτυροῦντες ἐν τῷ οὐρανῷ, ὁ πατήρ, ὁ λόγος καὶ τὸ ἅγιον πνεῦμα· καὶ οὗτοι οἱ τρεῖς ἕν εἰσιν —And there are three who give testimony in heaven, the Father, the Word, and the Holy Ghost. And these three are one."

24 Cfr. Franzelin, *De Deo Trino,* thes. 5.

25 *Analect. Eccles.,* 1897, pp. 99 sq.

and the Most Eminent Cardinals answered, *No.*"

a) As soon as this decree became known, the opinion was expressed, even by Catholic scholars, that it meant a definitive decision in favor of the authenticity of the *Comma Ioanneum,* which could not henceforth be doubted or denied without challenging the defined right and duty of Holy Church to watch over and authoritatively determine all questions connected with Sacred Scripture. Those who took this view forgot that a decree of the Holy Office, even when approved by the Pope "*in forma communi,*" does not partake of the nature of an infallible decision. That this is so, is manifest from the action of the same Congregation against Galilei, A. D. 1633.[26] The religious assent with which Catholics are bound to receive the decisions of the Holy Office,[27] is a duty growing out of Catholic respect for authority, and imposed by obedience. But it would be wrong to interpret it as forbidding deeper research into the soundness or unsoundness of a decision which does not *per se* claim to be infallible. The respect and obedience we owe to the Church will prompt us not to refuse our assent until it is positively certain, or at least highly probable, that the Sacred Congregation has made a mistake. The Pope in his capacity of supreme teacher can-

26 On the decision against Galilei, see Adolf Müller, S. J., *Der Galilei-Prozess (1632–1633) nach Ursprung, Verlauf und Folgen,* Freiburg 1909, pp. 191 sqq. This excellent work, together with the same author's *Galileo Galilei und das kopernikanische Weltsystem,* Freiburg 1909, is far and away the best account of this much-mooted historical incident. We hope both will soon find an English translator.

27 See the letter addressed by Pius IX to the Archbishop of Munich, under date of Dec. 21, 1863 (Denzinger-Bannwart, *Enchiridion,* n. 1684). Cfr. P. A. Baart, *The Roman Court,* pp. 111 sq., New York 1895.

not delegate his infallibility to any man or body of men; hence his approval of a congregational decree does not invest that decree with infallibility, unless indeed the Sovereign Pontiff sees fit, by an approbation "*in forma solemni*," to raise it to the rank of an *ex cathedra* decision solemnly binding all the faithful. This was not done in the present instance.

For the rest, it is well to remember that the decrees and decisions of the different Roman Congregations are as a rule disciplinary rather than doctrinal. They are for the most part designed to warn Catholic scholars against adopting doubtful theories until the reasons for and against have been thoroughly sifted. Thus it was in the early days of the Church in respect of the moot question regarding the existence of antipodes. Like value should be attached to the ecclesiastical decisions against the system of Copernicus, which has emerged victoriously from the violent conflict waged about it. Perhaps the decision of the Holy Office on the *Comma Ioanneum* belongs to the same category. In these parlous days, when Protestant and Rationalist critics are sapping the very foundations of sound Biblical science, and in their eagerness to frame new hypotheses are trotting out a horde of critical monsters which forthwith proceed to devour one another, there is danger that Catholic savants may venture too far along slippery paths, losing sight completely of the firm ground of ecclesiastical Tradition.[28] An immediate authoritative intervention in the controversy raging round the *Comma Ioanneum* seemed all the more advisable because a definitive solution of the problem on purely scientific grounds could hardly be expected for a long time to come. Though it seems at present a highly im-

28 Take, for example, the case of the unfortunate Abbé Loisy.

probable event, yet some ancient Greek or Latin palimpsest may yet be unearthed, containing the *Comma* in an undoubtedly genuine and original form. The absence of the passage from so many New Testament codices could then be satisfactorily explained by an oversight of the copyists. G. Schepss has lately found the mooted text cited in a work of Priscillian's newly discovered in 1889. At the present stage of the controversy, however, there is no blinking the fact that the critical arguments against the authenticity of the *Comma Ioanneum* considerably outweigh those adduced in its favor.

b) The most weighty objection raised against the authenticity of 1 John V, 7 is based on the circumstance that the text is missing in all the older Greek codices without exception. Not until the fifteenth century does it begin to make its appearance in the manuscript copies of St. John's First Epistle. Moreover, not one of the Greek Fathers who combated Arianism ever cited this strong passage, which would have dealt a death blow to the heresy of Subordinationism. In fact, when we observe how eagerly the Greek Fathers of the Nicene and Post-Nicene period conned their Bible for texts with which to refute the Arians, without ever lighting upon 1 John V, 7, the only rational explanation is that the *Comma Ioanneum* was not there. Nor were the Latin Fathers (if we disregard a few faint and doubtful traces) acquainted with the text of the three heavenly Witnesses. St. Augustine, *e. g.*, fails to cite it in his great work *De Trinitate*, in which with his customary ingenuity he turns to account practically all the Trinitarian texts found in the whole Bible.[29] He repeatedly quotes 1 John V, 8, but never once 1 John V, 7. What

29 The *Speculum Augustini "Audi Israhel"* is spurious. Cfr. Bardenhewer-Shahan, *Patrology*, p. 505.

is still more remarkable is that Leo the Great, in his dogmatic *Epistula ad Flavianum* (A. D. 451), quotes as Scriptural the verses that immediately precede, and several that follow the passage called *Comma Ioanneum,* but never alludes to the *Comma* itself. Nor was the *Comma* known to St. Jerome, who restored the Vulgate text by order of Pope Damasus. If the editors of the official edition, prepared under Pope Sixtus V and his predecessors, had recognized the spuriousness of the pseudo-Hieronymian prologue to the Catholic Epistles, now so apparent to all, the *Comma* would probably never have been incorporated in the Vulgate. The most ancient manuscript codices of the Vulgate — among them the Codex Fuldensis, the Codex Amiatinus, and the Codex Harleianus — and the oldest extant copies of the Greek Testament, do not contain the much discussed passage, which made its way very gradually since the eighth century. In England it was unknown to Saint Bede, who died in the year 735.

But how did the text of the three heavenly Witnesses find its way into the Vulgate? All explanations that have been advanced so far are pure guesswork. The circumstance that in certain manuscript codices the *Comma* occurs sometimes before and sometimes after verse 8, has suggested the hypothesis that it was originally a marginal note, which somehow crept into the text. Some think that a misunderstood remark by St. Cyprian first led to its reception. This would explain the early occurrence of the *Comma* in the African Church. St. Cyprian (+ 258) writes in his treatise *De Unitate Ecclesiae,* c. 6: "*Dicit Dominus: ego et Pater unum sumus, et iterum de Patre et Filio et Spiritu Sancto scriptum est: et tres unum sunt* — The Lord sayeth: I and the Father are one; and again it is written of the

Father and the Son and the Holy Ghost: And the Three are one." Of this passage, as Al. Schäfer points out, only the words "*et tres unum sunt*" can be looked upon as a quotation from Sacred Scripture, and they may have been borrowed from the genuine eighth verse of the fifth chapter of St. John's First Epistle.[30] Facundus of Hermiane (+ about 570), who had no inkling of the existence of the famous *Comma,* actually formulated this surmise: "*Tres sunt qui testimonium dant, spiritus, aqua et sanguis, et hi tres unum sunt . . . quod Ioannis testimonium B. Cyprianus de Patre, Filio et Spiritu Sancto intelligit.*"[31] Tertullian (born about 160) has a passage in his *Contra Praxeam* which sounds somewhat like the *Comma,*[32] but we may fairly doubt whether it is intended for a citation or merely expresses the author's personal opinion.

c) Against such arguments as these it is difficult to defend the authenticity of the *Comma Ioanneum,*[33] which undeniably did not find its way into the Vulgate until the ninth century, while the Greek codices contain no trace of it prior to the fifteenth century.[34] All that can be said for the other side is that since the apographs

30 Schäfer, *Einleitung in das N. T.*, p. 340, Paderborn 1898.

31 *Defens. Trium Capitul.*, I, 3.

32 *Contr. Prax.*, 25. The passage reads: "*Ita connexus Patris in Filio et Filii in Paracleto tres efficit cohaerentes, alterum ab altero, qui tres unum sunt, non unus.*"

33 But few attempts at such a defense have been made in English since Dr. Wiseman published his well-known *Letters on 1 John V, 7; e. g.*, by Lamy, in the *American Ecclesiastical Review*, 1897, pp. 449 sqq. Cfr. also Ch. Forster, *A New Plea for the Authenticity of the Text of the Three Heavenly Witnesses*, Cambridge 1867. J. Lebreton gives a brief and impartial summary of the present status of the controversy in an appendix (pp. 524–531) of his work *Les Origines du Dogme de la Trinité*, Paris 1910.

34 Of the Greek uncials every one that contains the First Epistle of St. John is without the *Comma Ioanneum.* Of the cursive MSS. of the Greek New Testament about one hundred and ninety do not include the passage, while only four contain it, and these four as text-witnesses are worthless. Cfr. W. L. Sullivan in the *New York Review*, Vol. II, (1906), No. 2, p. 180.

of the earliest period are nearly all lost, there remains a bare possibility that the *Comma Ioanneum* may have occurred in one or the other of the most ancient, especially African, codices. Some importance attaches to the fact that as early as 380 the Spanish heresiarch Priscillian cites as Scriptural the verse: "*Et tria sunt, quae testimonium dicunt in coelo, Pater, Verbum et Spiritus, et haec tria unum sunt.*"[35] The main argument for the authenticity of the *Comma* is based upon a passage in the "*Libellus Fidei,*" which the Catholic Bishops[36] who were cited by Hunneric, King of the Vandals, to meet the Arians in conference on Feb. 1, 484,[37] submitted in defense of their faith. The passage is as follows: "*Et ut adhuc luce clarius unius divinitatis esse cum Patre et Filio Spiritum Sanctum doceamus, Ioannis Evangelistae testimonio comprobatur. Ait namque: Tres sunt, qui testimonium perhibent in coelo: Pater, Verbum et Spiritus Sanctus, et hi tres unum sunt.*"[38] St. Fulgentius (468–533), Bishop of Ruspe, in the African province of Byzazena, undoubtedly knew of the verse and, rightly or wrongly, ascribed a knowledge of it to St. Cyprian: "*Beatus Ioannes Apostolus testatur dicens: Tres sunt, qui testimonium perhibent in coelo, Pater, Verbum, et Spiritus Sanctus, et tres unum sunt; quod etiam B. martyr Cyprianus in epistola de unitate ecclesiae confitetur.*"[39] The defense can also claim the

35 *Lib. Apologet.*, IV, ed. Schepss, p. 6. Schepss, as we have already intimated, discovered this lost work of Priscillian's in the Würzburg University Library in 1889.

36 They included Victor of Vita (cfr. his *Hist. Persecut.*, II, 56) and Vigilius of Tapsus.

37 Cfr. Alzog, *Manual of Universal Church History*, Vol. II, p. 28 sq. Cincinnati 1899; Sullivan in the *New York Review*, II, 2, 185 sq.

38 Quoted by Hardouin, *Conc.*, t. ii, p. 863.

39 *Resp. ad Obiect. Arianorum*, 10. The passage of St. Cyprian's, to which Fulgentius here refers, occurs in the sixth chapter *De Unitate Ecclesiae* and reads as follows: "*Dicit Dominus, ego et Pater unum sumus;*

authority of Cassiodorus, who, about the middle of the sixth century, with many ancient manuscripts at his elbow, revised the entire Vulgate of St. Jerome, especially the Apostolic Epistles, and deliberately inserted 1 John V, 7, which St. Jerome had left out. If we consider all these facts, in connection with the passage quoted above from Tertullian, which bears the earmarks of a direct citation from Holy Scripture, we are justified in assuming that the *Comma Ioanneum* was perhaps found in copies of the Latin Bible current in Africa as early as the third century.

d) The *dogmatic* authenticity of 1 John V, 7, is quite another matter. It can be satisfactorily established by a purely theological process of reasoning. The *Comma Ioanneum* played a prominent part at the Fourth Lateran Council, A.D. 1215, where Abbot Joachim of Flora adduced it in favor of his tritheistic vagaries. In the *Caput "Damnamus,"* which solemnly condemns his errors, we read: *"Non enim (ait Ioachim) fideles Christi sunt unum, i. e., quaedam una res, quae communis sit omnibus, sed hoc modo sunt unum, i. e., una ecclesia, propter catholicae fidei unitatem . . . quemadmodum in canonica Ioannis Apostoli epistula legitur: 'quia tres sunt, qui testimonium dant in coelo, Pater et Filius* [*sic!*] *et Spiritus Sanctus, et hi tres unum sunt.' Statimque subiungitur: Et tres sunt, qui testimonium dant in terra, spiritus, aqua et sanguis, et hi tres unum sunt: sicut in quibusdam codicibus invenitur."* [40] Though we have here the express testimony of a council of the

et iterum de Patre et Filio et Spiritu Sancto scriptum est: et tres unum sunt." It is, as Tischendorf has rightly observed, by far the weightiest proof for the *Comma Ioanneum*. But it does not prove decisively that St. Cyprian used a New Testament text which contained the "*Comma*"; and if it did, it would by no means follow that the verse was written by St. John. Cfr. Sullivan in the *New York Review*, II, 2, pp. 182 sq.

40 Quoted by Denzinger-Bannwart, *Enchiridion*, n. 431.

Church that the *Comma* occurs *only in certain codices,* it is to be noted that this council does not reject the text of the three heavenly witnesses as apocryphal or spurious, or as having been smuggled into the Bible.

The strongest dogmatical argument, according to Franzelin[41] and Kleutgen,[42] is that drawn from the Tridentine decree *De Canonicis Scripturis: "Si quis libros integros cum omnibus suis partibus, prout in ecclesia catholica legi consueverunt et in veteri vulgata latina editione habentur, pro sacris et canonicis non susceperit, . . . anathema sit."*[43] Franzelin and Kleutgen argue that since the *Comma Ioanneum,* being an important "dogmatic text," must be regarded as an integral part of Sacred Scripture, and as it undoubtedly formed part of the ancient Latin Vulgate, its canonical authenticity is fully covered by the Tridentine decree.

If this claim were well founded, the whole discussion would have been irrevocably closed in the sixteenth century. But Franzelin and Kleutgen overshoot the mark. The Tridentine decree settles nothing either for or against the authenticity of the *Comma Ioanneum.* For, as Schäfer points out,[44] the decree is distinctly limited by the phrases "*prout in ecclesia catholica legi consueverunt,*" and "*et in veteri vulgata latina editione habentur.*" Of these limitations the former does not fully apply to the *Comma Ioanneum,* and the latter can not affect the official edition of the Vulgate issued in 1592. Of the earlier editions many were notoriously without the *Comma.* Consequently, the clause "*omnibus suis partibus*" is not strictly applicable to 1 John V, 7. This argument is strengthened by the testimony

41 *De Deo Trino,* thes. 4.

42 *De Ipso Deo,* pp. 519 sqq.

43 Denzinger-Bannwart, *Enchiridion,* n. 784.

44 *Einleitung in das Neue Testament,* pp. 341 sqq., Paderborn 1898.

of the Fourth Lateran Council, which we have already quoted, to the effect that in the 13th century the *Comma Ioanneum* was found only in a few codices (*"in quibusdam codicibus invenitur"*). The fact that there still exist over fifty ancient manuscript codices of the Vulgate which lack the *Comma Ioanneum* is too remarkable to be brushed aside as irrelevant. The scientific aspect of the problem, therefore, is not touched by the Tridentine decree at all, and the *Comma* itself remains a doubtful text. Franzelin in another treatise admits this contention in principle.[45]

For the rest, it is plain that Rome does not wish to bolt the door to further critical research. Very soon after the Inquisition had promulgated its decree of Jan. 13, 1897, Cardinal Vaughan replied to a query from Mr. Wilfrid Ward: "I have ascertained from an excellent source that the decree of the Holy Office on the passage of the 'Three Witnesses,' which you refer to, is not intended to close the discussion on the authenticity of that text; the field of Biblical criticism is not touched by this decree." Availing himself of the liberty thus granted, Professor Karl Künstle, of the University of Freiburg in Baden, has lately attempted to throw new light on the origin of the *Comma*, and has succeeded in making it appear extremely probable that it was formulated by Priscillian, about A. D. 380, in the heretical wording: *"Et haec tria unum sunt in Christo Iesu,"* in support of his Sabellian Pan-Christism, and that it was recast in an orthodox mould by some

[45] *De Script. et Trad.*, ed. 4, p. 489, Romae 1896: *"Si de aliquo tali textu posset demonstrari, non esse ex veteri vulgata editione,"* he says, *"eius conformitas cum Scriptura primitiva non posset dici per decretum Concilii declarata. Qui ergo textum ita admittit vel non admittit, prout exstat vel non exstat in veteri vulgata editione, quae longo saeculorum usu in ecclesia probata est, is nihil agit contra decretum Concilii."*

Catholic theologian[46] (possibly pseudo-Vigilius of Tapsus) and inserted into the text of St. John's First Epistle by one "Peregrinus," who is believed to have been a monk named Bachiarius. The *Comma* is probably of Spanish origin.[47]

NOTE.—Our view of the controversy regarding the character of the decree of 1897 is confirmed by a declaration of the S. Congregation of June 2, 1927, printed in the *Documenta Ecclesiastica S. Scripturam Spectantia*, published by authority of the Biblical Commission (Romae, 1927, apud Librariam Vaticanam). The Declaration says: *"Decretum hoc latum est, ut coerceretur audacia privatorum doctorum ius sibi tribuentium authentiam commatis Ioannei aut penitus reiciendi aut ultimo iudicio saltem in dubium vocandi. Minime vero impedire voluit, quominus scriptores catholici rem plenius investigarent atque, argumentis hinc inde accurate perpensis, cum ea, quam rei gravitas requirit, moderatione et temperantia, in sententiam genuinitati contrariam inclinarent, modo profiterentur, se paratos esse stare iudicio Ecclesiae cui a Iesu Christo munus demandatum est, Sacras Literas non solum interpretandi, sed etiam fideliter custodiendi."* (Denzinger-Bannwart-Umberg, *Enchiridion*, 16th and 17th ed., n. 2198.)

READINGS: — *Scheeben, *Dogmatik*, Vol. I, §107 (Wilhelm-Scannell, *Manual*, I, pp. 265 sqq.).— Oswald, *Dogmatische Theologie*, Vol. II: Trinitätslehre, §3, Paderborn 1888.— J. Lebreton, *Les Origines du Dogme de la Trinité*, pp. 207 sqq., 524 sqq., Paris 1910.—IDEM, *Le Dieu Vivant: La Révélation de la S. Trinité dans le Nouveau Testament*, Paris 1919.—Brown, Stephen J., S. J., "The Dogma of the Trinity in the Synoptic Gospels," in the *American Ecclesiastical Review*, Sixth Series, Vol. II (LII), No. 5, May 1915, pp. 513–523. Other bibliographical references in the footnotes.

46 "Whether the celebrated passage . . . be genuine or not," says Newman, "it is felicitously descriptive of the Ante-Nicene tradition. . . ." *Tracts Theol. and Eccles.*, p. 159.

47 K. Künstle, *Das "Comma Ioanneum" auf seine Herkunft untersucht*, Freiburg 1905; summarized by W. L. Sullivan, C. S. P., in the *New York Review*, Vol. II (1906), No. 2, pp. 175–188. Cfr. also Chr. Pesch, S. J., *Praelect. Dogmat.*, 3rd ed., t. II, pp. 255 sqq., Friburgi 1906. Künstle's supposition that the *Comma* was invented by Priscillian himself is combatted by E. C. Babut, *Priscillien et le Priscillianisme*, pp. 267 sqq., Paris 1909. Other references may be found in Cornely's *Introd. in Utriusque Testamenti Libros Sacros*, Vol. III, pp. 668 sqq., Paris 1886.

SECTION 3

NEW TESTAMENT TEXTS TREATING OF THE DIVINE PERSONS SEVERALLY

In demonstrating the dogma of the Most Holy Trinity from those texts of Sacred Scripture which treat of the Divine Persons severally, we shall have to establish three distinct truths: (1) The *reality* of each Divine Person in contradistinction to mere personification; (2) the *non-coincidence* of each Person with the others, in contradistinction to the Sabellian heresy which confuses them; and (3) the *Divinity* of each Person, in opposition to the Arian and Macedonian doctrine that the Son or the Holy Ghost is a creature.

As "Logos" is manifestly synonymous with Son of God, and "Paraclete" with Holy Ghost, there cannot be five Divine Persons, but only three. To establish the hypostatic difference of these three is the purpose of the first two members of this argument, while the third shows forth the absolute unity of the Divine Nature possessed by the three Persons of the Blessed Trinity in common.

The most important part of our task in this Section is to establish the true Divine Sonship of Jesus Christ, a conception which fully harmonizes with the dogma of the Blessed Trinity and sets forth with great clearness its two fundamental marks, *viz.:* Trinity and Unity. For, as Gossler pertinently observes, "Belief in, and knowledge of, the Triune God is conditioned upon belief in, and knowledge of, the Son of God."[1] The combined results of exegetical research ultimately lead to the dogma of a real Trinity of Persons in one divine and indivisible Monad.

ARTICLE I

OF GOD THE FATHER

1. God's Fatherhood in the Figurative Sense of the Term.—The Biblical use of the name "Father" indicates that He to whom it is applied is a real person. It also proves His Divinity. But it does not necessarily argue that He is a father in the strict sense of the term, or that He is the "first" in a group of three Divine Persons.

There is a human fatherhood which is merely analogical and figurative.[2] Similarly Holy Scripture often refers to the Godhead, *i. e.*, the whole Blessed Trinity, as "Father" in a purely moral or metaphorical sense. Thus God is in a certain sense the Father of His creatures by the act of creation and the fact of His Divine Providence. Cfr. Job XXXVIII, 28: "God . . . the father of rain" (*"pater pluviae," i. e., auctor*

1 *Lehrb. d. kath. Dogmatik,* I, 2, p. 133, Ratisbon 1874.

2 Take for example the relation denoted by such terms as stepfather, father confessor, father of the Church.

pluviae). Hebr. XII, 9: "The father of spirits (*pater spirituum*)." He is called in a special manner "Father of men," or Father of the human race, because He created humankind out of pure benevolence and with paternal solicitude provides for their needs.[3] In the Old Testament Jehovah's relation to His Chosen People formed the basis of a particularly cordial and intimate kinship, which might well be styled fatherhood. Cfr. Deut. XXXII, 6: "*Numquid non ipse est Pater tuus, qui possedit te et fecit et creavit te* — Is not he thy father, that hath possessed thee, and made thee, and created thee?" Jer. XXXI, 9: "*Quia factus sum Israeli Pater et Ephraim primogenitus meus est* — For I am a father to Israel, and Ephraim is my first-born." It is a proof of the depth of feeling and the keen insight which distinguishes the Aryan nations that, though deprived of the benefits of supernatural Revelation, they fixed upon fatherhood as the characteristic note of God. Such appellations as the Sanskrit *Dyaus Pitar,* the Greek Ζεὺς πατήρ, and the Latin *Iupiter,* indicate that God impressed them above all else as the Father of men.

God's supernatural fatherhood with regard to man is related to the natural fatherhood of which we have just spoken, as light is related to shadow, or as being to nothingness. From the purely natural point of view God is our master rather than our father, and we are His slaves rather than His children.[4] But sanctifying grace elevates us to the supernatural rank of "children of God," inasmuch as it gives us "power to be made the sons of God," if we "believe in his name" and are

3 Cfr. Pohle-Preuss, *God: His Knowability, Essence, and Attributes*, pp. 260 sqq.

4 Cfr. Gal. IV, 7.

"born of God."[5] Rom. VIII, 15: "*Non enim accepistis spiritum servitutis iterum in timore, sed accepistis spiritum adoptionis filiorum, in quo clamamus: Abba, Pater* — For you have not received the spirit of bondage again in fear, but you have received the spirit of adoption of sons, whereby we cry: Abba (Father)." 1 Cor. VIII, 6: "Yet to us there is but one God, the Father (εἷς Θεός, ὁ πατήρ)." It is in this sense that we daily pray: "Our Father, who art in Heaven."[6]

2. God's Fatherhood in the Strict Sense of the Term.—Besides and above the figurative paternity of God, there is peculiar to Him another and higher fatherhood. This is based not on His (natural or supernatural) relations to His creatures, but on a mysterious vital process immanent in the Deity. Revelation tells us that God has from all eternity begotten a Son of the same substance with Himself, the "*unigenitus Filius, qui est in sinu Patris.*"[7] This physical, or, more correctly speaking, metaphysical, divine Sonship must have for its necessary correlative in the Godhead a true Fatherhood in the proper sense of the term. Hence the name "Father" is applied to God as a *nomen proprium,* or proper name, and it follows with logical necessity that there is a First Person in the Godhead. For, being a pure spirit, God the Father can have a natural, coessential son

5 John I, 12 sq.

6 Matth. VI, 9. In this as well as in many other Scriptural passages, "Father" is used merely as a *nomen appellativum s. commune.*

7 John I, 18.

(*filius naturalis*) only in so far as, by virtue of eternal generation, He communicates the fulness of His Divine Nature to a Second Person, who must in consequence be the true Son of God, and therefore Himself God. Cfr. 2 Pet. I, 17: "*Accipiens enim a Deo Patre honorem et gloriam, voce delapsa ad eum huiuscemodi a magnifica gloria: Hic est Filius meus dilectus, in quo mihi complacui, ipsum audite* — For he received from God the Father honor and glory: this voice coming down to him from the excellent glory: This is my beloved Son, in whom I am well pleased; hear ye him." No one felt the force of this argument more keenly than the unbelieving Jews. Cfr. John V, 18: "*Propterea ergo magis quaerebant eum Iudaei interficere, quia non solum solvebat sabbatum, sed et Patrem suum dicebat Deum, aequalem se faciens Deo* (πατέρα ἴδιον ἔλεγε τὸν Θεόν, ἴσον ἑαυτὸν ποιῶν τῷ Θεῷ) — Hereupon therefore the Jews sought the more to kill him, because he did not only break the sabbath, but also said God was his Father, making himself equal to God."

The sacred writers frequently emphasize God's peculiar and singular Paternity, and quite consistently depict it as the pattern and exemplar of all creatural fatherhood. Cfr. 2 Cor. I, 3: "*Benedictus Deus et Pater Domini nostri Iesu Christi* — Blessed be the God and Father of our Lord

Jesus Christ." Eph. III, 14 sq.: *"Flecto genua mea ad Patrem Domini nostri Iesu Christi, ex quo [scil. Patre] omnis paternitas in coelis et in terra nominatur* — I bow my knees to the Father of our Lord Jesus Christ, of whom all paternity in heaven and earth is named."

This inner-divine Paternity cannot be predicated of the Divine Nature or Essence as such— for the Divine Essence neither begets nor is begotten. Hence it must consist in a relative opposition between the Father and the Son. Consequently, the Father is a Person distinct from the Son; and inasmuch as paternity is notionally prior to sonship, He is the First Person of the Blessed Trinity.

It is to be noted that the Antitrinitarians never denied that the Father is a real person, or that He is true God. What they disputed was that the Father is the *First* Person of the Godhead. And in this they were quite consistent; for had they admitted that proposition, they would have been forced to admit also that there is a *Second* Person, namely, the Divine Son. It is this truth we now proceed to demonstrate from Holy Scripture.

READINGS: — On the theology of the Father, cfr. Heinrich, *Dogmat. Theologie,* 2nd ed., Vol. IV, pp. 139 sqq., Mainz 1885; Oswald, *Trinitätslehre,* § 4; Simar, *Dogmatik,* 4th ed., Vol. I, pp. 228 sqq., Freiburg 1899; Fr. H. Chase, *The Lord's Prayer in the Early Church,* Cambridge 1891. Also S. Thom., *S. Theol.,* 1a, qu. 33.

ARTICLE 2

OF GOD THE SON

In the sublime text John I, 14: "Καὶ ὁ Λόγος σὰρξ ἐγένετο — And the Word was made flesh," the dogma of the Blessed Trinity and the dogmatic teaching of the Church in regard to Jesus Christ run together into one. For this reason nearly all Scriptural passages that can be cited in proof of Christ's being the Only-begotten Son of God likewise offer solid arguments for the dogma that He is both the true Son of God and the Divine Logos, and consequently the Second Person of the Godhead. It will be sufficient to show, therefore, in this division of our treatise, (1) that Christ is the true Son of God, (2) that He is very God, and (3) that He is the Divine Logos. There is no need of a special demonstration to prove that Christ is a real person and not a mere personification.

A. Christ's Divine Sonship

1. THE TERM "SON OF GOD" AS USED IN A METAPHORICAL SENSE.—If, as we have shown, God can assume towards His rational creatures the relation of a father, these creatures must be capable of becoming, in a certain sense, sons or children of God.

a) Taking the term in a higher sense, man can become a son of God only in the supernatural order, as we shall show in the treatise on Grace, where we speak of Justification. Cfr. Matth. V, 9: "Blessed are the peacemakers: for they shall be called the children of God." But, as Holy Scripture clearly intimates, this supernatural sonship of the creature is not a sonship in the strict sense of the term; it is based on adoption.[8] Though this *filiatio adoptiva* is sharply contrasted with natural sonship,[9] inasmuch as the Bible traces it to the fact of the creature's "regeneration of God,"[10] nay, even calls it a participation in the Divine Nature,[11] it is to be remarked that the last-mentioned two notions never lose their accidental and analogous character, because they are conditioned by sanctifying grace, of which the *filiatio adoptiva* is the chief formal effect.

b) The important question we have here to solve is whether "Son of God" is applied to Christ merely as an analogous term. In that case, though He would still outrank God's other adopted children, Jesus would be no more than a *primus inter pares*. That He outranks all other men appears clearly enough from the fact that He alone is called in Holy Scripture, ὁ υἱὸς τοῦ Θεοῦ,— *the* Son of God. There are texts in which mere creatures are referred to as "sons of God," but in all these texts the subject is either in the plural,[12] or it is a col-

8 *Adoptio filiorum*, υἱοθεσία. On supernatural adoption, see Sollier in the *Catholic Encyclopedia*, I, 148 sqq.

9 *Filiatio naturalis.*

10 *Regeneratio*, Gr. παλιγγενεσία. Cfr. J. Pohle, *s. v.* "Wiedergeburt," in Herder's *Kirchenlexikon*, XII, 1468 sqq., Freiburg 1901.

11 Cfr. 2 Pet. I, 4: "θείας κοινωνοὶ φύσεως."

12 Cfr. Job I, 6: "*Filii Dei*," Hebr. אֱלֹהִים ; Rom. VIII, 15: "*Accepistis spiritum adoptionis filiorum Dei* — You have received the spirit of adoption of sons."

lective term,[13] or an indefinite singular really amounting to a plural.[14] The only passage which seems to offer an exception is 2 Kings VII, 15: "*Ego ero ei* [*scil. Salomoni*] *in patrem, et ipse erit mihi in filium* — I will be to him [Solomon] a father, and he shall be to me a son," but St. Paul expressly interprets this passage as referring typically to Christ: "*Cui dixit aliquando angelorum: . . . Ego ero illi in patrem, et ipse erit mihi in filium?* — For to which of the angels hath he said at any time: . . . I will be to him a father, and he shall be to me a son?"[15] In the light of these texts no one can deny that Christ is the Son of God in a higher sense than any angel or man. But there still remains a doubt as to whether *Filius Dei* is applied to Him as a proper name, or merely as an appellative; that is to say, whether He is the Son of God in the strict or merely in a figurative sense, *i. e.*, by adoption.

2. Christ the Son of God in the Strict Sense of the Term.—The Socinians and the Rationalists, Hugo Grotius among others, allege that *Filius Dei* is merely an official title of the Messias, bearing no intrinsic relation to any divine filiation; in other words, that Christ, in virtue of His supernatural birth from the Blessed Virgin Mary,[16] is called "Son of God" in a higher, though not in an essentially different sense than other rational creatures. The French Abbé Al-

13 Exod. IV, 22: "*Filius meus primogenitus Israel* — Israel is my son, my firstborn."

14 Ecclus. IV, 11: "*Et eris tu* [*scil. misericors*] *velut filius altissimi obediens* — And thou shalt be as the obedient son of the most High."

15 Heb. I, 5.

16 Modern Rationalists notoriously also deny the Virgin Birth.

fred Loisy adopts this Rationalist error when he writes: "The title 'Son of God' was accepted by the Jews, by the Disciples, and by the Saviour Himself as a synonym for 'Messias.'" [17] True, "Son of God" was the official title of the Messias; but it was a title based upon a reality, *i. e.*, Christ's Divine Sonship in the strict sense of the term. It is a mistake on the part of some Catholic theologians to concede the assertion of Rationalist exegetes that, while the true Divine Sonship of Jesus appears clearly enough from the Apostolic Letters and the Fourth Gospel, it cannot be proved from the Synoptics. The conduct of the Jews and our Saviour's own reiterated declarations, as recorded in the Gospels of St. Matthew, St. Mark, and St. Luke, clearly prove the contrary.

a) Though the Jews knew, and could not help knowing from their own sacred writings, that the future Messias would be God Himself, they were not accustomed to refer to Him of their own accord as "God," or "Son of God." They called Him either "son of David," [18] or "King of Israel," [19] or "the Prophet," [20] or "the Messias," that is Christ (מָשִׁיחַ = χριστός). Nevertheless

17 *L'Évangile et L'Église*, p. 62, Paris 1902. Against Loisy see M. Lepin's scholarly work *Christ and the Gospel, or Jesus the Messiah and Son of God*, Authorized English edition, Philadelphia 1910. See especially pp. 320 sqq. as bearing on the point here under consideration.

18 Cfr. Matth. IX, 27; XII, 23; XX, 30; XXI, 9; Mark XI, 10.

19 Matth. XXVII, 42.

20 John I, 21: VI, 14; VII, 40.

they logically concluded from Christ's repeated references to Himself as Son of God, that He claimed consubstantiality with the Godhead, in other words, true Divinity.[21] Similarly the Synoptics, by weaving into their story sayings that can apply to none other than the Son of God in the strictest sense of the term, or by accompanying their profession of faith in the "true Son of God" with a latreutic act of adoration, plainly demonstrate that they mean to apply the name to Jesus in its proper, not in a figurative, sense. When He was baptized in the Jordan,[22] "there came a voice from heaven, saying: This is my beloved Son, in whom I am well pleased." The Greek text has: Οὗτός ἐστιν ὁ υἱός μου ὁ ἀγαπητός, repeating the definite article to emphasize the unique rôle of the Son. Before the institution, or, more correctly, before the promise of the primacy, Peter had first to profess his faith in the Divine Sonship of Jesus. Matth. XVI, 15 sqq.: "Whom do you say that I am? Simon Peter answered and said: Thou art Christ, the Son of the living God (σὺ εἶ ὁ Χριστός, ὁ υἱὸς τοῦ Θεοῦ τοῦ ζῶντος)." Like the other Apostles, Peter had long before believed in the Messianic mission and dignity of his Master; hence his profession of faith as recorded in Matth. XVI, 16, can only

21 John V, 18; X, 33.

22 Matth. III, 13 sqq.; Mark I, 9 sqq.; Luke III, 21 sqq.

mean: "Thou art not only the Christ, *i. e.*, the Messias, but likewise the true Son of God." This view is confirmed by our Saviour's reply: "*Beatus es, Simon Bar Iona, quia caro et sanguis non revelavit tibi, sed Pater meus, qui in coelis est* — Blessed art thou, Simon Bar-Jona, because flesh and blood [*i. e.*, human reason] hath not revealed it to thee, but my Father who is in heaven." That is to say, Peter's knowledge and his profession of faith in Christ's Divine Sonship was owing to a direct revelation and the grace of faith.[23] When the Disciples "in the midst of the sea" saw Jesus stretching out His hand and saving Peter, who at His Master's bidding had ventured upon the angry waves, they were overpowered by the glorious miracle and "adored Him, saying: Indeed thou art the son of God."[24]

b) This argument is supported by Christ's own testimony. The Synoptics tell us as distinctly as do SS. John and Paul, that not only did He always and everywhere assert His Divine Sonship, but He finally sealed it with His blood. When Caiphas adjured Him by the living God, saying: "Tell us if thou be the Christ the son of God,"[25] Jesus solemnly replied: "Thou hast

[23] Cfr. Schanz, *Kommentar über das Evangelium des hl. Matthäus*, p. 375, Mainz 1879.

[24] Matth. XIV, 33: "*Qui autem in navicula erant, venerunt et adoraverunt eum dicentes: Vere Filius Dei es* (ἀληθῶς Θεοῦ υἱὸς εἶ)."

[25] Εἰ σὺ εἶ ὁ Χριστός, ὁ υἱὸς τοῦ Θεοῦ.

said it."[26] And when, in confirmation of His oath, the Saviour significantly assured His questioner that he would yet see Him sitting on the right hand of the power of God, and coming in the clouds of heaven to judge mankind, "the high priest rent his garments, saying: He hath blasphemed."[27] In asserting His Divine Sonship, therefore, Christ asserted His Divinity, and the Sanhedrin, regarding this assertion as blasphemous, acted with perfect consistency when they condemned Him to an ignominious death. According to the Gospel of St. Luke, they "brought him into their council, saying: If thou be the Christ, tell us — *Si tu es Christus, dic nobis,*"[28] and when Jesus had assured them that He would sit "on the right hand of the power of God," they asked Him: "Art thou then the Son of God? (σὺ οὖν εἶ ὁ υἱὸς τοῦ Θεοῦ) ?" and He firmly and definitely answered: "You say that I am (ὑμεῖς λέγετε, ὅτι ἐγώ εἰμι)." Whereupon He was led to Pilate, and they accused Him of claiming that He was "Christ the king,"[29] and that "He made Himself the Son of God."[30] It is not too much to say, therefore, that Christ laid down His life for the truth of His solemn affirmation that He was really and truly "the Son of God." The

26 Σὺ εἶπας = Yes.

27 Matth. XXVI, 63 sqq.

28 Luke XXII, 66 sq.

29 Luke XXIII, 2: "*Dixit se Christum regem esse.*"

30 John XIX, 7: "*Filium Dei se fecit.*"

Fourth Gospel and the Epistles of St. Paul verify, continue, and complete the story of the Synoptics.[31]

3. THE TEACHING OF ST. JOHN AND ST. PAUL ON CHRIST'S DIVINE SONSHIP.—The Saviour's favorite disciple, the meek and gentle John, both in character and temperament differed radically from the fiery Paul; yet their teaching in regard to Christ agrees in every essential detail, and it may be truly said that the Johannine Christology is characterized by a Pauline depth of thought, while the teaching of St. Paul has a distinctly Johannean tinge. Both Apostles are at one in affirming that the Divine Sonship of Christ is a true sonship in the strict sense of the term, and therefore essentially different from the sonship predicated of angels and men.

a) The epithets applied to Jesus by both SS. John and Paul are with quite evident intent so chosen as to exclude absolutely the "*sensus improprius.*"

Both call Christ His Heavenly Father's "own Son" (*Filius proprius*, ἴδιος υἱός). Rom. VIII, 32: "*Qui proprio Filio suo* (τοῦ ἰδίου υἱοῦ) *non pepercit*—He spared not even his own Son." John V, 18: "*Patrem suum* (πατέρα ἴδιον) *dicebat Deum, aequalem se faciens Deo*—Jesus also said God was his Father, making himself

31 Cfr. B. Bartmann, *Das Himmelreich und sein König nach den Synoptikern*, pp. 107 sqq., Paderborn 1904; M. Lepin, *Christ and the Gospel*, pp. 394 sqq.

equal to God." He is the Father's "beloved Son," into whose kingdom we are translated.[32] He is "the only begotten Son, Who is in the bosom of the Father — *Unigenitus Filius* (ὁ μονογενὴς υἱός), *qui est in sinu Patris,*" [33] the Son begotten by the eternal Father.[34] This note of unicity, which is especially accentuated by St. John, plainly implies that the Father has no other son but Christ.[35] Consequently Christ is truly the Son of God in precisely the same sense in which God is "true God." Cfr. 1 John V, 20: "*Scimus quoniam Filius Dei* (ὁ υἱὸς τοῦ Θεοῦ) *venit, et dedit nobis sensum, ut cognoscamus verum Deum* (τὸν ἀληθινὸν Θεόν) *et simus in vero Filio eius* — And we know that the Son of God is come: and he hath given us understanding that we may know the true God, and may be in his true Son."

b) These texts appear still more significant if collated with certain other Scriptural passages, which expressly declare that the Divine Sonship of Christ is a sonship in the strict and proper sense of the term.

If there existed any higher beings who, as "sons of God," might claim precedence of Christ, they would certainly be the angels of Heaven. Now we have the distinct teaching of St. Paul that the angels are bound to adore Christ as "the Son of God" and "the first-born of the Father." Hebr. I, 5 sq.: "*Cui enim dixit aliquando angelorum: Filius meus es tu, ego hodie genui te? . . . Et cum iterum introducit primogenitum* (πρωτό-

32 Cfr. Col. I, 13: "*Qui nos transtulit in regnum Filii dilectionis suae*" (a Hebraism for: "*Filii dilecti sui*"; cfr. 2 Pet. I, 17).

33 John I, 18; cfr. Lepin, *op. cit.*, pp. 330 sqq.

34 Hebr. V, 5. Cfr. Ps. II, 7.

35 Cfr. John I, 14; III, 16, 18; 1 John IV, 9.

τοκον) *in orbem terrae, dicit: Et adorent eum* [*sc. Christum*] *omnes angeli Dei*—For to which of the angels hath he said at any time: Thou art my Son, today I have begotten thee. . . . And when he again bringeth in the first begotten into the world, he saith: And let all the angels of God adore him." Among the many favored children of grace, especially the prophets and the Lord's anointed, whom Sacred Scripture sometimes calls "sons of God," or even "gods," because of their exalted dignity, in the opinion of the Jews and of St. Paul none was greater than Jehovah's favorite servant, Moses.[36] And yet St. Paul, comparing him with Christ, says that Moses is merely a "faithful servant in the house of God," while Jesus is "as the Son in his own house."[37] It is only in the light of these facts that we are able fully to appreciate the further teaching of SS. John and Paul, that, as the heavenly Fatherhood of God is the prototype of all created paternity, so the Divine Sonship of Christ is the exemplar of all derived or adoptive sonship. Cfr. John I, 12: "*Dedit eis potestatem filios Dei fieri, his qui credunt in nomine eius* [*scil. unigeniti a Patre*]—He gave them power to be made the sons of God, to them that believe in his name" (*i. e.*, in the name of the Only-begotten of the Father. John I, 14). Gal. IV, 4 sq.: "*Misit Deus Filium suum* (τὸν υἱὸν αὐτοῦ) . . . *ut adoptionem filiorum* (τὴν υἱοθεσίαν) *reciperemus*—God sent his son . . . that we might receive the adoption of sons."

c) The teaching of St. John culminates in the notion of the Divine Logos; that of St. Paul in

36 Cfr. Deut. XXXIV, 10; Heb. III, 1 sqq.

37 Heb. III, 5 sq.: "*Et Moyses quidem fidelis erat in tota domo eius* [*sc. Dei*] *tamquam famulus* (ὡς θεράπων), . . . *Christus vero tamquam Filius in domo sua* (ὡς υἱὸς ἐπὶ τὸν οἶκον αὐτοῦ)."

the cognate conception of Christ as the image of God and splendor of His glory. Cfr. 2 Cor. IV, 4: *"Imago Dei* (εἰκὼν Θεοῦ);" Col. I, 15: *"Imago Dei invisibilis."* With an unmistakable allusion to St. John's teaching on the Divine Logos, the Apostle of the Gentiles defines this "image of the invisible God" as *splendor gloriae* (ἀπαύγασμα τῆς δόξης) and as *figura substantiae eius* (χαρακτὴρ τῆς ὑποστάσεως αὐτοῦ)—"the brightness of the glory of God" and "the figure of his substance." [38]

Of these two terms the former expresses the consubstantiality (*homoousia*), the latter the personal self-existence of the Son side by side with the Father. Both these truths are also taught in the Fourth Gospel: [39] "The Word was God" and "the Word was with God." That St. Paul [40] employs the phrases "brightness of his glory" and "figure of his substance" not in any creatural sense, but absolutely, is made manifest by the second part of the sentence in which they occur.[41] There he ascribes to Christ none but divine attributes: "*Portansque omnia verbo virtutis suae, purgationem peccatorum faciens, sedet ad dexteram maiestatis in excelsis*—Upholding all things by the word of his power, making purgation of sins, [Christ] sitteth on the right hand of the majesty on high." [42] Therefore Christ is the "image of the Divine Substance" in so far as He is strictly and truly the "Son of God," which further

38 Heb. I, 3.

39 John I, 1.

40 Heb. I, 3.

41 On the terms ἀπαύγασμα and χαρακτήρ, cfr. Lebreton, *Les Origines du Dogme de la Trinité*, p. 348.

42 Heb. I, 3.

appears from Heb. I, 2: "*Diebus istis* [*Deus*] *locutus est nobis in Filio, . . . per quem fecit et saecula*—In these days [God] hath spoken to us by his Son, . . . by whom he also made the world."[43] While the term ἀπαύγασμα τῆς δόξης represents the Father as "light," and the Son as the reflection of this light (for this reason He is called *lumen de lumine* as well as *Deus de Deo*),[44] the locution χαρακτὴρ τῆς ὑποστάσεως αὐτοῦ complements the former by emphasizing the independent subsistence of the Son of God (*i. e.,* Christ) in His relative opposition to God the Father,—a point which the Fathers of the Church did not fail to insist upon in their early conflicts with Photinus and Sabellius.

d) The Scriptural teaching so far developed furnishes us with a key for interpreting those numerous texts which speak of the primogeniture of Christ.

The "only begotten Son" (*unigenitus,* μονογενής) alone is and always remains the "firstborn" (*primogenitus,* πρωτότοκος).[45] No creature can claim to be His equal in birth or dignity. St. Paul's teaching on this head is most clearly developed in his Epistle to the Colossians. There he distinguishes in Christ a twofold "right of the firstborn": the one divine, the other human; the former based upon the title of creation, redemption, and final

43 Cfr. John I, 10, 3.

44 Cfr. W. Humphrey, S. J., "*His Divine Majesty,*" pp. 433 sq., London 1897.

45 "Πρωτότοκος is not an exact translation of *Primogenitus,* though Homer, as Petavius says, may use τίκτω for *gigno.* It is never used in Scripture for Only-begotten. We never read there of the First-born of God, or of the Father; but First-born of the creation, whether the original creation or the new."—Newman, "Causes of the Rise and Successes of Arianism" in *Tracts Theol. and Eccles.,* p. 204 n., London 1895.

end; the latter on Christ's prerogative as the mystic head and reconciler of His Church, which consists of sinful men. From the first-mentioned viewpoint He is "*primogenitus omnis creaturae* (πρωτότοκος πάσης κτίσεως)"; from the point of view mentioned in the second place, He is "*primogenitus ex mortuis* (πρωτότοκος ἐκ τῶν νεκρῶν)."[46] In both respects Christ is no mere creature, but very God. For like unto the Hypostatic Wisdom of the Old Testament,[47] He possesses, as "the firstborn of every creature," an eternal, divine existence, and is equipped with creative power, whereby He has created and upholds the universe together with the realm of angels.[48] As the "firstborn from the dead," on the other hand, He is "the head of the body [of] the church," absolute "beginning," the one "who holds in all things the primacy," the possessor of "the fullness of all perfection," and lastly "the reconciling mediator through the blood of His cross, of the things that are on the earth and the things that are in heaven,"—all of which can be true only on the supposition that Christ as the Firstborn is at the same time the true and genuine Son of God, and therefore Himself God.[49] According to St. Paul, therefore, Christ's human primogeniture is based upon His divine primogeniture, which in turn coincides with His unigeniture (*primogenitus* = *unigenitus*).[50]

4. THE CONSUBSTANTIALITY OF THE SON OF GOD WITH GOD.—In the Scriptural texts we

46 Col. I, 13 sqq. On the term πρωτότοκος see Lebreton, *op. cit.*, pp. 302 sqq.

47 Cfr. Ecclus. XXIV, 5: "*Primogenita ante omnem creaturam* — Wisdom, the firstborn before all creatures."

48 Col. I, 15–17.

49 Col. I, 18–20.

50 Cfr. Heb. I, 5 sqq.; Apoc. I, 5. Cfr. J. Lebreton, *Les Origines du Dogme de la Trinité*, pp. 302 sqq., 397 sqq.

have cited, the Divinity which is communicated to the Son by His divine γέννησις from the Father is not founded upon Ditheism, or the existence of two coequal gods, but on the numerical identity of the Divine Nature.

This conclusion, which flows so manifestly from the monotheistic character of both the Old and the New Testament, is expressly confirmed in the Epistle to the Philippians,[51] where St. Paul draws a neat distinction between the "form of a servant" (*forma servi*, μορφὴ δούλου) and the "form of God" (*forma Dei*, μορφὴ Θεοῦ). By the former he means the truly human, and by the latter the truly divine nature of Jesus Christ, in the possession of which the Son of God is consubstantial or coequal with God (*aequalis Deo*, ἴσα Θεῷ). "*Qui* [*scil. Christus*] *cum in forma Dei esset, non rapinam arbitratus est, esse se aequalem Deo, sed semetipsum exinanivit formam servi accipiens . . . et habitu inventus ut homo* — Christ Jesus, being in the form of God, thought it not robbery to be equal with God: but emptied himself, taking the form of a servant . . . and in habit found as a man."—"*Forma servi*" in this context can mean nothing else than the human nature which the Son of God "assumed,"[52] and in virtue of which He was "found as a man." "*Forma Dei*," on the other hand, plainly signifies the Divine Nature, which Christ possessed before he "took the form of a servant" and before He "emptied Himself," and which to claim He did not need to think robbery, *i. e.*, unjust usurpation. It is immaterial whether we take "*rapina*"

51 Phil. II, 5 sqq.

52 John I, 14: "And the Word was made flesh, and dwelt among us."

in its active sense as "*actus rapiendi,*" or objectively as "*res rapta.*"[53]

B. The Divinity of Christ

If Christ is truly the Son of God, no special argument is required to show that He is Divine. Yet as Holy Scripture, aside from those passages which prove Christ's Divine Sonship, also contains a number of texts which expressly assert His Divinity, it will be well to study these separately and to show how they confirm our thesis. We shall divide them into three distinct groups.

1. THE DIVINE ATTRIBUTES OF CHRIST.—A being that possesses divine attributes and performs divine acts, is truly divine. Christ, according to the New Testament Revelation, possesses divine attributes and performs divine acts. Consequently He is true God. The major premise of this syllogism, being merely a descriptive definition of God, needs no proof. From out of the profusion of Scriptural texts which can be cited in support of the minor, we select the following.

[53] Cfr. St. Chrysostom, *Hom. in Philip.*, 7, n. 2: "*Hoc, inquam, esse aequalem Deo, non ex rapina habuit, sed a natura, quamobrem seipsum exinanivit.*" For a full elucidation of Phil. II, 5 sqq., see K. J. Müller, *Brief des hl. Paulus an die Philipper*, Freiburg 1899.—The dogma of Christ's Divine Sonship is ably defended against the attacks of the Modernists by M. Lepin, *Christ and the Gospel* (English tr.), pp. 263 sqq., Philadelphia 1910.

a) The New Testament predicates self-existence, which is the fundamental attribute of the Godhead, in the same terms of Christ in which the Old Testament predicates it of Jehovah. Jesus said to St. John:[54] "*Noli timere, ego sum primus et novissimus* (ὁ πρῶτος καὶ ὁ ἔσχατος) *et vivus et fui mortuus* — Fear not, I am the first and the last, and alive, and was dead."[55] As *causa prima* the αὐτούσιος is *per se* and by intestine necessity the *finis ultimus* of all creation. Now Christ says of Himself:[56] "*Ego sum α et ω, primus et novissimus, principium et finis* — I am Alpha and Omega, the first and the last, the beginning and the end." Similarly St. Paul:[57] "Τὰ πάντα δι' αὐτοῦ καὶ εἰς αὐτὸν ἔκτισται — All things were created by him and in him."

Because of His aseity God is incomprehensible to the created intellect. Christ shares in this incomprehensibility. On the other hand He possesses a truly comprehensive knowledge of the Father. Cfr. Matth. XI, 27: "*Nemo novit* (ἐπιγινώσκει) *Filium nisi Pater, . . . neque Patrem quis novit* (ἐπιγινώσκει) *nisi Filius, et cui voluerit Filius revelare* — No one knoweth the Son but the Father: neither doth any one know the Father but the Son, and he to whom it shall please the Son to reveal him." Note that the verb ἐπιγινώσκειν is stronger than simple γινώσκειν; it denotes that comprehensive knowledge which is proper to the infinite God.[58]

b) Chief among God's transcendental attributes of being is His absolute truth. Now Christ is the absolute, living Truth, as He Himself testifies: "*Ego sum via et veritas et vita* (ἡ ἀλήθεια καὶ ἡ ζωή) — I am the

54 Apoc. I, 17 sqq.

55 Cfr. Apoc. II, 8. For comparison also read Is. XLI, 4: "*Ego* יְהוָה *primus et novissimus ego sum* — I the Lord, I am the first and the last."

56 Apoc. XXII, 13.

57 Col. I, 16.

58 Cfr. 1 Cor. XIII, 12

way, and the truth, and the life."[59] This (truth-) life is communicated to Him in virtue of His eternal generation by the Father; hence it is a divine life, and as such self-existent in character. John V, 26: "*Sicut enim Pater habet vitam in semetipso* (ἐν ἑαυτῷ), *sic dedit* [*i. e., generando communicavit*] *et Filio habere vitam in semetipso* (ἐν ἑαυτῷ) — For as the Father hath life in himself, so he hath given to the Son also to have life in himself." This process of communication, therefore, results in a differentiation, not of nature or essence, but of persons only. Cfr. 1 John I, 2: "*Annuntiamus vobis vitam aeternam* (τὴν ζωὴν τὴν αἰώνιον), *quae erat apud Patrem* (πρὸς τὸν πατέρα) *et apparuit nobis* — We declare unto you the life eternal, which was with the Father, and hath appeared to us." As the living truth, the Saviour must also be the author of life,[60] especially in the supernatural order of grace. Cfr. John XI, 25: "*Ego sum resurrectio et vita* (ἡ ζωή); *qui credit in me, etiam si mortuus fuerit, vivet* — I am the resurrection and the life: he that believeth in me, although he be dead, shall live." Again, "*Qui habet Filium, habet vitam* (τὴν ζωήν) — He that hath the Son, hath life."[61]

God's attributes of veracity and fidelity are rooted in His absolute truth. In this absolute sense Christ, too, is veracity itself; for He "testifieth" only "what he hath seen and heard" of His father in Heaven. Cfr. John III, 31 sq.: "*Qui de coelo venit, super omnes est. Et quod vidit et audivit, hoc testatur* — He that cometh from heaven, is above all. And what he hath seen and heard, that he testifieth." John VIII, 26: "*Qui me*

59 John XIV, 6.

60 Acts III, 15: "But the author of life (ὁ ἀρχηγὸς τῆς ζωῆς) you killed, whom God hath raised from the dead."

61 1 John V, 12.

misit, verax (ἀληθής) *est; et ego, quae audivi ab eo, haec loquor in mundo* — He that sent me is true: and the things I have heard of him, these same I speak in the world."

For this reason, too, He is absolute fidelity. Cfr. Matth. XXIV, 35: "Heaven and earth shall pass away, but my words shall not pass away." Apoc. XIX, 11: "*Fidelis et verax* — Faithful and true." Apoc. III, 14: "*Haec dicit Amen, testis fidelis et verax, qui est principium creaturae Dei* — These things saith the Amen, the faithful and true witness, who is the beginning of the creation of God."

Christ's substantial sanctity coincides with His ethical goodness and is based on His Divine Sonship. Cfr. Luke I, 35: "*Quod nascetur ex te Sanctum, vocabitur Filius Dei* — The Holy which shall be born of thee shall be called the Son of God." [62] In virtue of the Hypostatic Union His divine sanctity overflows into the human race. Cfr. Heb. VII, 26: "*Talis enim decebat, ut nobis esset pontifex, sanctus, innocens, impollutus, segregatus a peccatoribus et excelsior coelis factus* — For it was fitting that we should have such a high priest, holy, innocent, undefiled, separated from sinners, and made higher than the heavens." [63]

c) Among God's categorical attributes of being is omnipotence, which in the natural order manifests itself in the creation and preservation of the universe, while in the supernatural sphere it works miracles by its own power. In both respects Christ has given irrefragable proofs of His Divinity. He is, in the first place, the creator and preserver of the universe. Col. I, 16 sq.:

62 Cfr. Apoc. III, 7: "*Sanctus et verus* — The Holy one and the True one."

63 This subject will be treated at length in Christology.

"*In ipso* (ἐν αὐτῷ) *condita sunt universa in coelis et in terra, visibilia et invisibilia, sive throni sive dominationes sive principatus sive potestates: omnia per ipsum* (δι' αὐτοῦ) *et in ipso* (εἰς αὐτόν) *creata sunt, et ipse est ante omnes* (πρὸ πάντων) *et omnia in ipso constant* — For in him were all things created in heaven and on earth, visible and invisible, whether thrones, or dominations, or principalities, or powers: all things were created by him and in him, and he is before all, and by him all things consist." This text contains three separate and distinct propositions: (1) All things were created *in* the Son; that is to say, according to the counsels of Christ and in virtue of His omnipotence. (2) All things were made through the Son (*per ipsum*), *i. e.*, the Son was not merely the instrument of creation, but its true creative cause.[64] (3) All things were made in reference to the Son (εἰς αὐτόν), that is to say, He is the final end of the whole created universe. Consequently He is true God, and as such "before all" (*ante omnes*) *i. e.*, eternal, and at the same time the preserver of the universe. Heb. I, 3: "*Portans omnia verbo virtutis suae* — Upholding all things by the word of his power." Holy Scripture throughout both Testaments regards the working of signs and miracles in one's own name and by one's own power as a sure proof of omnipotence. The miracles of Christ proceed from His own omnipotence, not from any derived or communicated power; — except in this sense that God the Father has communicated this power to Him as His Son by a truly divine γέννησις from everlasting. Cfr. John V, 19: "*Non potest Filius a se facere quidquam, nisi quod viderit Patrem facientem; quaecumque enim ille fecerit, haec et Filius similiter facit*

[64] Cfr. Heb. I, 2: "*Per quem fecit et saecula* — By whom also he made the world." Cfr. also Heb. I, 10.

— The Son cannot do any thing of himself, but what he seeth the Father doing: for what things soever he doth, these the Son also doth in like manner." In this sense Christ possesses the power of raising the dead. John V, 21: "*Sicut Pater suscitat mortuos et vivificat, sic et Filius, quos vult, vivificat* — For as the Father raiseth up the dead and giveth life: so the Son also giveth life to whom he will." Therefore He is able to say: "*Et ego resuscitabo eum* (ἀναστήσω αὐτὸν ἐγώ) *in novissimo die* — And I will raise him up in the last day." [65] When the leper adored him, Christ did not object. Matth. VIII, 2 sqq.: "*Et ecce leprosus veniens adorabat eum* (προσεκύνει αὐτῷ), *dicens: Domine, si vis, potes me mundare. Et extendens Iesus manum, tetigit eum dicens: Volo, mundare* — And behold a leper came and adored him, saying: Lord, if thou wilt, thou canst make me clean. And Jesus stretching forth his hand, touched him, saying: I will, be thou made clean." Christ's omnipotence is the source of the universal sovereignty to which He lays claim. As God alone is Lord of life and death, heaven and hell, so Christ holds "the keys of death and of hell." Apoc. I, 18: "*Et habeo claves mortis et inferni.*" [66] He is the παντοκράτωρ [67] to whom all creatures, including the angels, are subject,[68] and as such is "the Lord of lords, and King of kings." Apoc. XVII, 14: "*Agnus vincet illos, quoniam dominus dominorum est et rex regum.*" [69] As we have but one God the Father, so we have but one Lord Jesus Christ. 1 Cor. VIII, 6: "*Nobis tamen unus est Deus Pater, ex quo omnia et nos in illum, et unus Dominus* (εἷς κύριος) *Iesus Christus, per quem omnia et nos per ipsum* (δι' οὗ τὰ

65 John VI, 40.

66 Cfr. also Apoc. III, 7.

67 Apoc. I, 8.

68 1 Pet. III, 22.

69 Cfr. also Apoc. XIX, 16.

πάντα καὶ ἡμεῖς δι' αὐτοῦ) — Yet to us there is but one God, the Father, of whom are all things, and we unto him; and one Lord Jesus Christ, by whom are all things, and we by him."

Two other divine attributes not shared by any creature are absolute immutability, and eternity which flows therefrom. Both of these are ascribed by Holy Scripture to Christ. What the Psalmist says of the immutability of Jehovah,[70] "*Ipsi peribunt, tu autem permanes* — They shall perish, but thou remainest," St. Paul applies without limitation to Jesus.[71] That Christ is eternal can be deduced from the Scriptural teaching that He existed before time. John the Baptist confessed:[72] "He was before me (πρῶτός μου ἦν)," and Christ Himself confirmed this assertion by His solemn declaration:[73] "*Antequam Abraham fieret, ego sum* (πρὶν Ἀβραὰμ γενέσθαι, ἐγώ εἰμι) — Before Abraham was made, I am." St. Augustine commentates this text as follows: "*Non dixit: antequam Abraham esset, ego eram, sed: antequam Abraham fieret, qui nisi per me non fieret, ego sum. Neque hoc dixit: antequam Abraham fieret, ego factus sum. In principio enim fecit Deus coelum et terram; nam in principio erat Verbum. Antequam Abraham fieret, ego sum. Agnoscite creatorem, discernite creaturam* — He said not, Before Abraham *was*, I was; but, Before Abraham *was made* (and he could not be made but by Me), I am. Neither said he this: Before Abraham was made, I was made. For, In the beginning God created the heaven and the earth: namely, in the beginning was the Word. Before Abraham was made, I am. Acknowledge the Creator, discern the creature."[74] Cfr.

70 Ps. CI, 27 sqq.

71 Heb. I, 10 sqq.

72 John I, 15.

73 John VIII, 58.

74 *Tractatus in Ioa.*, 43, n. 17. Browne's translation, I, 586.

also the famous passage in Christ's prayer for His disciples:[75] *"Et nunc clarifica me tu, Pater, apud temetipsum claritate, quam habui prius, quam mundus esset, apud te* (τῇ δόξῃ, ᾗ εἶχον πρὸ τοῦ τὸν κόσμον εἶναι, παρὰ σοί)—And now glorify thou me, O Father, with thyself, with the glory which I had, before the world was, with thee." As Cardinal Toletus pertinently observes, this passage has reference to the divine glory which Christ enjoyed as God together with His Father from all eternity. Therefore His Ascension was merely a return to "where he was before,"[76] or, more correctly, where "He always is." Cfr. John III, 13: *"Nemo ascendit in coelum, nisi qui descendit de coelo, Filius hominis, qui est in coelo*—And no man hath ascended into heaven, but he that descendeth from heaven, the Son of man who is in heaven."[77] Hence for Christ to be "in Heaven" means to be "in the bosom of the Father," *i. e.*, to be the true Son of God from all eternity. Eternity for Him is merely the past, present, and future combined in an unchanging life. Heb. XIII, 8: *"Iesus Christus heri et hodie, ipse et in saecula*—Jesus Christ, yesterday, and to-day, and the same for ever."

In His relation to space, and to the world of pure spirits, Christ is endowed with omnipresence, and particularly with that power of indwelling in the souls of the just which is peculiar to God. St. Paul probably means to emphasize His omnipresence when he says:[78] *"Qui descendit, ipse est et qui ascendit super omnes coelos, ut impleret omnia* (ἵνα πληρώσῃ τὰ πάντα)—He that descendeth is the same also that ascended above all heavens, that he might fill all things;"—unless indeed

75 John XVII, 5.

76 John VI, 63: *"Ubi erat prius."*

77 Cfr. also John XVI, 28; I, 18.

78 Eph. IV, 10.

the phrase to "fill all things" is meant to indicate the fulfilment of the prophecies relating to Christ's Ascension. Cfr. John XIV, 23: "*Pater meus diliget eum, et ad eum veniemus et mansionem apud eum* (μονὴν παρ' αὐτῷ) *faciemus* — My Father will love him, and we will come to him, and will make our abode with him." No mere creature could, without committing blasphemy, thus put himself on a level with God, and promise to indwell with God in the souls of the just; and none but God Himself could solemnly promise: "*Et ecce ego vobiscum sum omnibus diebus usque ad consummationem saeculi* — And behold I am with you all days, even to the consummation of the world.[79] Only a believer in the Divinity of Jesus can exclaim with St. Paul: "*Vivit vero in me Christus* — But Christ liveth in me."[80]

d) Among the operative attributes of God the most important is probably omniscience. As God alone can adequately comprehend His own Essence, so likewise only a truly divine Son can adequately comprehend the divine Father. Cfr. John X, 15: "*Sicut novit* (γινώσκει) *me Pater, et ego agnosco* (γινώσκω) *Patrem* — As the Father knoweth me, I know the Father." And again: "*Ego scio eum* (ἐγὼ οἶδα αὐτόν), *quia ab ipso sum* (παρ' αὐτοῦ εἰμί), *et ipse me misit* — I know him, because I am from him, and he hath sent me."[81] This argues an intimate knowledge such as no creature can possess. John VI, 46: "*Non quia Patrem vidit quisquam, nisi is qui est a Deo* (εἰ μὴ ὁ ὢν παρὰ τοῦ Θεοῦ), *hic vidit Patrem* (οὗτος ἑώρακε τὸν πατέρα) — Not that any man hath seen the Father; but he who is of God, he hath seen the Father." This intuitive vision has its source in

79 Matth. XXVIII, 20. Cfr. also John XIV, 16; XV, 5 sqq.; XVI, 13 sqq.

80 Gal. II, 20.

81 John VII, 29.

Christ's divine γέννησις. Cfr. John I, 18: "*Deum nemo vidit unquam; unigenitus Filius, qui est in sinu Patris, ipse enarravit* — No man hath seen God at any time: the only begotten Son who is in the bosom of the Father, he hath declared him." Christ's divine self-comprehension necessarily implies an adequate knowledge of all things external to the Godhead. For if, as St. Paul assures us, "in him dwelleth all the fulness of the Godhead corporeally,"[82] it is evident that "in him are hid all the treasures of wisdom and knowledge."[83] It is by this standard, therefore, that His knowledge of all things, even the most hidden, must be gauged. Thus He was able to assure Nathanael: "Before that Philip called thee, when thou wast under the fig tree, I saw thee."[84] Whereupon the new Apostle, struck by Christ's wonderful knowledge, exclaimed: "Thou art the Son of God, thou art the King of Israel."[85]

If cardiognosis is an exclusive prerogative of the Godhead,[86] Christ is true God. For He applied to Himself the words of Jeremiah: "I am the Lord who search the heart,"[87] when He said: "All the churches shall know that I am he that searcheth the reins and hearts."[88] More than once in fact did He demonstrate that He possessed this attribute of Divinity. Cfr. Luke IX, 47: "*At Iesus videns cogitationes cordis illorum*

82 Col. II, 9: "*In ipso inhabitat omnis plenitudo divinitatis corporaliter* (ἐν αὐτῷ κατοικεῖ πᾶν τὸ πλήρωμα τῆς θεότητος σωματικῶς)."

83 Col. II, 3: "*In quo* [*Christo*] *sunt omnes thesauri sapientiae et scientiae absconditi.*"

84 John I, 48: "*Priusquam te Philippus vocaret, cum esses sub ficu, vidi te.*"

85 John I, 49: "*Tu es Filius Dei, tu es rex Israel.*"

86 As we have shown in the first volume of this series, *God: His Knowability, Essence, and Attributes*, pp. 359 sqq.

87 Jer. XVII, 10: "*Ego Dominus* יְהוָה *scrutans cor et probans renes.*"

88 Apoc. II, 23: "*Et scient omnes ecclesiae, quia ego sum scrutans renes et corda.*"

(ἰδὼν τὸν διαλογισμὸν τῆς καρδίας αὐτῶν) — But Jesus seeing the thoughts of their heart." With vision wondrous clear He foresees free future events, as, *e. g.*, His betrayal at the hands of Judas, Peter's denial, the flight of His disciples, His Passion, Resurrection, and Ascension, the destruction of Jerusalem, etc. His "Woe to thee, Corozain, woe to thee, Bethsaida"[89] shows that He also possesses the *scientia futuribilium*.[90]

2. Christ's Title to Divine Honors.—No mere creature can claim divine honors without incurring the awful crime of idolatry. But Christ claims and receives divine honors. Therefore, He is true God. This syllogism rests on the supposition—which it is the business of apologetics to prove—that Christ was neither an impostor nor a megalomaniac, but, on the contrary, a morally altogether superior and physically normal being. We also assume it as a datum furnished by fundamental theology,[91] that His Apostles and Disciples were neither fools nor knaves, but men who knew the facts of Christ's career and who were sincere in worshipping Him as God.

a) Christ laid claim to divine honors.

John V, 22 sq.: "*Pater . . . omne iudicium dedit Filio, ut omnes honorificent Filium, sicut honorificant Patrem* (ἵνα πάντες τιμῶσι τὸν υἱόν, καθὼς τιμῶσι τὸν πατέρα)

89 Matth. XI, 21 sqq.

90 On the "*scientia futuribilium*," as a divine attribute, see Pohle-Preuss, *God: His Knowability, Essence, and Attributes*, pp. 361 sqq.

91 Cfr. Pohle-Preuss, *op. cit.*, pp. 7 sq.

— The Father . . . hath given all judgment to the Son, that all men may honor the Son, as they honor the Father." Here Jesus plainly exacts for Himself, as Son, the same worship which He demands for His Father. The context proves that the adverb καθώς is meant to express not merely similitude but equality; for in the same chapter of St. John's Gospel from which the passage is taken, Christ distinctly asserts and defends His coequality with the Father, and "the Jews sought the more to kill him, because he . . . said God was his Father, making himself equal to God."[92] He never was known to refuse divine worship when offered to Him, but accepted it without protest.[93] His Apostles, too, particularly St. Paul and St. John, insist that Christ is entitled to divine honors. Rom. XIV, 10 sq.: "*Omnes enim stabimus ante tribunal Christi; scriptum est enim: Vivo ego, dicit Dominus, quoniam mihi flectetur omne genu et omnis lingua confitebitur Deo* — We shall all stand before the judgment seat of Christ. For it is written: As I live, saith the Lord, every knee shall bow to me, and every tongue shall confess to God."[94] This can only mean that all men will one day appear before the judgment seat of Jesus Christ and be compelled to worship Him as God. The same thought is expressed yet more effectively in another Pauline text:[95] "*Donavit illi nomen, quod est super omne nomen, ut in nomine Iesu omne genu flectatur coelestium, terrestrium et infernorum; et omnis lingua confiteatur, quia Dominus Iesus Christus in gloria est Dei Patris* — God hath given him a name which is above all names: that in the name of Jesus every knee should bow, of those that are in heaven, on

92 John V, 18.

93 Cfr. Matth. XIV, 33; VIII, 2 *et al.*

94 Cfr. Is. XLV, 23 sq.

95 Phil. II, 9 sqq.

earth, and under the earth; and that every tongue should confess that the Lord Jesus Christ is in the glory of God the Father."[96]

If Christ is true God, then the prayers directed to Him must be equally efficacious as those addressed to the Father. Holy Scripture plainly teaches that they are. John XIV, 13: "*Quodcunque petieritis Patrem in nomine meo, hoc faciam* [not: *faciet*], *ut glorificetur Pater in Filio* — Whatsoever you shall ask the Father in my name, that will I do: that the Father may be glorified in the Son." John XIV, 14: "*Si quid petieritis me in nomine meo, hoc faciam* — If you shall ask me any thing in my name, that will I do." In the hour of death no man may, without grievous sin, commend his soul to any creature. Christ commends *His* into the hands of His Heavenly Father. Luke XXIII, 46: "Father, into thy hands I commend my spirit." And the dying protomartyr Stephen unhesitatingly cries out: "*Domine Iesu, suscipe spiritum meum* — Lord Jesus, receive my spirit."[97]

b) The Godhead is the sole formal object of the three theological virtues. But Holy Scripture represents Christ as a Supreme Being, to whom all men owe faith, hope, and charity. Consequently, He is true God.

Jesus Himself requires men to believe in Him with the same faith which they have in God. In this connection it is well to remember that there is an important distinction between *credere alicui* and *credere in aliquem*. We may

[96] On the adoration of the "slain Lamb," *i. e.*, Christ in Heaven, cfr. Apoc. V, 11-13.

[97] Acts VII, 58.

believe a creature, but we *believe in* God alone. Cfr. John XIV, 1: "*Creditis in Deum, et in me credite* (πιστεύετε εἰς τὸν Θεόν, καὶ εἰς ἐμὲ πιστεύετε)—You believe in God, believe also in me." Faith in Christ is productive of eternal life. John VI, 47: "*Amen, amen, dico vobis: qui credit in me* (εἰς ἐμέ) *habet vitam aeternam*—Amen, amen I say unto you: He that believeth in me, hath everlasting life." For belief in Jesus Christ is nought else than faith in the true Son of God. 1 John IV, 15: "*Quisquis confessus fuerit, quoniam Iesus est Filius Dei* (ὁ υἱὸς τοῦ Θεοῦ), *Deus in eo manet et ipse in Deo*—Whosoever shall confess that Jesus is the Son of God, God abideth in him, and he in God."

Christ is also the object of theological hope, as the story of the Atonement clearly shows. If St. Paul calls himself "an apostle of Jesus Christ, . . . our hope,"[98] this is neither an empty phrase nor a hyperbole. For, as St. Peter tersely says: "*Non est in aliquo alio* (ἐν ἄλλῳ οὐδενί) *salus; nec enim aliud nomen est sub coelo datum hominibus, in quo oporteat nos salvos fieri*—Neither is there salvation in any other; for there is no other name under heaven given to men, whereby we must be saved."[99]

Christ is likewise the object of that theological charity ("*amor super omnia*") to which God alone can lay claim. Matth. X, 37: "He that loveth father or mother more than me, is not worthy of me." Whatever interferes with the love of Christ is to be treated as an obstacle in the way of salvation. Luke XIV, 26: "*Si quis venit ad me et non odit patrem suum et matrem et uxorem et filios et fratres et sorores, adhuc autem et ani-*

98 1 Tim. I, 1: "*Paulus, apostolus Iesu Christi, . . . spei nostrae.*"

99 Acts IV, 12. For further information on this point we must refer the student to the dogmatic treatise on Grace.

mam suam, non potest esse meus discipulus — If any man come to me and hate not his father, and mother, and wife, and children, and brethren, and sisters, yea and his own life also, he cannot be my disciple." The Father rewards us with His love if we love Christ. Cfr. John XIV, 23: "*Si quis diligit me, . . . et Pater meus diliget eum, et ad eum veniemus et mansionem apud eum faciemus* — If any one love me, . . . my father will love him, and we will come to him and make our abode with him."[100] St. Paul's anathema against all those who "love not our Lord Jesus Christ,"[101] would be wantonly criminal if Christ were not true God. And it is only on this same assumption that the love of Christ can be called "a life in Christ." Phil. I, 21: "*Mihi enim vivere Christus est, et mori lucrum* — For to me, to live is Christ: and to die is gain." 2 Cor. V, 14 sq.: "*Caritas enim Christi urget nos, . . . ut et qui vivunt, iam non sibi vivant, sed ei, qui pro ipsis mortuus est et resurrexit* — For the charity of Christ presseth us, . . . that they also who live, may not now live to themselves, but unto him who died for them and rose again." St. Paul boldly identifies "*caritas Christi*" with "*caritas Dei,*" and says, nothing should separate us from it. Rom. VIII, 35 sqq.: "*Quis ergo nos separabit a caritate Christi? Tribulatio, an angustia, an fames, an nuditas, an periculum, an persecutio, an gladius? . . . Certus sum enim, quia neque mors neque vita neque angeli . . . neque creatura alia poterit nos separare a caritate Dei, quae est in Christo Iesu Domino nostro* — Who then shall separate us from the love of Christ? Shall

100 Cfr. also John XIV, 21.

101 1 Cor. XVI, 22: "*Si quis non amat Dominum nostrum Iesum Christum, sit anathema* — If any man love not our Lord Jesus Christ, let him be anathema."

tribulation? or distress? or famine? or nakedness? or danger? or persecution? or the sword? . . . For I am sure that neither death nor life nor angels . . . nor any other creature, shall be able to separate us from the love of God, which is in Christ Jesus our Lord." Consequently Christ and God are one.

c) Christ's adorableness, and consequently His Divinity, can be demonstrated also from the fact that Baptism is conferred in His name conjointly with that of the Father and the Holy Ghost.

We shall not enter into the Scholastic controversy whether by a special privilege the Apostles baptized in the name of Christ only, instead of employing the Trinitarian formula which Jesus Himself gave to them, as recorded in the twenty-eighth chapter of St. Matthew's Gospel.[102] This and other similar questions do not concern us here. They belong to the dogmatic treatise on Baptism. The very fact that Baptism used to be called "Baptism in Christ's name" is proof that the early Christians believed in the Divinity of our Lord. Nor does it make the slightest difference whether the Sacrament was originally administered "ἐπὶ τῷ ὀνόματι Ἰησοῦ Χριστοῦ εἰς ἄφεσιν ἁμαρτιῶν,"[103] or "ἐν τῷ ὀνόματι τοῦ Ἰησοῦ Χριστοῦ,"[104] for both formulas clearly emphasize the authority and power of Christ to forgive sins; — or "εἰς τὸ ὄνομα τοῦ κυρίου Ἰησοῦ,"[105] which particularly accentuates the consecration and devotion of the

102 A brief account of this controversy will be found in Fr. Fanning's article on "Baptism" in the *Catholic Encyclopedia*, Vol. II, p. 263.

103 Acts II, 38.

104 Acts X, 48.

105 Acts VIII, 16.

baptized convert to Jesus as man's final end. In matter of fact no man could without committing idolatry allow himself to be baptized "in the name" of any creature; for no one but God can forgive sins and exact absolute subjection and divine worship. Cfr. 1 Cor. I, 13: "*Numquid Paulus crucifixus est pro vobis? Aut in nomine Pauli baptizati estis?* — Was Paul crucified for you? or were you baptized in the name of Paul?"

3. Holy Scripture Expressly Calls Christ "God."—Having demonstrated the Divinity of Christ, it will serve to confirm our argument to note that Holy Scripture in several places expressly refers to Him as God.

a) If the Tetragrammaton יְהוָה is God's incommunicable proper name, which expresses His Divine Essence,[106] then a Being that is identical with the Old Testament Yahweh must be true God. Now Jesus Christ is identical with the Old Testament Yahweh. Therefore He is true God.

In his Epistle to the Hebrews, St. Paul says: "*Et cum iterum introducit primogenitum* [*sc. Christum*] *in orbem terrae, dicit: Et adorent eum omnes angeli* — And, when he again bringeth in the first begotten into the world, he saith: And let all the angels of God adore him."[107] This text not only proves that Christ is true God; it also proves that He is Yahweh. For, in the passage which St. Paul here quotes,[108] the

106 See Pohle-Preuss, *God: His Knowability, Essence, and Attributes*, pp. 135 sqq.

107 Heb. I, 6.

108 Ps. XCVI, 7.

Psalmist describes how Yahweh appeared on earth for the purpose of founding a kingdom; how He reappears as the terrible Judge; how the heavens declare His justice and all the people behold His glory, and how those are confounded who adore graven things and glory in their idols. Then there follows the exhortation (verse 7): "Adore him (*i. e.*, יְהוָה), all you angels." Consequently Christ is the Jehovah of whom David speaks in this Psalm.

We read in the Messianic Psalm XLIV, which is ascribed to the sons of Core: "*Sedes tua, Deus* (אֱלֹהִים) *in saeculum saeculi*—Thy throne, O God, is for ever and ever."[109] The Rationalist exegetes, who take the word *Deus* in this text for a nominative instead of a vocative, disregard both the dignity of God and Scriptural usage. If their interpretation were correct, the meaning of the text would be: Thy seat, or throne (*i. e.*, according to the Rationalist conception, the throne of an earthly king), is God Himself for ever and ever. Though Holy Scripture sometimes refers to creatures (*e. g.*, heaven and hell, angels and men) as the seat or throne of God, it nowhere designates God as the seat or throne of man, *e. g.*, of an earthly prince. This interpretation is positively untenable in the light of Heb. I, 8: "*Ad Filium* [*scil. Christum*] *autem dicit: Thronus tuus, Deus, in saeculum saeculi* (ὁ θρόνος σου, ὁ Θεός, εἰς τὸν αἰῶνα τοῦ αἰῶνος)," where the text Ps. XLIV, 7 is used to show Christ's superiority over the angels. That St. Paul intends ὁ Θεός for a vocative is plain from New Testament Greek usage, as the student may see from a comparison of such texts as Matth. XI, 26;

109 Ps. XLIV, 7. On this passage, and the whole Psalm of which it forms a part, cfr. A. J. Maas, S. J., *Christ in Type and Prophecy*, Vol. II, pp. 36 sqq., New York 1895.

Mark V, 41; Luke VIII, 54; John XIX, 3; Eph. VI, 1; Col. III, 18; Heb. X, 7; Apoc. VI, 10. Consequently Ps. XLIV, 7, can only mean: "Thy throne, O God אֱלֹהִים, stands for ever." Since the sons of Core never employ the term "Elohim" except when they wish to designate the true God, it follows that Christ bears the Divine Name אֱלֹהִים, *i. e.*, θεός = God.

The hardness of heart which the Jews manifested in spite of the many wonderful miracles wrought by our Saviour, St. John attributes to the prophecy of Isaias [110] and adds: "*Haec dixit Isaias, quando vidit gloriam eius et locutus est de eo* — These things said Isaias, when he saw his glory and spoke of him [Christ]." [111] Turning to the sixth chapter of Isaias, we read: "*Vidi Dominum* (אֲדֹנָי) *sedentem super solium excelsum. . . . Seraphim clamabant alter ad alterum et dicebant: Sanctus, Sanctus, Sanctus Dominus exercituum* (יְהוָה צְבָאוֹת), *plena est omnis terra gloria eius* — I saw the Lord sitting upon a throne high and elevated. . . . The seraphims . . . cried to one another: Holy, holy, holy, the Lord God of hosts, all the earth is full of his glory." [112] Hence, according to St. John, Christ is "God" (*Dominus*, אֲדֹנָי) and "Lord of hosts" (*Dominus exercituum*, יְהוָה צְבָאוֹת).

It should also be noted that St. Mark, in the beginning of his Gospel,[113] refers the well-known exhortation of Isaias:[114] "*Parate viam Domini* — Prepare ye the way of the Lord," to John the Baptist, as the precursor of the "Lord," thereby acknowledging the latter to be "Jehovah." In Mark I, 2, we have a citation from Malachias (attributed to Isaias), in which Jehovah

110 Is. VI, 9 sqq.
111 John XII, 41.
112 Is. VI, 1 sqq.
113 Mark I, 3.
114 Is. XL, 3.

Himself is quoted as prophesying: "*Ecce ego mitto angelum meum et praeparabit viam ante faciem meam* — Behold I send my angel, and he shall prepare the way before my face." [115] Now this angel is none other than John the Baptist, who, as a precursor, is to "prepare the way before the face of Jehovah," *i. e.*, Christ. As Christ [116] also applies this text to the Baptist, resp. to Himself, we have a double warrant for the assertion that the Jehovah of Malachias is identical with Jesus.

b) Christ is expressly called "God" in at least four New Testament texts. A fifth occurs in the prologue of St. John's Gospel, but we defer the discussion of it to the next Section, where we shall treat explicitly of the Logos.

α) The first of the four passages just alluded to is John XX, 28. The Evangelist describes how Christ reproached the incredulous Thomas for his unbelief, whereupon "Thomas answered and said to Him: My Lord and my God—(ὁ Κύριος μου καὶ ὁ Θεός μου) *Dominus meus et Deus meus.*" Theodore of Mopsuestia and Nestorius represented this reply as a mere exclamation of surprise; but the text plainly says: "*dixit ei* (εἶπεν αὐτῷ)—[Thomas] said to him." These words also exclude the Rationalist theory which asserts that the Apostle, in exclaiming "My Lord and my God!" did not address Jesus, who

115 Mal. III, 1. On this prophecy cfr. Maas, *op. cit.*, Vol. I, pp. 435 sqq.

116 Luke VII, 27 and Matth. XI, 10.

stood before him, but Almighty God in Heaven.

It is obvious from the context that Thomas desired to make a profession of faith not simply in the Resurrection of Christ, but also in His Divinity, for which the Resurrection furnishes such a triumphant argument. It is in this sense that Christ replies to him: "*Quia vidisti me, Thoma, credidisti; beati, qui non viderunt et crediderunt* — Because thou hast seen me, Thomas, thou hast believed; blessed are they that have not seen, and have believed."[117]

β) Christ is again expressly called God in Tit. II, 13: "*Exspectantes beatam spem et adventum gloriae magni Dei et Salvatoris nostri Iesu Christi* (τοῦ μεγάλου Θεοῦ καὶ σωτῆρος ἡμῶν Ἰησοῦ Χριστοῦ) — Looking for the blessed hope and coming of the glory of the great God and our Saviour Jesus Christ."

St. Paul does not mean to distinguish two separate persons — the "great God," or Father, and "Our Saviour Jesus Christ." He is speaking solely of Christ, who is both "the great God" and "our Saviour;" else he would repeat the definite article and express himself like this: **Τοῦ μεγάλου Θεοῦ καὶ τοῦ σωτῆρος ἡμῶν Ἰησοῦ Χριστοῦ.** Whenever St. Paul wishes to distinguish between the different Persons of the Most Holy Trinity, he always repeats the article. On the other hand, he never repeats the article when heaping several predicates on one and the same Person. Cfr. 2 Cor. I, 3: "**Εὐλογητὸς ὁ Θεὸς καὶ πατὴρ τοῦ Κυρίου** — Blessed be the God and Father of our Lord Jesus Christ."[118] The

117 John XX, 29.

118 Cfr. also Eph. I, 3.

Ethiopian translation has dropped the καὶ without in the least changing the signification of the text. But there is also a strong objective reason for applying the phrase "the great God" to Jesus Christ. For in speaking of the "coming of the glory of the great God," the Apostle can only mean Christ, because Holy Scripture tells us nothing of an epiphany of the Father, and we know that the second coming (*parousia*) of Christ will coincide with the Last Judgment.

γ) An equally cogent argument can be construed from 1 John V, 20: *"Scimus quoniam Filius Dei venit et dedit nobis sensum, ut cognoscamus verum Deum et simus in vero Filio eius: hic est verus Deus et vita aeterna* — And we know that the Son of God is come: and he hath given us understanding that we may know the true God, and may be in his true Son. This is the true God and life eternal." Here the Divinity of Christ, which is logically deducible from the fact that He is a true Son of the true God, is expressly reaffirmed in the concluding phrase: This is the true God—ἀληθινὸς Θεὸς.

It is contrary to the rules of logic and grammar alike to refer the phrase "This is the true God and life eternal," not to the immediately preceding word "*Filio,*" but to the more remote "*verum Deum*" (*i. e., Patrem*). In that case *ille* — ἐκεῖνος should be the pronoun used, not *hic* — οὗτος. To refer the demonstrative pronoun *hic* — οὗτος to the determinative pronoun *eius* would offend against the idiom of the Latin language. If

Erasmus were right in his assumption that the phrase, "The true God and life eternal" designates the Father, not the Son, St. John would have made himself guilty of an insufferable tautology, *viz.: "Verus Deus est verus Deus."* Moreover, the aim of St. John's First Epistle, which was written as a prologue to his Gospel, is not to demonstrate the Godhead of the Father, which no one denied, but the Divinity of the Son, who had appeared corporeally in Christ. It is furthermore to be noted that the "true God" whom St. John has in mind, is also called "eternal life" (οὗτός ἐστιν ὁ ἀληθινὸς Θεὸς καὶ ζωὴ αἰώνιος). Now St. John never means the Father but invariably the Son when he uses the phrase "eternal life." Consequently Christ is as certainly *"verus Deus"* as is His Father. Cfr. 1 John I, 2: "*Annuntiamus vobis vitam aeternam, quae erat apud Patrem et apparuit nobis* — We declare unto you the life eternal, which was with the Father, and hath appeared to us."[119] 1 John V, 11: "*Vitam aeternam dedit nobis Deus, et haec vita in Filio eius est. Qui habet Filium, habet vitam; qui non habet Filium, vitam non habet* — God hath given to us eternal life. And this life is in his Son. He that hath the Son, hath life. He that hath not the Son, hath not life." The last vestige of possible doubt is removed by the Greek text, which reads thus: "Καὶ ἔσμεν ἐν τῷ ἀληθινῷ ἐν τῷ υἱῷ αὐτοῦ Ἰησοῦ Χριστῷ· οὗτός ἐστιν ὁ ἀληθινὸς Θεὸς καὶ ζωὴ αἰώνιος." The demonstrative pronoun clearly points to Jesus Christ.

δ) The *"crux Rationalistarum"* is the famous doxology, Rom. IX, 5: *"Ex quibus* [*scil. Isra-*

119 Cfr. also John I, 4; XI, 25; XIV, 6.

elitis] *est Christus secundum carnem, qui est super omnia Deus benedictus in saecula* (καὶ ἐξ ὧν ὁ Χριστὸς τὸ κατὰ σάρκα ὁ ὢν ἐπὶ πάντων Θεὸς εὐλογητὸς εἰς τοὺς αἰῶνας)." Whoever reads this sentence without prepossession will unhesitatingly refer the predicate *Deus super omnia* (ἐπὶ πάντων Θεὸς) to Christ.

The Greek manuscript codices present the New Testament text without punctuation marks, and it would seem to be the business of exegesis rather than of textual criticism to determine whether there should be a comma or a period after the word σάρκα. If a comma, then the whole doxology plainly refers to Christ; if a period, it would be most natural to refer it to the Father or to the Deity in general. Similarly, in the Latin text of the Vulgate, the Rationalists place a period after "*carnem*" and reconstruct the passage thus: ". . . *ex quibus est Christus secundum carnem. Qui est super omnia Deus* [= *Pater*], *benedictus* [*sit*] *in saecula*."[120] But this punctuation is arbitrary. There is no intrinsic reason whatever for inserting such an abrupt hymn of praise in honor of the Father into a context which treats solely of the Son. Conversely, the Apostle had excellent reasons for connecting the doxology with the name of Christ, whose descent according to the flesh from the Jews he had accentuated immediately before. This interpretation of the passage is so natural and plausible that the early writers were unanimous in referring the doxology to the Son and not to the Father. To the fifteen witnesses whom Petavius[121] was able to mar-

120 Thus Erasmus, Westen, Griesbach, and others.
121 *De Trinitate*, II, 7.

shal in confirmation of this statement, Cardinal Franzelin [122] added thirty others, while Hurter [123] enriched the list with fourteen more. This practically unanimous consent of the Fathers loses none of its force by the circumstance that some of them (in a very correct sense) assert that the epithet ὁ ἐπὶ πάντων Θεός belongs solely to the Father, because the Father alone, as the First Person of the Blessed Trinity, is unoriginate (ἄναρχος) and at the same time the principle of the Son (ἀρχὴ τῆς ἀρχῆς). Thus Athanasius,[124] Basil,[125] and Gregory of Nyssa.[126] However, since these Fathers did not have in mind the Epistle to the Romans, but that to the Ephesians, in which St. Paul writes: "*Unus Deus et Pater omnium qui est super omnes* (ὁ ἐπὶ πάντων)—One God and Father of all, who is above all," [127] we can reasonably assume that they do not mean to contradict the other Fathers. This assumption is rendered still more probable by the fact that these same apparently dissentient Fathers elsewhere expressly interpret the doxology as referring to Christ.[128] For the rest, such unsuspected witnesses as Rosenmüller and the editor of the new edition of H. A. W. Meyer's voluminous commentary on the various books of Sacred Scripture, B. Weiss, admit that the Rationalist interpretation involves a violation of the rules of Greek grammar. In fact it would be just as unnatural and ungrammatical to write ὁ ὢν ἐπὶ πάντων Θεός, instead of ὁ Θεὸς ὁ ὢν ἐπὶ πάντων, as it would be natural and gram-

122 *De Verbo Incarnato*, thes. 9.

123 *Opuscula Patrum*, XVI, p. 240, 2nd ed., Oeniponte 1895.

124 *Ad Serap.*, Ep. 1, n. 28.

125 *Ep.*, 38, n. 4.

126 *Contr. Apoll.*, n. 77.

127 Eph. IV, 6. Cfr. Newman, *Athanasius*, II, 348 sq., 9th ed., London 1903.

128 Athanas., *Ep. ad Epict.*, n. 10; Basil, *Contr. Eunom.*, IV, n. 2; Greg. Nyss., *Contr. Eunom.*, l. X.

matical to resume by ὁ ὢν the immediately preceding subject, namely, ὁ Χριστός.

Be it noted in conclusion that Christ's standing epithet in the pages of the New Testament is not "God" (*Deus,* Θεός), but rather "Lord" (*Dominus,* Κύριος), as can easily be gathered from a perusal of the Apostolic Epistles. But inasmuch as *"Dominus"* corresponds exactly to the Hebrew יְהוָה and אֲדֹנָי, the texts in which Jesus is called "Lord" prove His Divinity quite as cogently as those in which He is called "God."

C. The Logos

Whereas the Synoptics portray Christ mainly on His human side, St. Paul emphasizes the Godman, and St. John, who was the Saviour's favorite disciple, raising his eagle eye to the very Heavens, shows us Christ subsisting before all time in His Divine Nature as the "Word of God" (*Verbum,* ὁ Λόγος). This term[129] is of the utmost importance for the proper understanding of the mystery of the Blessed Trinity. The use of the term "Logos" is peculiar to St. John.[130] The attempt to trace the Johannine Logos to the teaching of the Jewish philosopher Philo has proved abortive. Aside

129 "*Logos, verbum,* being a term already used in the schools of heathen philosophy, was open to various misunderstandings on its appearance in the theology of revealed teaching. In the Church it was both synonymous with and corrective of the term 'Son'; but heretics had almost as many senses of the term as they had sects."— Newman, *Athanasius,* II, 337, 445 sqq., 9th ed., London 1903. Cfr. J. Lebreton, *Les Origines du Dogme de la Trinité,* Book 1, Paris 1910; E. Krebs, *Der Logos als Heiland im ersten Jahrhundert,* Freiburg 1910.

130 Cfr. John I, 1 sqq.; 1 John I, 1; V, 7; Apoc. XIX, 13.

from the name there is absolutely no similarity between the two conceptions; rather an irreconcilable opposition. It is far more reasonable to regard the teaching of St. John on the Logos as an inspired development of the doctrine of "Uncreated Wisdom" which is set forth in the Sapiential Books of the Old Testament. May we not also assume that St. John was directly enlightened by Him on whose bosom he was privileged to lean?[131]

The most important portion of the Johannean Gospel, as bearing on the dogma of the Blessed Trinity, is the prologue, which distinctly asserts the personality, the hypostatic difference, and the Divinity of the Logos, who is Christ, the Son of God made flesh.

1. The Logos a Real Person.—The Fourth Gospel begins thus: "In the beginning was the Word, and the Word was with God (ἐν ἀρχῇ ἦν ὁ Λόγος καὶ ὁ Λόγος ἦν πρὸς τὸν Θεόν)." Inasmuch as St. John distinguishes very clearly between the "Word" and "God," the "Word with God" (*apud Deum*) cannot be an absolute divine attribute, *e. g.*, personified wisdom or omnipotence; for wisdom and omnipotence are not "with God" but "in God." This is clearly apparent from the whole context of the prologue, especially I, 14: "And the Word was made flesh." It would be impossible for the Divine Nature, or for any one of its attributes, to "become flesh," because the Divine Nature, as such, is incapable of entering into union with a finite substance, and

131 John XIII, 23. On the sources of St. John's Logos doctrine see F. Clarke, in the *Irish Eccl. Record*, Vol. XXI, Nos. 2 sqq.; Felder-Stoddard, *Christ and the Critics*, Vol. I, pp. 390 sqq.

hence cannot form an undivided synthesis with human nature. Consequently the Logos is truly a person and not a mere personification.

2. THE LOGOS AS SECOND PERSON OF THE BLESSED TRINITY, DISTINCT FROM THE FATHER. —That the Logos must be conceived as the Second Person of the Divine Trinity, appears from the opposition between Θεός and πρὸς τὸν Θεόν. The one is "God," the other is "with God" as His Logos, and as such is likewise God.[132] But the Evangelist continues: "He came unto his own (εἰς τὰ ἴδια), and his own (οἱ ἴδιοι, *i. e.*, the children of Israel) received him not." Whence it again appears, first, that the Logos is a real Person, and, secondly, that He cannot be the Father, because the Father never "came into this world."[133] Consequently, the Logos must be a different Person from the Father. This conclusion is made certain by verses 14 and 18, in which the Logos is identified with the Son of God. John I, 14: *"Et Verbum* (ὁ Λόγος) *caro factum est et habitavit in nobis; et vidimus gloriam eius* [*scil. Verbi*], *gloriam quasi unigeniti a Patre* (ὡς μονογενοῦς παρὰ πατρός) — And the Word was made flesh, and dwelt among us, and we saw his glory, the glory as it were of the only begotten of the Father." John I, 18: *"Unigenitus Filius* (ὁ μονογενὴς υἱός), *qui est in sinu*

132 John I, 1.

133 John I, 9.

Patris, ipse enarravit — The only begotten Son who is in the bosom of the Father, he hath declared him." If the Logos is identically the same Person as the "Son in the bosom of the Father," there is between the Logos and the Father the same relative opposition which exists between the Son and the Father, and consequently the Logos cannot be identical with the Father. He must be an independent Hypostasis.

3. THE LOGOS AS A DIVINE PERSON, OR GOD. —The fifth of the Scriptural texts [184] in which the Logos is expressly called "God," is John I, 1: *"In principio erat Verbum, et Verbum erat apud Deum, et Deus erat Verbum* — In the beginning was the Word, and the Word was with God, and the Word was God." In the last clause of this sentence *"Verbum"* is the subject and *"Deus"* the predicate, as a glance at the Greek text: καὶ Θεὸς ἦν ὁ Λόγος, tells. Therefore the meaning of the clause is: "The Logos was God." But why did St. John thus transpose subject and predicate? His reason for doing so appears from the context: Ὁ Λόγος ἦν πρὸς τὸν Θεὸν, καὶ Θεὸς ἦν ὁ Λόγος. By bringing τὸν Θεόν and Θεός into juxtaposition, the Evangelist desired to emphasize the consubstantiality of the Logos with God the Father, "with" whom He was "from the beginning." Positively to exclude the

184 Cfr. *supra*, p. 82.

thought that the two might be identical in Person, St. John insists:[135] Οὗτος (*i. e.*, ὁ Λόγος) ἦν ἐν ἀρχῇ πρὸς τὸν Θεόν; that is to say, the Logos is indeed "God"; but He is likewise "with God."

Even if the Logos were not expressly called "God," His Divinity could be inferred from the divine attributes ascribed to Him by the Evangelist.

a) The Logos is the Creator of all things without exception. John I, 3: "*Omnia per ipsum facta sunt, et sine ipso factum est nihil, quod factum est* — All things were made by him: and without him was made nothing that was made." John I, 10: "*In mundo erat, et mundus* (ὁ κόσμος) *per ipsum factus est* — He was in the world, and the world was made by him." He who created the world must be God. "*Peccatum quidem non per ipsum factum est,*" beautifully observes St. Augustine, ". . . *et idolum non per Verbum factum est, sed . . . omnis omnino creatura ab angelo usque ad vermiculum. Quid praeclarius angelo in creaturis? Quid extremius vermiculo in creaturis? Per quem factus est angelus, per ipsum factus est vermiculus* — Sin indeed was not made by the Word . . . an idol too was not made by the Word, but . . . every created thing whatever, from an angel to a worm. What created being more excellent than an angel? What lower than a worm? Yet He who made the angel, the very same made the worm also."[136] As Creator of the world the Logos is an uncreated Substance, *ens a se*. As if to refute the later Arian notion that the Logos who created the world was Himself a mere creature, St. John stresses

135 John I, 2.

136 *Tract. in Ioannem*, I, n. 13.

the fact that "all things were made by him" by adding: "And without him was made nothing that was made."[137] If absolutely nothing was created without the Logos, the Logos Himself must either be increate, or His own creator, which would involve a contradiction. "*Quomodo potest fieri*," says St. Augustine, "*ut Verbum Dei factum sit, quando Deus per Verbum fecit omnia? Si et Verbum Dei ipsum factum est, per quod aliud Verbum factum est? . . . Non enim per se ipsum fieri potuit, per quod facta sunt omnia. Crede ergo Evangelistae. Poterat enim dicere: In principio fecit Deus Verbum, quomodo dixit Moyses: In principio fecit Deus coelum et terram* — How could the Word of God be made, when by the Word God made all things? If the Word of God was itself also made, by what other Word was it made? . . . For that by which all things are made, could not be made by itself. Believe then the Evangelist. For he might have said: In the beginning God made the Word; just as Moses said: In the beginning God made the heavens and the earth."[138]

b) The Logos is eternal. Cfr. John I, 1 sq.: "In the beginning (ἐν ἀρχῇ) was the Word. . . . The same was in the beginning (ἐν ἀρχῇ) with God." A preexistence which antedates time and creation is equal to absolute eternity. To say that the Logos began to be "with God" at some certain time, would be tantamount to asserting that the Father began out of His own substance to beget "the only begotten Son in His bosom."[139] Consequently the Son must be coeternal with the Father. This is further confirmed by a con-

[137] John I, 3: Πάντα δι' αὐτοῦ ἐγένετο, καὶ χωρὶς αὐτοῦ ἐγένετο οὐδὲ ἕν (*nihil* = nothing whatever), ὃ γέγονεν. On this passage, cfr. Card. Newman, *Athanasius*, II, 275 sqq.

[138] *Tract. in Ioannem*, I, n. 11.

[139] John I, 18.

sideration of that attribute of the Divine Logos which may be designated as His divine immanence. By "Word of God" (*Verbum,* Λόγος) we may understand either the external word of God (*verbum oris s. externum*), *i. e.,* Divine Revelation; or His internal, immanent word (*verbum mentis s. internum*). The former, which is something impersonal, accidental, created, temporal, extra-divine, is not mentioned by St. John in the prologue of his Gospel. The Word of which he speaks is manifestly the internal Word, which, being an intrinsic product of generation, immanent in the intellect of the begetting Father, forms part of the Divine Essence. Consequently the Logos is coeternal with the Essence of the Godhead.

c) Lastly, the Logos is the author of the Supernatural, and as such must be God. In Himself "the true light"[140] and "the life,"[141] He is in His external manifestation "the light [that] shineth in the darkness,"[142] and the principle of our adopted sonship.[143] John I, 12: "*Quotquot autem receperunt eum, dedit eis potestatem filios Dei fieri* (ἔδωκεν αὐτοῖς ἐξουσίαν τέκνα Θεοῦ γενέσθαι), *his qui credunt in nomine eius* (εἰς τὸ ὄνομα αὐτοῦ)— But as many as received him, he gave them power to be made the sons of God, to them that believe in his name." Belief in the Logos is a necessary condition of salvation and eternal beatitude. Consequently the Logos is God. From the fulness of His grace we must all draw; it is from Him we receive grace and truth. Cfr. John I, 16 sq.: "*Et de plenitudine eius nos omnes accepimus, et gratiam pro gratia; quia lex per Moysen data est, gratia et veritas* (ἡ χάρις

140 John I, 4, 7, 9.

141 John I, 4.

142 John I, 5, 9.

143 Cfr. the article "Adoption, Supernatural," in the *Catholic Encyclopedia,* Vol. I, pp. 148 sqq.

καὶ ἡ ἀλήθεια) *per Iesum Christum facta est* — And of his fulness we have all received, and grace for grace. For the law was given by Moses; grace and truth came by Jesus Christ." The Logos is the author both of nature and of the Supernatural, and therefore very God.

The Logos appeared corporeally on earth in Jesus Christ, for it is to Him and to Him alone that we can apply such Scriptural passages as: "He came unto his own,"[144] "He was in the world,"[145] "John . . . gave testimony of [Him],"[146] and, lastly,[147] "The Word was made flesh, and dwelt among us."[148] This "Word made flesh," which is for the first time called "Jesus Christ" in John I, 17, is "the only begotten Son of God."[149] Hence Christ is both the Logos and the Son of God. With John I, 15, therefore, begins the story of the life of Jesus Christ.[150]

Readings: — J. E. Stadler, *Uber die Identität der Idee der Weisheit mit der des Wortes,* Münster, 1832; E. Bougaud, *The Divinity of Christ* (tr. by Currie) New York 1906; *L. Atzberger, *Die Logoslehre des h. Athanasius,* München 1880; M. Beyr, *Trinitatis in Unitate Dei Salus Mundi,* Graz 1875; K. Müller, *Göttliches Wissen und göttliche Macht des johanneischen Christus,* Freiburg 1882; *P. Keppler, *Die Komposition des Johannesevangeliums,* Freiburg 1884; G. A. Müller, *Christus bei Josephus Flavius,* 2nd ed., Innsbruck 1896; Simar, *Theologie des h. Paulus,* 2nd ed., Freiburg 1883; *Franzelin, *De Verbo Incarnato,* thes. 2–9, ed. 4, Romae 1893; G. B. Tepe, *Instit. Theolog.,* Vol. II, pp. 234 sqq., Parisiis 1895; J. B. Bartmann, *Das Himmelreich und sein König,* Paderborn 1904; H. Schell, *Jahwe und Christus,* Pader-

144 John I, 11.

145 John I, 10.

146 John I, 6 sq.

147 John I, 6 sqq.

148 John I, 14.

149 John I, 14, 18.

150 Cfr. K. Weiss, *Der Prolog des hl. Johannes,* Freiburg 1899; Belser, "Der Prolog des Johannesevangeliums" in the *Theologische Quartalschrift* of Tübingen, 1903, pp. 483 sqq.; J. Lebreton, *Les Origines du Dogme de la Trinité,* pp. 382 sqq., Paris 1910.

born 1905; St. Thomas, *Contr. Gent.*, IV, 7 (Rickaby, *Of God and His Creatures*, pp. 344 sqq., London 1905); Bellarmine, *Controv. de Christo*, l. I; J. Perrone, *De D. N. I. Chr. Divinitate adv. huius Aetatis Incredulos*, 3 Vols., Taurini 1870; H. P. Liddon, *The Divinity of Our Lord and Saviour Jesus Christ*, London 1867; M. Lepin, *Christ and the Gospel*, Philadelphia 1910; A. J. Maas, S. J., *Christ in Type and Prophecy*, 2 vols., New York 1893–5; C. C. Martindale, S. J., "The 'Word' of God: Pagan and Jewish Background," in the *Month*, No. 570 sqq.; G. R. Roche, S. J., *The Divinity of Jesus Christ*, London 1916; A. L. Williams (Prot.), *The Hebrew-Christian Messiah*, London 1917; J. Tixeront, *Apologetical Studies*, St. Louis 1917, pp. 39–65; F. Clarke, "Sources of St. John's Logos Doctrine," in *Irish Eccles. Record*, 1922, Nos. 658 sqq.—Idem, "The Logos of St. John in Holy Writ," *ibid.*, 1924, No. 680, pp. 177–202; Felder-Stoddard, *Christ and the Critics*, 2 vols., London 1924 sq.

ARTICLE 3

OF GOD THE HOLY GHOST

The term "Holy Ghost," or "Spirit of God," does not imply opposition so clearly as "Father" and "Son." In demonstrating this dogma, therefore, we shall have to emphasize the personality of the Holy Ghost and the fact that He is an independent Hypostasis, distinct from both the Father and the Son. His Divinity can be proved with comparative ease. Accordingly, this article will fall into three divisions. In the first division we shall demonstrate that the Holy Ghost is a real Person; in the second, that He is a Person distinct from the Father and the Son; and in the third, that He is a truly Divine Person, or God Himself. Once these three points are established from Holy Scripture, no further proof will be needed to show the existence of a Third Person in the Godhead.

A. The Personality of the Holy Ghost

1. The Word Ghost (Spirit) in its Impersonal Sense.—The Bible not infrequently uses the terms "God the Father" and "sons of God" in a figurative sense. Similarly it also employs the word "spirit of God" in a way that does not always suggest the idea of a real personality.

When we read, for instance, that "the spirit of God moved over the waters,"[151] we understand that the sacred writer personifies the breath of divine omnipotence. At least there is no cogent reason for thinking that Moses here meant the Person of the Holy Ghost. In those texts, too, which tell of supernatural effects wrought by grace, or of the workings of the spirit, it is not always obvious that Holy Scripture means to describe something more than an external divine effect which might be figuratively termed "holy spirit." In the Fiftieth Psalm the words "*Spiritum rectum innova in visceribus meis,*"[152] and "*Spiritu principali confirma me,*"[153] evidently denote a supernatural spirit of rectitude and self-control, *i. e.*, a good disposition. "*Et spiritum sanctum tuum ne auferas a me,*"[154] must likewise be interpreted impersonally. The "holy spirit" here referred to is the spirit of sanctity. There are still other texts in which "spirit" does not designate a Person, but the absolute Divine Nature, which is essentially spiritual. Cfr. John IV, 24: "God is a spirit (*spiritus*, πνεῦμα), and they that adore him, must adore him in

151 Gen. I, 2.

152 "Renew a right spirit within my bowels." Ps. L, 12.

153 "Strengthen me with a perfect spirit." Ps. L, 14.

154 "Take not thy holy spirit from me." Ps. L, 13.

spirit and in truth." In the eighth verse of the third chapter of St. John's Gospel, Christ Himself employs the word "spirit" in its original impersonal and material sense of "wind." For *spiritus* is derived from *spirare,* which means *to blow, to breathe,* as the Greek πνεῦμα is derived from πνεῖν, which has the same meaning.[155]

2. The Word Spirit in its Hypostatic Sense.—Aside from the texts already quoted, there is a considerable number of other Scriptural passages in which the Holy Ghost is clearly described as a real and individual person.

a) There are in the first place certain epithets designed to restrict the concept of spirit and to show that it is not a mere impersonal abstraction. Holy Scripture very frequently speaks not merely of the "spirit of God," but of the "Holy Spirit" (τὸ ἅγιον πνεῦμα), and this personal appellation in some texts is individualized even more strongly by the reduplication of the definite article τὸ, as *e. g.* in John XIV, 26: τὸ πνεῦμα τὸ ἅγιον. In some instances the Divine Spirit is spoken of as "the Spirit of the Father," or "the Spirit of the Son," or "the Spirit of Christ," which clearly intimates opposition to the Father and the Son.[156] 1 Cor. II, 12: "*Spiritus qui ex Deo est* (τὸ πνεῦμα τὸ ἐκ τοῦ Θεοῦ)—The Spirit that is of God," distinctly recalls John I, 1: "*Et Verbum erat apud Deum*—And the Word was with God."

155 On the rôle of the Holy Ghost in the Old Testament, see *supra*, p. 18 sq. On the whole subject of this subdivision, Newman, *Athanasius*, II, pp. 304 sqq.; Lebreton, *Les Origines du Dogme de la Trinité*, pp. 74 sqq.

156 Acts XVI, 7; Cfr. Rom. VIII, 9; Gal. IV, 6; Phil. I, 19, 1 Pet. I, 11.

b) The Holy Ghost is also called Paraclete (*Paraclitus*, παράκλητος). This term is as peculiar to St. John as the term Logos. Like Logos and Son of God, Paraclete and Holy Ghost denote one identical Person.

Paraclete is not, however, predicated of the Holy Spirit so exclusively as Logos is applied to the Son. Thus, in the First Epistle of St. John, Christ is called Paraclete.[157] The Saviour Himself in the Fourth Gospel repeatedly refers to the Holy Ghost as the Paraclete. What, then, is the meaning of Paraclete? The word is used in three different senses, all derived from the root-verb παρακαλεῖν. The first and original sense is "advocate" (*advocatus*, from παρακαλεῖν = *in auxilium advocare*). But the operations which Jesus ascribes to the Paraclete manifestly cannot be brought within the limits of this definition. Some exegetes derive Paraclete from παρακαλεῖσθαι (*i. e., consolari*) and take it to mean "comforter" (*consolator*). But if that derivation were correct, the noun should spell παρακλήτωρ, not παράκλητος. Moreover, it is plain from our Lord's discourse after the Last Supper,[158] that the office of the Paraclete is far superior to that of a mere comforter. He is formally to take the place of the departing Son of God, and to represent Him in His Church in the same manner in which Christ had represented the Father. The Paraclete is to complete the work begun by the Saviour and to assist the newly founded Church unto the consummation of the world, filling it with His sanctifying

157 1 John II, 1: "*Si quis peccaverit, advocatum* (παράκλητον) *habemus apud Patrem, Iesum Christum iustum* — If any man sin, we have an advocate with the Father, Jesus Christ the just."

158 John XIV–XVI.

power and with the spirit of truth. Paraclete may also mean "representative," from παρακαλεῖν = *aliquem in locum alterius accire.*[159]

From these verbal definitions it is clear that the "Paraclete" or "Holy Spirit" is not a mere personification but a real person.

c) The correctness of this interpretation is borne out by the characteristic description which Christ Himself has given of the Paraclete, His operations, and His relation to the Father and the Son. He is an "other" (*alius,* ἄλλος) than the Father who "sends" Him,[160] and He is also distinct from the Son, who sends Him "from the Father."[161]

Between Him who sends (*mittens*) and Him who is sent (*missus*) there is logically the same relative opposition as between Father and Son. This distinction furnishes a safeguard against the modalistic error which conceives the Holy Spirit as a mere mode of manifestation of the Godhead. It is also useful in refuting the Rationalist contention that the name *Spiritus Sanctus* merely shelters a poetical prosopopœia or personification. An impersonal being could not "teach all truth," "give testimony," "bring all things to [the Apostles'] mind," remind them of what Christ had told them, and so forth. There are many other texts of Sacred Scripture in which the Holy Spirit is described as possessing all the marks of a real personality. Thus He has a free will, for St. Paul speaks of Him as

159 Cfr. Oswald, *Trinitätslehre,* pp. 73 sqq., Paderborn 1888.

160 John XIV, 16.

161 John XV, 26.

"*Dividens singulis, prout vult*—(the Spirit worketh), dividing to every one according as he will."[162] He appoints the bishops: "*Attendite vobis et universo gregi, in quo vos Spiritus sanctus posuit episcopos regere ecclesiam Dei, quam acquisivit sanguine suo*—Take heed to yourselves and to the whole flock, wherein the Holy Ghost hath placed you bishops, to rule the church of God, which he hath purchased with his own blood."[163] He prays for us "with unspeakable groanings,"[164] like as Christ "always lives to make intercession for us."[165] Nay, He formally ascribes to Himself subsistent personality by commanding: "*Segregate mihi* (μοι) *Saulum et Barnabam in opus, ad quod assumpsi* (προςκέκλημαι) *eos*—(The Holy Ghost said to them): Separate me Saul and Barnabas, for the work whereunto I have taken them."[166]

B. The Hypostatic Difference Between the Holy Ghost and the Father and the Son

1. St. Paul and the Disciples of John the Baptist at Ephesus.—On one occasion, when St. Paul came to Ephesus, he found there about twelve disciples of John the Baptist, and thinking that they had already received Baptism, he asked them: "Have you received the Holy Ghost (πνεῦμα ἅγιον) since ye believed?" They answered: "We have not so much as heard that there be a Holy Ghost (ἀλλ' οὐδέ, εἰ πνεῦμα ἅγιον ἔστιν ἠκούσαμεν)." And when the Apostle queried further: "In what then were you baptized?" they replied: "In John's baptism." . . . "Having heard these

162 1 Cor. XII, 11.
163 Acts XX, 28.
164 Rom. VIII, 26.
165 "*Semper vivit ad interpellandum pro nobis.*" Heb. VII, 25.
166 Acts XIII, 2.

things, they were baptized in the name of the Lord Jesus." And when St. Paul "had imposed his hands on them, the Holy Ghost (τὸ πνεῦμα τὸ ἅγιον) came upon them."[167] This account makes it certain beyond a peradventure that Jesus and the Holy Ghost are two distinct Persons. For the initial ignorance of the disciples of John the Baptist did not refer to the Godhead as such (concerning which they must have been sufficiently instructed), but to that particular Divine Person who, in contradistinction to Jesus, the Son of God, is called Holy Ghost. In accordance with this marked difference between the two Divine Persons, John's disciples at Ephesus received two distinct sacraments, *viz.*, Baptism (*i. e.*, the Baptism of Jesus) and Confirmation.

2. Christ's Last Discourse.—In His discourse to His Disciples after the Last Supper,[168] Christ clearly distinguishes between the Father, and the Son, and the Holy Ghost. "*Ego rogabo Patrem et alium Paraclitum* (ἄλλον παράκλητον) *dabit vobis, ut maneat vobiscum in aeternum* — I will ask the Father, and he shall give you another Paraclete, that he may abide with you for ever."[169] The "*alius*" so distinctly differentiates the Paraclete from both Christ Himself and the Father, that a blending of the Three Persons into one, or into two, is entirely out of question. The Father "gives"; the Paraclete "is given"; and Christ "asks the Father to give" the Paraclete. It is futile to object that God may give

167 Acts XIX, 1-6.

168 John XIV-XVI.

169 John XIV, 16.

Himself to His creatures; for the Father is asked by the Son to give to the Apostles, not Himself, nor His Son, but the Paraclete, or Holy Ghost. The hypostatic difference between the Three Persons of the Divine Trinity is still more clearly marked in John XIV, 26: *"Paraclitus autem Spiritus sanctus, quem mittet Pater in nomine meo, ille vos docebit omnia* (Ὁ δὲ παράκλητος, τὸ πνεῦμα τὸ ἅγιον, ὃ πέμψει ὁ πατὴρ ἐν τῷ ὀνόματί μου, ἐκεῖνος [not: ἐκεῖνο] ὑμᾶς διδάξει πάντα) — But the Paraclete, the Holy Ghost, whom the Father will send in my name, he will teach you all things." In this passage, too, it is impossible to confound the Paraclete with the Father, because it is the Father who sends Him; or with Christ, because it is in Christ's name that He is sent. Consequently the Paraclete is a different Person than either the Father or the Son.

3. The Immanent Origin of the Holy Ghost.—The Holy Ghost is "of God," and, like the Logos, Himself a Divine Person, who owes His Personality to His eternal procession from the Father. Sacred Scripture calls the Holy Ghost "the Spirit that is of God," [170] and distinctly declares that He "proceedeth from the Father." [171] Consequently the Holy Ghost is a different Person from the Father. But is He

170 1 Cor. II, 12: τὸ πνεῦμα τὸ ἐκ τοῦ Θεοῦ.

171 John XV, 26: παρὰ τοῦ πατρὸς ἐκπορεύεται.

likewise personally distinct from the Son? The context plainly shows that that is what St. John means to inculcate. "*Cum autem venerit Paraclitus, quem ego mittam vobis a Patre, spiritum veritatis qui a Patre procedit* (τὸ πνεῦμα τῆς ἀληθείας, ὃ παρὰ τοῦ πατρὸς ἐκπορεύεται), *ille testimonium perhibebit de me*—But when the Paraclete cometh, whom I will send you from the Father, the Spirit of truth, who proceedeth from the Father, he shall give testimony of me."[172] Here the Paraclete, or "Spirit of truth," who "proceedeth from the Father," and who cannot therefore be identical with the Father, is sharply distinguished from the Son, who sends Him; for no one can send Himself. Besides, St. John distinctly affirms that the Paraclete is sent to give testimony of Christ. From all of which it is as plain as the light of day that the Bible makes a sharp distinction between the Holy Ghost and the Father and the Son, and that each must therefore be a separate and distinct Hypostasis.

C. *The Divinity of the Holy Ghost*

Although the Divinity of the Holy Ghost is logically deducible from the texts already quoted, the Pneumatomachian and Socinian heresies demand a special refutation. In formulating the Scriptural argument for the Divinity of the

172 John XV, 26.

Holy Ghost, we shall follow the same method which we employed in elaborating that for the Divinity of Christ.

1. THE DIVINE ATTRIBUTES OF THE HOLY GHOST.—Sacred Scripture ascribes to the Holy Ghost divine attributes both of being and of life. Therefore the Holy Ghost is God.

a) Of the transcendental attributes of being, truth is frequently ascribed to the Holy Ghost. He is called the substantial "Spirit of truth," who "teaches all truth." John XVI, 13: "*Cum autem venerit ille Spiritus veritatis* (τὸ πνεῦμα τῆς ἀληθείας), *docebit vos omnem veritatem* (πᾶσαν τὴν ἀλήθειαν)—But when he, the Spirit of truth, is come, he will teach you all truth." This substantial Spirit of truth by virtue of His "procession from the Father" must be increate and divine; else He could not be called the Inspirer of God's infallible word.[173]

A second characteristic prerogative of the Holy Ghost, which is indicated by His very name, is His substantial holiness or sanctity. The epithet *sanctus* (ἅγιος) describes the very essence of the Third Person of the Divine Trinity. Not as if the Father and the Son were not also substantially holy,[174] but the Holy Ghost proceeds from Sanctity or Love as His principle, and is therefore Hypostatic Holiness or Personal Love.[175] It is for this reason that He is represented, *per appropriationem*, as "the Sanctifier," *i. e.*, the principle of all created holiness. Cfr. Rom. V, 5: "*Caritas Dei*

173 2 Pet. I, 21.

174 God as such must be holy by His very nature.—Cfr. Pohle-Preuss, *God: His Knowability, Essence, and Attributes*, pp. 251 sqq.

175 *Infra*, Chapters III and IV.

diffusa est in cordibus nostris per Spiritum Sanctum, qui datus est nobis — The charity of God is poured forth in our hearts, by the Holy Ghost, who is given to us."

The omnipotence of the Holy Ghost is more clearly defined in the supernatural sphere than in the domain of nature. St. Paul sublimely demonstrates it in his First Epistle to the Corinthians, where the Holy Ghost is eulogized as the author of the supernatural gifts of grace, such as wisdom, knowledge, the working of miracles, prophecy, "interpretation of speeches," etc.[176] The Holy Ghost wrought His own theophany (or visible manifestation) in the form of "parted tongues of fire" on Pentecost Day, when, as Sacred Scripture tells us, the Apostles "were filled with the Holy Ghost, and . . . began to speak with divers tongues, according as the Holy Ghost gave them to speak."[177] But the greatest miracle of His omnipotence was the Incarnation, when the Blessed Virgin Mary "conceived [her Divine Son] of the Holy Ghost."[178]

Omnipresence and indwelling are likewise distinctly divine attributes. Now, the Holy Ghost is everywhere in Sacred Scripture represented as the penetrating, transforming, purifying, sanctifying, and vivifying principle of supernatural life; so much so that the Nicaeno-Constantinopolitan Creed expressly designates Him as the Vivifier.[179] Cfr. John VI, 64: "*Spiritus est, qui vivificat* — It is the Spirit that quickeneth." 2 Cor. III, 6: "Τὸ δὲ πνεῦμα ζωοποιεῖ — But the Spirit quickeneth." This vivifying and sanctifying omnipresence implies the divine prerogative of indwelling in the souls of the just.

176 1 Cor. XII, 4-11.

177 Acts II, 4.

178 Cfr. Matth. I, 20: "*Quod in ea natum est, de Spiritu Sancto est* — That which is conceived in her, is of the Holy Ghost."

179 *Vivificator* (ζωοποιός), *i. e.*, He who gives life.

The Saints are temples of the Holy Ghost. John XIV, 17: "You shall know him; because he shall abide with you, and shall be in you." 1 Cor. III, 16: "Know you not that you are the temples of the Holy Ghost, and that the Spirit of God dwelleth in you?" 1 Cor. VI, 19: "Know you not that your members are the temple of the Holy Ghost, who is in you, whom you have from God?"

b) Of the attributes of divine life, omniscience belongs to the Holy Ghost in the same measure as it belongs to the Logos. He is the "searcher of the deep things of God," which "no man knoweth, but the Spirit of God." 1 Cor. II, 10–11: "*Spiritus omnia scrutatur, etiam profunda Dei. Quis enim hominum scit, quae sunt hominis, nisi spiritus hominis, qui in ipso est. Ita et ea quae Dei sunt, nemo cognovit nisi Spiritus Dei* — For the Spirit searcheth all things, yea, the deep things of God. For what man knoweth the things of a man, but the spirit of a man that is in him? So the things also that are of God no man knoweth but the Spirit of God." In virtue of this Divine Knowledge He is the revealer of the mysteries of God. "*Spiritu loquitur mysteria.*"[180] Out of His perfect knowledge of the future free acts of rational creatures, the Holy Ghost inspires the prophets and predicts the future. John XVI, 13: "*Quae ventura sunt, annuntiabit vobis* — The things that are to come, he shall shew you."[181]

Besides these attributes, there are His external divine operations. Continuing the work of the Redemption, the Holy Ghost is perpetually remitting sins in the Church. John XX, 22 sq.: "*Accipite Spiritum Sanctum: quorum remiseritis peccata, remittuntur eis*

180 1 Cor. XIV, 2; cfr. 2 Pet. I, 21.

181 Cfr. also 1 Pet. I, 10 sqq.; 2 Pet. I, 21.

— Receive ye the Holy Ghost. Whose sins you shall forgive, they are forgiven them."—"The charity of God is poured forth in our hearts by the Holy Ghost,"[182] and it is the Holy Ghost through whom the just are adopted as children of God. Rom. VIII, 14: "*Quicumque enim Spiritu Dei aguntur, ii sunt filii Dei* — For whosoever are led by the Spirit of God, they are the sons of God." He is, lastly, the seal of supernatural life stamped on our souls. Eph. I, 13: "*Credentes signati estis Spiritu promissionis sancto* [*i. e., Spiritu a Deo promisso*]— Believing, you were signed with the Holy Spirit of promise" (that is to say, with the Spirit promised by God).

2. THE HOLY GHOST ENTITLED TO DIVINE WORSHIP.—The Trinitarian form of benediction puts the Holy Ghost on a par with the Father and the Son. This general argument for His adorability can be fortified by a special proof, drawn from the peculiar malice involved in blaspheming the Person of the Holy Ghost.

Cfr. Matth. XII, 31–32: "*Omne peccatum et blasphemia remittetur hominibus; Spiritus autem blasphemia non remittetur. Et quicunque dixerit verbum contra Filium hominis* [*i. e., Christum*] *remittetur ei; qui autem dixerit contra Spiritum Sanctum, non remittetur ei neque in hoc saeculo neque in futuro* — Every sin and blasphemy shall be forgiven men, but the blasphemy of[183] the Spirit shall not be forgiven. And

182 Rom. V, 5.

183 Better, *against*, as Fr. Spencer renders it in *The Four Gospels, A New Translation*, New York 1898.

whosoever shall speak a word against the Son of man, it shall be forgiven him: but he that shall speak against the Holy Ghost, it shall not be forgiven him, neither in this world, nor in the world to come." Therefore blasphemy against the Holy Ghost is a more grievous offence than ordinary blasphemy; which could not be were not the Holy Ghost at least coequal in majesty and adorableness with the Father and the Son. As for Christ's dictum in the text just quoted, we need hardly say that it is only *as man* that He subordinates Himself to the Holy Ghost, in the same sense in which He elsewhere says:[184] "The Father is greater than I." This argument is confirmed by all those Scriptural texts which contain the phrase "temple of the Holy Ghost," for a temple is reared for the worship of the Divinity.

3. The Name "God" Applied to the Holy Ghost.—Although the Bible nowhere expressly calls the Third Person of the Blessed Trinity "God," the appellation occurs frequently in contexts where "God" can be legitimately substituted for "Holy Ghost."

a) To begin with, the Old Testament contains a number of passages which are directly referred to the Holy Ghost in the New. Is. VI, 8–9, we read: "*Et audivi vocem Domini* (אֲדֹנָי) *dicentis: . . . Vade et dices populo huic: audite audientes et nolite intelligere* — And I heard the voice of the Lord, saying: . . . Go and thou shalt say to this people: Hearing, hear and understand not." Now St. Paul teaches:[185] "*Bene Spiritus Sanctus locutus est per Isaiam prophetam: Vade et dices,*

[184] John XIV, 28.

[185] Acts XXVIII, 25.

etc. — Well did the Holy Ghost speak to our fathers by Isaias the prophet, saying: Go to this people and say to them, etc." According to St. Paul, therefore, the Holy Ghost is identical with the Old Testament אֲדֹנָי, that is to say, with the one true God, to whom alone this name is attributable as a *quasi nomen proprium.*[186] A similar substitution of names takes place whenever a prophecy is alternately ascribed to the Father, to the Son, and to the Holy Ghost.[187] If the Father is God, and the Son is God, the Holy Ghost, too, must be God.

b) In many passages of the New Testament the word "God" can be directly substituted for "Holy Ghost." Thus St. Peter addresses Ananias in these words: "*Cur tentavit Satanas cor tuum, mentiri te Spiritui Sancto. . . . Non es mentitus hominibus, sed Deo* — Why hath Satan tempted thy heart, that thou shouldst lie to the Holy Ghost. . . . Thou hast not lied to men, but to God." [188] By substitution we get the proposition: "The Holy Ghost is God." St. Paul, when he asks: [189] "*Nescitis quia templum Dei estis et Spiritus Dei habitat in vobis?* — Know you not that you are the temple of God and that the Spirit of God dwelleth in you?"— plainly intimates that the Holy Ghost dwelling in "the temple of God" is identical with God Himself.[190] A comparison of John I, 13: "*Ex Deo nati sunt* — They are born of God," with John III, 5: "*Nisi quis renatus fuerit ex aqua et Spiritu Sancto* — Unless a man be born again of water and the Holy Ghost," shows that "Holy Ghost" = "God." Finally St. Paul says in his Epistle to the Hebrews: "*Multifariam*

186 Compare Ps. XCIV, 8–11 with Heb. III, 7–11.

187 *Vide supra*, pp. 29 sq.

188 Acts V, 3–4.

189 1 Cor. III, 16.

190 Cfr. 1 Cor. VI, 19; 2 Cor. VI, 16.

multisque modis olim Deus loquens patribus in prophetis — God . . . at sundry times and in divers manners spoke in times past to the fathers by the prophets,"[191] and St. Peter assures us: "*Non enim voluntate humana allata est aliquando prophetia, sed Spiritu Sancto inspirati locuti sunt sancti Dei homines* — For prophecy came not by the will of man at any time: but the holy men of God spoke, inspired by the Holy Ghost."[192]

The synthesis of the Three Divine Persons in the complete concept of the Trinity is most perfectly consummated in the so-called *ordo subsistendi*,[193] by virtue of which the Three observe a constant order and follow one another in an immutable sequence. The members of this formula can not be transposed. The Father must be conceived strictly as the First, the Son as the Second, and the Holy Ghost as the Third Person of the Godhead. Yet this is not to be understood as implying a sequence of time or dignity, a before or after, a more or less; for in virtue of their absolute consubstantiality or *homoousia* all Three Divine Persons are coequal in rank, eternity, and power.[194] The numerical sequence

191 Heb. I, 1.

192 2 Pet. I, 21. For a fuller elucidation of the topic of this paragraph, cfr. Heinrich, *Dogmat. Theologie*, IV, § 228; Kleutgen, *De Ipso Deo*, pp. 489-509.

193 Ἀκολουθία κατὰ τὴν τάξιν.

194 Cfr. the Athanasian Creed: "*Et in hac Trinitate nihil prius aut posterius, nihil maius aut minus, sed totae tres personae coaeternae et coaequales* — And in this Trinity none is afore or after other, none is greater or less than another, but the whole Three Persons are co-eternal together, and co-equal."

of the Three Divine Persons in the Trinity, therefore, simply implies a succession with regard to origin, the Father being the principle of the Son, and the Father and the Son together the principle of the Holy Ghost. In our Lord's baptismal mandate, in the form of baptism which He Himself dictated, in the *Comma Ioanneum,* in the Christian doxologies, and wherever else the Bible formally enumerates the Three Divine Persons, this order is unvaried. When Holy Scripture seems to make an exception (as, *e. g.,* 1 Cor. XII, 1 sqq.), it is easy to see that no formal enumeration is intended.

READINGS: — St. Athanasius, *De Trinit. et Spiritu Sancto Libri III;* Didymus Alex., *De Spiritu Sancto* (in Migne, *Patr. Gr.,* 39, 1031 sqq.); St. Ambrose, *De Spiritu Sancto ad Gratianum August.;* S. Thom., *Contr. Gent.,* IV, 16 sqq. (Rickaby, *l. c.,* pp. 349 sqq.) and the commentators; Petavius, *De Trinit.,* II, 6, 13 sqq., VII, 5; Th. Schermann, *Die Gottheit des hl. Geistes nach den griechischen Vätern des vierten Jahrhunderts,* Freiburg 1901; Cardinal Manning, *The Temporal Mission of the Holy Ghost,* Am. reprint, New York 1905; J. Lebreton, *Les Origines du Dogme de la Trinité,* pp. 251 sqq., 283 sqq., 325 sqq., 371 sqq., 418 sqq., Paris 1910; E. W. Winstanley, *Spirit in the New Testament: An Enquiry into the Use of the word πνεῦμα in all Passages, and a Survey of the Evidence Concerning the Holy Spirit,* Cambridge 1908; H. B. Swete, *The Holy Spirit in the New Testament,* London 1909; J. Forget, art. "Holy Ghost" in the *Catholic Encyclopedia,* Vol. VII, pp. 409 sqq.; H. A. Barry, *God the Holy Ghost,* Boston 1901; W. F. Stadelman, C. S. Sp., *Glories of the Holy Ghost,* Techny, Ill., 1919, pp. 6 sqq.; J. R. M. Landrieux, *The Forgotten Paraclete,* London 1924; G. Menge, O. F. M., *Der hl. Geist,* Hildesheim 1927.

CHAPTER II

THE BLESSED TRINITY IN TRADITION

The dogma of the Blessed Trinity was defined by the Council of Nicaea, A. D. 325. The ensuing Antitrinitarian controversies, which marked the period ending with the year 381, came to a head at the Second Ecumenical Council, which safeguarded the doctrine against various heretical incursions. In the precise formulation which it received at Nicaea and Constantinople, the dogma has come down to our time, and we can consequently, in demonstrating it from Tradition, confine our attention to the first four centuries of the Christian era. Since the condemnation of various heretical perversions affords the best insight into the genuine ecclesiastical Tradition, we shall preface our positive exposition by a brief account of the Antitrinitarian heresies up to the beginning of the fifth century.

SECTION 1

THE ANTITRINITARIAN HERESIES AND THEIR CONDEMNATION BY THE CHURCH

There are two logical processes whereby the dogma of the Blessed Trinity can be essentially perverted; *per defectum, i. e.,* by exaggerating the notion of unity and eliminating that of Trinity (Monarchianism); or *per excessum, i. e.,* by exaggerating the concept of the Trinity, making it a Trinity of Divine Natures and thereby denying the unity of Persons (Tritheism). Tritheism will receive due consideration in the second part of this volume, in which we shall expound the doctrine of Unity in the Trinity (*Unitas in Trinitate*).

Monarchianism, or the doctrine of the *Monarchia,* as it is called by an assumption of exclusive orthodoxy like that which has led to the adoption of the term "Unitarianism" at the present day,[1] denies the distinction of Persons in the Divine Nature. It is threefold: (1) crass Monarchianism, in its present-day form called Unitarianism, which denies all distinction of persons in God. (2) Modalism, so-called, which admits a Trinity of Persons, but holds that the difference between them

1 Cfr. Newman, *The Arians of the Fourth Century,* p. 117.

is not real, but merely nominal or modal; this heresy is called Sabellianism from its chief champion, Sabellius. (3) Subordinationism, which, while it readily grants that the three Divine Persons are really distinct, insists that they are not coequal, but subordinate one to the other (Arianism, Macedonianism). This logical division of Monarchianism substantially coincides with the successive phases of its historic development.

READINGS: — The various text-books of Church History, especially Alzog (Pabisch-Byrne's translation), Vol. I, pp. 348 sqq., 5th ed., Cincinnati 1899; Funk-Cappadelta, *A Manual of Church History*, Vol. I, London 1910; *Hefele, *A History of the Councils of the Church*, Vols. I sqq.; *Oswald, *Trinitätslehre*, §§ 8–9, Paderborn 1888; H. Couget, *La SS. Trinité et les Dogmes Antitrinitaires*, Paris 1905; F. J. Hall, *The Trinity*, pp. 63 sqq.. New York 1910.

ARTICLE 1

CRASS MONARCHIANISM

1. THE HERESY OF MONARCHIANISM.—This is an ancient heresy, the beginnings of which can be traced to the second century of the Christian era. It is either Dynamistic or Patripassian. Dynamistic Monarchianism asserts that the Father alone is true God, and that the divine element in Christ was merely a power (δύναμις) indwelling in Him as an impersonal divine spirit. Patripassian Monarchianism completely identifies the Son with the Father, asserting that the Person of the Father was made flesh and suffered on the Cross. The Patripassian is superior to the

Dynamistic form of Monarchianism in so far as it acknowledges Christ to be a manifestation of the Divine Essence.

a) Dynamistic Monarchianism was championed by the Ebionites, the Cerinthians, and the Carpocratians, who all held that Christ was a mere man, though endowed with divine powers or energies, after the manner of the Old Testament prophets or the pagan soothsayers. The chief representatives of this heresy were Theodotus of Byzantium (about A. D. 192), a tanner by trade, and his pupil Theodotus the Younger. The latter, surnamed the Money-Changer, asserted that a divine power had indeed descended upon the man Jesus at his baptism, but that the same Divine Power (λόγος, υἱός) had appeared in Melchisedech, who had been mediator and intercessor for the angels in the same sense in which Christ was for men, and whose followers were therefore called Melchisedechians.[2] A somewhat later protagonist of this heresy was the notorious Paul of Samosata, an extremely clever man, who died as Bishop of Antioch, about A. D. 260. He taught that Christ, though supernaturally begotten and born of a virgin, was nevertheless a mere man, and that the Divine Logos (*i. e.*, the impersonal wisdom of God) was not united to Him substantially, but simply as a quality or power; whence His deification was foreordained. Thus "the Logos was greater than Christ; the Logos was from above, Christ from below; Christ suffered in His nature and wrought miracles by grace." It was

2 Alzog, *Universal Church History*, English tr., Vol. I, 350; Blunt's *Dictionary of Sects, Heresies, etc.*, new impression, London 1903, pp. 304 sq. On Theodotus the tanner, and his pupil the money-changer, cfr. Eusebius, *Hist. Eccles.*, V, 28; Theodoretus, *Haeret. Fab.*, II, 5.

only by means of divine grace and His own co-operation therewith, that Christ ultimately became God.[3]

A kindred heresy was that of Photinus, Bishop of Sirmium (d. 366), who "increased the scandal, by advocating, and with greater boldness, an almost Unitarian doctrine."[4] He taught that the Logos is the impersonal intellect, while the Holy Ghost is the impersonal power of God, in whom there is but one Person, *viz.*, the Father. Hence Θεός = λογοπάτωρ. Christ, according to Photinus, was a simple man, in whom the Logos dwelt as efficient power (ἐνέργεια δραστική), and who earned for himself the name of "God" by his obedience.

The main argument of all these heretics was this. If the Father were other than the Son, and each were nevertheless true God, it would be necessary to assume the existence of two Gods (Ditheism). Consequently Christ, though endowed with divine power (δύναμις), is a mere man. Paul of Samosata quoted in support of his heresy John XVII, 3; XIV, 28; Matth. XI, 27; Luke II, 52.

b) The Patripassian form of Monarchianism, according to the *Philosophoumena*,[5] seems to have had for its author Noëtus of Smyrna, a philosopher of the school of Heraclitus. He denied the distinction of Persons in the Godhead and taught that the Father was born, suffered, and died in Christ.[6] Another leader of the

3 Cfr. Alzog, I, 350 sq.; Hergenröther, *Kirchengeschichte*, 3rd ed., Vol. I, p. 222. There is some difficulty in determining what were the opinions of the Samosatene. Cfr. Newman, *Select Treatises of St. Athanasius*, II, 237 sqq.; IDEM, *The Arians of the Fourth Century*, pp. 3 sqq.

4 Newman, *The Arians of the Fourth Century*, p. 313.

5 IX, 7 sqq., ed. Miller, p. 284, Oxon. 1851. Cfr. Bardenhewer-Shahan, *Patrology*, pp. 209 sqq.

6 "*Pater passus est.*" In a fragment of the writings of Hippolytus Noëtus's teaching is stated in these terms: "Τὸν Χριστὸν εἶναι τὸν πατέρα καὶ αὐτὸν τὸν πατέρα γεγεννῆσθαι καὶ πεπονθέναι καὶ ἀποτεθνηκέναι." (*Fragm. contr. Noët.*, c. 1.) On Noëtus and the

Patripassian heretics was Praxeas (about A. D. 192), a contemporary of Tertullian, by whom he was denounced as one of the "*vanissimi Monarchiani*" who boasted, "*Monarchiam habemus.*"[7] Regardless of the distinction between Nature and Person, Praxeas taught that the Divine Substance has but one Hypostasis. As Father, God is a spirit, but He is called Son in so far as He has assumed human flesh (without a soul)—"*Ipse se filium sibi fecit.*" Consequently Christ is indeed true God, but He is not the Son of God; and inasmuch as Christ was the Father incarnate, it was the Father who suffered and died on the Cross. In confirmation of his error Praxeas quoted John X, 30: "*Ego et Pater unum sumus*—I and the Father are one;" and John XIV, 9: "*Philippe, qui videt me, videt et Patrem*—Philip, he that seeth me, seeth the Father also." Praxeas and his adherents were therefore also called υἱοπάτορες.[8]

2. Attitude of the Church Towards Monarchianism.—The Church strenuously opposed all these heresies even before she began to hold ecumenical councils.

The iniquitous Theodotus of Byzantium was excommunicated by Pope Victor I (189–198). Paul of Samosata was called to account by several synods,[9] but, clever sophist that he was, escaped conviction until Malchion, a learned presbyter of Antioch, was able to expose the drift of his errors and tore the mask from his

Noëtians, cfr. Blunt, *Dictionary of Sects, Heresies*, etc., pp. 373 sqq., new impression, London 1903.

7 *Contr. Praxeam*, c. 3.

8 On this term, see Newman, *Select Treatises of St. Athanasius*, II, 475 sq.

9 A. D. 264 sqq.

face at a council held in Antioch A. D. 269.[10] Paul was deposed and excommunicated, but tenaciously held on to his see until the Emperor Aurelian put an end to the reign of Queen Zenobia, into whose favor he had insinuated himself.[11]

Noëtus, when cited before a council in Asia Minor, sought to conceal his Patripassian leanings by emphasizing his monotheism, and pathetically exclaimed: "What wrong have I done? I adore the One God, I know but One God, and none beside Him, who was born, suffered, and died!"[12] The assembled bishops (called *presbyteri*) did not reply that they were Ditheists. They simply declared: "We, too, adore the One God, but in a manner in which we know that He is adored rightly. And we likewise possess the One Christ, . . . the Son of God, who suffered and died."[13] Noëtus was excommunicated A. D. 170. Praxeas had to recant his errors in writing. He went to Africa, where he found a staunch opponent in Tertullian, who employed the Apostles' Creed as the most effective weapon against the Patripassian heresy.[14]

Against the later "Unitarianism" of the Socinians, who also denied the Blessed Trinity and the Divinity of Jesus Christ, and taught a sort of abstract monotheism, Pope Paul IV (A. D. 1555) issued his dogmatic Constitution "*Cum quorundam.*"[15]

10 Cfr. Bardenhewer-Shahan, *Patrology*, p. 165.

11 A. D. 272. Cfr. Newman, *The Arians of the Fourth Century*, pp. 3 sqq.; Edm. Venables in the *Dictionary of Christian Biography, s. v.* "Paulus of Samosata"; Hefele, *History of the Councils* (Engl. ed.), Vol. I, pp. 118 sqq. The authenticity of the "*Epistola Synodica Anni 269*" is doubtful. Cfr. Bardenhewer-Shahan, *Patrology*, p. 165.

12 Quoted by Epiphanius, *Haeres.*, 57, 1.

13 Epiph., *l. c.*

14 Tertull., *Contr. Prax.*, c. 2.

15 Denzinger-Bannwart, *Enchiridion*, n. 993. On modern Antitrinitarianism, see Chapter IV, § 1, *infra*.

READINGS: — *Hagemann, *Die römische Kirche und ihr Einfluss auf Disziplin und Dogma in den drei ersten Jahrhunderten*, Freiburg 1864; Hergenröther-Kirsch, *Kirchengeschichte*, 4th ed., Vol. I, pp. 245 sqq., Freiburg 1902; Schwane, *Dogmengeschichte*, 2nd ed., Vol. I, Freiburg 1892; A. Harnack, art. "Monarchianism" in the *New Schaff-Herzog Encyclopedia of Religious Knowledge*, Vol. VII, pp. 453–461, New York 1910; J. Tixeront, *History of Dogmas*, English tr., Vol. I, 290 sqq., St. Louis 1910; J. Chapman, O. S. B., art. "Monarchians" in the *Catholic Encyclopedia*, Vol. X, pp. 448 sqq.

ARTICLE 2

THE MODALISM OF SABELLIUS

1. THE HERESY OF SABELLIUS.—Sabellius (about A. D. 250) was not an extreme Monarchianist; he recognized the existence of a Trinity, though an imperfect one, in the Godhead.[16]

The Sabellian Triad is no true, real, immanent Trinity. It is merely a modal, external, and transitive distinction, based upon the relation of God (in Whom the Sabellians admit but one Person) to the created universe. In other words, the Trinity of the Sabellians is a merely external Trinity of manifestation, not an internal one of life. Father, Son, and Holy Ghost, they argue, are three distinct modes (πρόσωπα) by which the one Person of the Godhead manifests Himself, and which are interrelated as body, soul, and spirit in man, or light, warmth, and sphericity in the sun. The undifferentiated Divine Monad has in course of time developed and "dilated" into a Triad. In its rôle of Creator it is

16 Cfr. Newman, *The Arians of the Fourth Century*, Ch. I, § 5: "Sabellianism," pp. 116–132; see also Chapman's article "Monarchians" in the *Catholic Encyclopedia*, Vol. X. 448 sqq.

called Father; as the Redeemer it is called Son; and as the Sanctifier, enlightening and regenerating the faithful, it is called Holy Ghost. Hence the Modalist formula: "Τρεῖς ὀνομασίαι ἐν μιᾷ ὑποστάσει," or, still more sharply: "Μία ὑπόστασις καὶ τρεῖς ἐνέργειαι."

Although the Trinity of Sabellius was not a real Trinity of Persons, but merely a triple differentiation of office and external manifestation, he nevertheless adopted, for the sake of perverting it, the orthodox formula of τρία πρόσωπα. He dishonestly played upon the ambiguity of the word πρόσωπον, which etymologically may signify a person, outward appearance, a countenance, or a character in a play.[17] It was on this account that the later Oriental theologians avoided the term πρόσωπον (*persona* = mask) for person; or, when they did employ it, defined it most carefully as πρόσωπον ἐνυπόστατον, in order to exclude the Sabellian interpretation of πρόσωπον ἀνυπόστατον.

2. ITS CONDEMNATION.—Sabellius, after having been treated with considerate kindness by Pope Zephyrin, was finally excommunicated by Callistus (217–222). We know this from the *Philosophoumena* of St. Hippolytus (first complete edition by Miller, Oxford 1851).

After his excommunication Sabellius retired to the Lybian Pentapolis (about A. D. 257), and there continued to propagate his errors. He was opposed by Dionysius the Great, Bishop of Alexandria, who wrote several dogmatic epistles in refutation of Sabellianism, but in his zeal for the truth went to the other extreme,

17 Alzog, *Universal Church History* (English tr.), Vol. I, p. 355.

so that he was accused of teaching Ditheism.[18] The most objectionable passage[19] in the latter's writings was probably this: "The Son of God is a work or creature (ποίημα) and something that has come into being; He is not distinct according to His nature, but foreign to the Father in substance" [οὐσία undoubtedly is here the same as ὑπόστασις, both terms being used promiscuously for a time to signify nature or person]. At this juncture (A. D. 262) Pope Dionysius issued a truly epoch-making decision, of which St. Athanasius has preserved some fragments. In his epistle the sovereign teacher of Christendom distinctly condemns the Sabellian heresy, but at the same time censures the ditheistic expressions used by the Bishop of Alexandria. It is not too much to say that this Apostolic letter condemned not only Monarchianism and Sabellianism, but likewise, in advance, Subordinationism and Tritheism, which were the products of a later age.[20] The energetic and loyal Bishop of Alexandria, who in his zeal had overshot the truth, readily submitted and satisfied the Pope of his good faith by means of an explicit statement which he forwarded to Rome. This important document embodies two points of particular interest. In the first place Denis explains that he had employed the unfortunate term ποίημα not in the meaning of "creature," but in the hypostatic sense of *productus, i. e., genitus,* in order to emphasize the reality and self-existence of the Person of the Logos against Sabellius. Secondly, he cordially accepts the new locution ὁμοούσιος τῷ Θεῷ, used

18 Newman, *The Arians of the Fourth Century,* pp. 126 sq.

19 Quoted by St. Athanasius, *De Sententia Dionysii Alex.,* Migne, *P. G.,* XXV, 465. Cfr. Newman, *Select Treatises of St. Athanasius,* I, pp. 45 sq.

20 The Latin text of such parts of Pope Dionysius's epistle as have come down to us, can be found in Scheeben's *Dogmatik,* Vol. I, p. 746.

by Pope Dionysius in his dogmatic epistle, though, as he takes pains to remark, he had "not found this term anywhere in Holy Scripture." [21] This goes to show that the term was coined and circulated long before the Council of Nicaea; in other words, the heresy of Arius was condemned before it was ever hatched. The phrase ὁμοούσιος τῷ Θεῷ embodies all the essential elements of the dogma:— Christ's Divine Sonship, His Divinity, and His Consubstantiality with the Father.[22]

READINGS:— Worm, *Historia Sabelliana* 1796; *Döllinger, *Hippolyt und Callistus,* Ratisbon 1853 (English translation, *Hippolytus and Callistus,* Edinburg 1876); Newman, *The Arians of the Fourth Century,* pp. 116 sqq., New Ed., London 1901. —B. J. Otten, S. J., *History of Dogmas,* Vol. I, pp. 153 sqq.

ARTICLE 3

THE SUBORDINATIONISM OF ARIUS AND MACEDONIUS

1. THE HERESY OF SUBORDINATIONISM.—This heresy involved the Church in many terrific conflicts. It started with an attack on the co-equality of the Son with the Father (Arianism), and ultimately impugned the dogma of the Consubstantiality of the Holy Ghost with the Father and the Son (Macedonianism, Pneumatomachians).

21 Cfr. Newman, *Select Treatises of St. Athanasius,* I, p. 44.

22 Cfr. St. August., *Contr. Maxim.,* II, 14, 3: "*Hoc est illud* ὁμοούσιον, *quod fides antiqua pepererat* — This is that famous term ὁμοούσιος, to which the ancient faith had given birth."

a) The salient tenets of Arianism [23] are these: The Logos began His existence in time. Consequently there was a time when the Son of God was not (ἦν ποτε, ὅτε οὐκ ἦν). He is not begotten out of the substance of the Father, but made by the free will of the Father "out of nothing" (ἐξ οὐκ ὄντων γέγονεν ὁ λόγος). Though He existed before all creatures, *i. e.*, before the beginning of time, the Logos does not exist from everlasting, and consequently He is not God, but a creature of the Father (ποίημα, κτίσμα τοῦ πατρός), exalted indeed above all other creatures, because God's instrument in creating the world. Therefore He is "God" by grace (θέσει, μετοχῇ, καταχρηστικῶς), an intermediary being between God and the world (μέσος γενόμενος). Although it was possible for the Logos to sin, and His will was therefore alterable (τρεπτός, ἀλλοιωτός), still by a perfect use of free will and grace He actually became sinless.

To deceive the unsuspecting faithful, and to veil his errors, Arius played fast and loose with the words γενητός (*i. e., creatus, factus*) and γεννητός (*i. e., genitus*) and their contradictories ἀγένητος (*i. e., increatus*) and ἀγέννητος (*i. e., ingenitus*), just as the Semi-Arians later did with ὁμοούσιος (*i. e.,* consubstantial) and ὁμοιούσιος (*i. e.,* of like substance).

b) The heresy of Macedonius and Marathon was an offshoot of Semi-Arianism. Macedonius, who was Bishop of Constantinople about A. D. 360, taught that the Holy Ghost is a creature of the Logos, by whom, according to the Arian theory, all things were created. This completed the essential subordination of the Three Persons of the Divine Trinity, whom these heretics ranked as follows: A Great One = the Holy Ghost; a

23 Cfr. Newman, *The Arians of the Fourth Century*, pp. 201 sqq.

Greater One = the Logos; Greatest of all = God the Father.

Some Semi-Arians were willing to admit the Divinity of Christ; but they refused to forswear the heretical conceit that the Holy Ghost is a mere creature. It was for this reason that St. Athanasius called them "enemies of the Spirit" (πνευματόμαχοι).

2. ITS CONDEMNATION.—For the first time since the Council of the Apostles at Jerusalem, the infallible Church exercised her teaching authority against Subordinationism at two ecumenical synods, of which the first condemned Arianism, while the second dealt a death blow to the heresy of the Macedonianists.

a) The First Ecumenical Council, held at Nicaea A. D. 325, in the reign of Constantine,[24] solemnly rejected the heresy of Arius. It did this in a twofold manner: positively, by enlarging and expounding the Apostles' Creed; negatively, by anathematizing Arius and his followers.

The famous Nicene Creed revolves about the term ὁμοούσιος, which was rejected by the Arians as "unscriptural." The symbol itself is equivalent to a dogmatic definition, and its history is highly instructive for any one who would trace the development of the Catholic conception of the dogma of the Most Holy Trinity.

24 For a brief account of its history, its transactions, and its consequences, see Newman, *The Arians of the Fourth Century*, pp. 237–270. More detailed information in Hefele's *History of the Councils*, Vols. I and II of the English translation.

At first the Fathers of the Council thought it sufficient to adopt the formula "*Filius ex Deo*" against the Arian ἐξ οὐκ ὄντων. But when the friends of Arius, particularly Bishop Eusebius of Cæsarea, in order to conceal the real question at issue, willingly accepted this formula on the ground that all things are "from God," the ἐκ τοῦ πατρός was amplified into ἐκ τῆς οὐσίας τοῦ πατρός. Finally, in order to baffle the Eusebians, the phrase ὁμοούσιος τῷ πατρί (consubstantial with the Father) was added. This proved the utter condemnation of the Arian heresy. The decisive passages of the Nicene Creed finally took this shape: "*Et in unum Dominum, Iesum Christum, Filium Dei, qui ex Patre unigenitus generatur* (τὸν υἱὸν τοῦ Θεοῦ γεννηθέντα ἐκ τοῦ πατρὸς μονογενῆ), *hoc est ex substantia Patris* (ἐκ τῆς οὐσίας τοῦ πατρός), *Deum ex Deo* (Θεὸν ἐκ Θεοῦ), *lumen de lumine, Deum verum ex Deo vero, genitum, non factum,* (γεννηθέντα, οὐ ποιηθέντα), *consubstantialem Patri* (ὁμοούσιον τῷ πατρί)—And in one Lord Jesus Christ, the Son of God, begotten of the Father, Only-begotten, that is, from the substance of the Father; God from God, Light from Light, Very God from Very God, begotten not made, consubstantial with the Father."[25] This clear-cut definition irrevocably established the dogma of Christ's Divine Sonship, His Divinity, and His Consubstantiality with the Father.[26]

The heretical antitheses of Arius were condemned in a special anathematism appended to the Creed, which reads as follows: "*Eos autem qui dicunt: erat [tempus] quando non erat* (ἦν ποτε, ὅτε οὐκ ἦν) *et*

25 Newman's translation. Cfr. *Select Treatises of St. Athanasius in Controversy with the Arians,* Vol. I, p. 57.

26 Cfr. St. Athanasius, *De Decret. Nicaen. Syn.*, reproduced in Migne, *P. G.*, XXV, 415 sqq.

priusquam gigneretur, non erat, et aiunt Filium Dei ex non exstantibus factum (ὅτι ἐξ οὐκ ὄντων ἐγένετο) *vel ex alia substantia vel essentia esse* (ἐξ ἑτέρας ὑποστάσεως ἢ οὐσίας εἶναι) *vel mutabilem vel vertibilem* (ἀλλοιωτὸν ἢ τρεπτόν) *esse, hos anathematizat Ecclesia catholica* — But those who say, 'Once he was not,' and 'Before His generation He was not,' and 'He came into being from nothing,' or those who pretend that the Son of God is 'of other subsistence or substance,' or 'created,' or 'alterable,' or 'mutable,' the Catholic Church anathematizes." [27] In this passage the Holy Synod reaffirms the Consubstantiality of the Son of God (*i. e.*, Christ), by rejecting the doctrine of the *Heterousia*, and asserts His Divinity by emphasizing that He possesses the attributes of eternity, uncreatedness, and immutability.[28]

b) Pope Damasus, at a synod held in Rome, A. D. 380,[29] so thoroughly repudiated the heresy of Macedonius that the twenty-fourth in his series of anathemas has been justly styled "a summary of the contents of all the others, and the keystone of all previous dogmatic formulas." [30] The Second Ecumenical Council, convoked by the Emperor Theodosius I at Constantinople, A. D. 381, formally defined the Divinity of the Holy Ghost in these words: "*Et*

27 Newman's translation. (*Select Treatises of St. Athanasius,* Vol. I, p. 57.)

28 The Fathers of Nicaea use ὑπόστασις as synonymous with οὐσία. The two terms, as Cardinal Newman points out, at that time "had not their respective meanings so definitely settled and so familiarly received as afterwards." (*Select Treatises of St. Athanasius,* Vol. II, p. 455.)

29 Cfr. Denzinger-Bannwart, *Enchiridion,* Nos. 58 sqq.

30 Scheeben, *Dogmatik,* I, p. 748.

in Spiritum Sanctum, Dominum et vivificantem (εἰς τὸ πνεῦμα τὸ ἅγιον, τὸ κύριον, τὸ ζωοποιόν), *qui ex Patre procedit* (τὸ ἐκ τοῦ πατρὸς ἐκπορευόμενον), *qui cum Patre et Filio simul adoratur et conglorificatur, qui locutus est per prophetas* — And in the Holy Ghost, the Lord and Life-giver, who proceedeth from the Father, who is adored and glorified together with the Father and the Son, who has spoken through the prophets."

Apart from the significant appellation "Lord" (τὸ κύριον) the Divinity of the Holy Ghost is defined in this passage indirectly rather than directly. He is not formally called God, but certain divine attributes are ascribed to Him; *viz.*, vivification or the giving of life, adoration and glory such as is due to the Father and the Son, and the illumination of the prophets. In ascribing these attributes to the Third Person, the Council manifestly meant to assert the Consubstantiality of the Holy Ghost with the Father and the Son. The hypostatic difference is sufficiently indicated by the clause, "*Qui ex Patre procedit* — Who proceedeth from the Father," which combines the two Scripture texts John XV, 26, and 1 Cor. II, 12. The reason why the Council of Constantinople did not define the Procession of the Holy Ghost from the Son (*Filioque*), is that the Macedonians had not denied, but, on the contrary, maintained it, though they erred in holding that the Holy Ghost proceeded from the Son as a mere creature (ποίημα, *factura*).[31] The schismatic Greeks, therefore, have no right to quote this Council

31 It was not even fitting or advisable for the Council to mention the Procession from the Son. (Cfr. Wilhelm-Scannell, *A Manual of Catholic Theology*, I, 296 sq.)

in favor of their heretical teaching that the Holy Ghost proceeds from the Father alone. The Second Council of Constantinople, A. D. 381, was not originally a general council, and the fact that it later came to rank as such, is due to its subsequent reception by the Universal Church rather than to the formal approbation of its decrees by Pope Damasus. This Council completed the preliminary formulation of the dogma of the Blessed Trinity. The so-called Athanasian Creed, which belongs to the sixth century, merely restates the ancient teaching of the Church in clearer terms and expounds it more at length. The most perfect Trinitarian formula, from a technical point of view, and also the most comprehensive, as we have already intimated, is that drawn up by the Eleventh Council of Toledo, A. D. 675.[32] The later synodical decisions do not concern us here.

The dogmatic importance of the Constantinopolitan Creed, which has been adopted into the liturgy of the Mass, cannot be too strongly emphasized, though in the light of recent researches this symbol may no longer be regarded as a mere amplification of the Nicene Creed. It seems that the Fathers assembled at Constantinople did not have before them the Creed of Nicaea, but a different symbol which had been adopted by a provincial synod of Jerusalem held about the same time.[33] The schismatic Greeks cherish the so-called Creed of Nicaea-Constantinople with an almost superstitious reverence as their inviolable and sole norm of faith. They call it *τὸ ἱερώτατον σύμβολον*, because it embodies all "twelve articles of belief" in a formula which is as immutable as it is definitive. "The Nicene Creed [in the ampli-

32 Cfr. Denzinger-Bannwart, *Enchiridion*, nn. 275 sqq.

33 Cfr. E. F. K. Müller, *Symbolik*, pp. 46 sqq., Erlangen and Leipzig 1896.

fied form believed to have been given to it by the Council of Constantinople]," says W. Gass,[34] "is the jewel of their faith, a brief but exhaustive précis of their dogmatic teaching. Its letters are woven into the vestments of their highest ecclesiastical dignitaries at Moscow. Their liturgy culminates in its recitation, and the great bell of the Kremlin is rung during its recital, which also forms part of the ceremony when the Czar is crowned in the presence of his people. It is for this reason that the faithful are so familiar with its text, which is furthermore constantly recalled to their mind by numerous symbolic pictures circulated among them."

Readings: — On Arianism, Walch, *Ketzergeschichte,* Vol. II, pp. 385 sqq., Leipzig 1764; *Möhler, *Athanasius der Grosse und die Kirche seiner Zeit im Kampfe mit dem Arianismus,* Mainz 1844; Dorner, *Entwicklungsgeschichte der Lehre von der Person Christi,* 2nd ed., Vol. I, pp. 806 sqq., Stuttgart 1845 (English translation, *History of the Development of the Doctrine of the Person of Christ,* 5 vols., Edinburgh 1861–63); *Kuhn, *Christliche Lehre von der göttlichen Dreieinigkeit,* §§ 25 sqq., Tübingen 1857; Franzelin, *De Deo Trino,* thes. 8, Romae 1881; J. Marquardt, *Cyrilli Hierosolym. De Contentionibus et Placitis Arianorum Sententia,* Braunsberg 1881; Lauchert, *Die Lehre des hl. Athanasius,* München 1895; Gwatkin, *Studies of Arianism,* 2nd ed., London 1900; Newman, *The Arians of the Fourth Century,* New Impression, London 1901; Idem, *Select Treatises of St. Athanasius in Controversy with the Arians,* 9th ed. (Vol. II, Being an Appendix of Illustrations), London 1903; Idem, *Tracts Theological and Ecclesiastical,* New Ed., pp. 137 sqq., London 1895.

On modern Antitrinitarianism, or Unitarianism, cfr. Trechsel, *Die protestantischen Antitrinitarier vor Faustus Socin,* Heidelberg 1839–44; F. S. Bock, *Historia Antitrinitariorum, maxime Socinianismi et Socinianorum,* 2 vols., Regiomont. 1774–5; Th. Parker, *A Discourse of Matters Pertaining to Religion,* London

34 *Symbolik der griechischen Kirche,* p. 119, Berlin 1872.

1846; *Burnat, *Lelio Socin,* Vevey 1894; *Ph. Huppert, *Der deutsche Protestantismus zu Beginn des 20. Jahrhunderts,* 3rd ed., Köln 1902; J. H. Allen, *Historical Sketch of the Unitarian Movement Since the Reformation,* New York 1894; R. Wallace, *Antitrinitarian Biography,* 3 vols., London 1850; T. R. Slicer, art. "Unitarianism in the United States," in the *Encyclopedia Americana,* Vol. XV, New York 1904.

On the Macedonian heresy see B. J. Otten, S. J., *A Manual of the History of Dogmas,* Vol. I, St. Louis 1917, pp. 248 sqq.

SECTION 2

THE POSITIVE TRADITION OF THE FIRST FOUR CENTURIES

The Trinitarian belief of the Christian Church during the first four centuries is manifested partly by her official liturgy and the private prayers of the faithful; partly by the doctrinal discussions of the Fathers, whom, for convenience sake, we may group in two categories, *viz.*, Ante-Nicene and Post-Nicene. The Council of Nicaea forms a sort of dividing line between the two, in so far as before its formal definition of the dogma, the Fathers were laboriously groping for accurate terms and not infrequently failed to formulate the teaching of the Church with sufficient theological precision.[1] We cannot reasonably assume that they deviated from this teaching, except in the few cases in which the fact is clearly apparent from their writings. One of these exceptional cases is that of Hippolytus, who is charged with entertaining Ditheistic views; another, that of Origen, whose language on the subject of the Blessed

1 Cfr. J. Chapman, O. S. B., in the *Catholic Encyclopedia*, Vol. X, p. 450.

Trinity lays him open to the suspicion of heterodoxy.

General Readings: — *Ruiz, *De Trinitate*, Lugduni 1625; Werner, *Geschichte der apologetischen und polemischen Literatur der christlichen Theologie*, Vol. I, Schaffhausen 1861; Réville, *Histoire du Dogme de la Divinité de Jésus-Christ*, 2nd ed., Paris 1876; Dorner, *History of the Development of the Doctrine of the Person of Christ*, Edinburgh 1861–3; 5 vols. (to be used with caution); Schwane, *Dogmengeschichte*, 2nd ed., Vols. I and II, Freiburg 1892, 1895; Th. de Régnon, *Études de Théologie Positive sur la Sainte Trinité*, 4 vols., Paris 1892 sqq.; J. Tixeront, *History of Dogmas* (Engl. tr.), Vol. I, St. Louis 1910; F. J. Hall, *The Trinity*, pp. 50 sqq., New York 1910.— B.J. Otten, S. J., *History of Dogmas*, Vol. I, St. Louis 1917, pp. 260 sqq.

ARTICLE 1

THE HOLY TRINITY IN THE OFFICIAL LITURGY OF THE EARLY CHURCH AND THE PRIVATE PRAYERS OF THE FAITHFUL

1. The Apostles' Creed.—The belief of the early Christians found its natural utterance in the so-called Apostles' Creed, which is undoubtedly as old as the Church herself. In all of its various recensions this symbol voices simple faith in the Divine Trinity.[2] St. Irenæus,[3] Origen,[4] and Tertullian[5] testify to its antiquity. The salient passages concerning the Blessed

2 Cfr. Denzinger-Bannwart, *Enchiridion*, nn. 1–14.

3 *Adv. Haer.*, I, 10, Migne, *P. G.*, VII, 550 sq.

4 *De Princip.*, Preface, Migne, *P. G.*, XI, 117 sq.

5 *De Praescr.*, 13, Migne, *P. L.*, II, 26.

Trinity are as follows: *"Credo in Deum* [not: *deos*], *Patrem omnipotentem . . . et in Iesum Christum, Filium eius unicum . . . et in Spiritum Sanctum* — I believe in God [not: gods], the Father, Almighty, . . . and in Jesus Christ, His only Son . . . and in the Holy Ghost."

It is safe to regard the Apostles' Creed as an expansion of the form of Baptism; in fact it is *the* baptismal symbolum. The constant practice of the Church in the administration of Baptism is of itself convincing proof that the dogma of the Divine Trinity always formed part and parcel of the original deposit of faith. In the *Didache* or *Teaching of the Twelve Apostles*,[6] which, according to the late Dr. F. X. Funk, was written towards the end of the first century, when Nerva ruled the Roman Empire, we read: *"Baptizate in nomine* (εἰς τὸ ὄνομα) *Patris et Filii et Spiritus Sancti* — Baptize in the name of the Father, and of the Son, and of the Holy Ghost." [7]

An interesting counterpart of the baptismal symbolum of the early Church is the private profession of faith

6 Rediscovered by Philotheus Bryennios and edited by him in 1883. Cfr. Bardenhewer-Shahan, *Patrology*, pp. 19 sqq.; Tixeront, *History of Dogmas*, Vol. I, pp. 135 sqq.; C. Taylor, *An Essay on the Doctrine of the Didache*, Cambridge 1889.

7 *Doctrina Duodecim Apostolorum*, 7, 1; ed. Funk, pp. 21 sq., Tubingae 1884. For an English translation of the *Didache*, see *The Ante-Nicene Fathers*, American Reprint, Vol. VII, pp. 377 sqq., New York 1907. On the Apostles' Creed cfr. Bäumer, *Das Apostolische Glaubensbekenntnis, seine Geschichte und sein Inhalt*, Mainz 1893, and Herbert Thurston, S. J., in the *Catholic Encyclopedia*, Vol. I, pp. 629–632, who also gives copious bibliographical references.

ascribed to St. Gregory Thaumaturgus (d. 270). This document tersely, clearly, and completely expounds the Catholic teaching on the Blessed Trinity. Defending the faith against Paul of Samosata, the Wonder-worker professes: "*Unus Deus Pater Verbi viventis. . . . Unus Dominus solus ex solo, Deus ex Deo. . . . Unus Spiritus Sanctus ex Deo subsistentiam* (ὕπαρξιν) *habens. . . . Trinitas perfecta* (τριὰς τελεία), *quae gloria et aeternitate et regno non dividitur nec alienatur* — There is one God, Father of the Living Word. . . . One Lord, sole from sole, God from God. . . . One Holy Ghost having His being from God. . . . A perfect Triad not separated nor dissociated in glory, eternity, and reign."[8] Gregory of Nyssa tells us that his grandmother Macrina had received this formula from Thaumaturgus himself and handed it down to her grandchildren in Cappadocia.[9] We are able to obtain a glimpse into the popular belief of the early Christians from an ancient evening hymn, which concludes with a doxology to "Father, Son, and Holy Ghost."[10]

2. THE ANCIENT CHRISTIAN DOXOLOGIES.— The public and private doxologies, which may be looked upon as the common property of the faithful in the early Church,[11] distinctly voice belief in the Blessed Trinity. In fact these an-

8 Migne, *P. G.*, X, 984 sqq. Newman's translation, *Tracts Theol. and Eccles.*, pp. 155 sq.

9 Migne, *P. G.*, XLVI, 913. Gregory of Nyssa's Life of St. Gregory Thaumaturgus is, however, "of little historical value because of its highly legendary character." Cfr. Bardenhewer-Shahan, *Patrology*, p. 170.

10 Ἐλθόντες ἐπὶ τοῦ ἡλίου δύσιν, ἰδόντες φῶς ἑσπερινόν, ὑμνοῦμεν πατέρα καὶ υἱὸν καὶ ἅγιον πνεῦμα Θεοῦ. Quoted by Routh, *Reliqu. Sacr.*, 2nd ed., Vol. III, p. 515, Oxon. 1846.

11 For a brief historical account of them, see Fortescue's article "Doxology" in the *Catholic Encyclopedia*, Vol. V, pp. 150 sq.

cient hymns, or psalms of praise, seem to be a development of the Trinitarian forms of benediction contained in the New Testament Epistles, and they doubtless reflect the publicly professed faith of the early Christians, unaffected by extraneous elements of abortive speculation. The coordinative form *"Gloria Patri et Filio et Spiritui Sancto* (or *cum Spiritu Sancto*) — Glory be to God the Father, and to the Son, and to the Holy Ghost (or, together with the Holy Ghost)," and the subordinative form, *"Gloria Patri per Filium in Spiritu Sancto* — Glory be to the Father through the Son in the Holy Ghost" are probably of equal antiquity, and the assertion of the Arian historian Philostorgius,[12] that the first-mentioned formula had been introduced into the liturgy by Bishop Flavian of Antioch, must be received with suspicion. It is certain that already Justin Martyr was acquainted with it.[13] Because the Arians showed a decided predilection for the formula *"Gloria Patri per Filium in Spiritu Sancto,"* (Διὰ τοῦ υἱοῦ ἐν τῷ ἁγίῳ πνεύματι), St. Basil substituted therefor, as equally correct, the formula μετὰ τοῦ υἱοῦ σὺν τῷ πνεύματι τῷ ἁγίῳ, which threw into stronger relief the consubstantiality and coequal adorableness of the Son and of the Holy Ghost with the Father.[14]

12 *Hist. Eccles.*, III, 13, Migne, *P. G.*, LXV, 502.

13 *Apol.*, I, c. 65, Migne, *P. G.*, VI, 427.

14 Cfr. C. M. Kaufmann, *Handbuch der Altchristl. Epigraphik.* Freiburg 1917, pp. 146 sq., 165 sqq.

3. THE CONFESSIONS OF THE MARTYRS.—The confessions of faith that have come down to us from the lips of the early martyrs, furnish another important contribution to the positive Tradition of the primitive Church concerning the Blessed Trinity. Being the formal pronouncements of holy men and women, made before pagan magistrates in the face of cruel death, they are rightly held in high esteem. The oldest document of this kind which we possess is the confession of St. Polycarp, Bishop of Smyrna, who laid down his life for his faith A. D. 156. Its salient passages are as follows: *"Verax Deus, . . . te glorifico per sempiternum et coelestem pontificem Iesum Christum, dilectum Filium, per quem tibi cum ipso et in Spiritu Sancto gloria et nunc et in futura saecula*—O truthful God, . . . I glorify Thee, through the Eternal and Heavenly High Priest, Jesus Christ, [Thy] beloved Son, through whom be glory to Thee, with Him in the Holy Ghost, both now and for the ages to come."[15] Some martyrs in their profession of faith laid special stress on the Divinity of Jesus Christ. Thus St. Epipodius of Lyons (+ 178): *"Christum cum*

[15] *Acta Martyr. Polyc.*, XIV, 3. "Here," says Newman, "the Three are mentioned, as in the baptismal form; as many as Three, and no more than Three, with the expression of a still closer association of the Three, one with another, than is signified in that form, *viz.*, as contained in the words, 'through,' 'with,' and 'in.'" *Tracts Theol. and Eccles.*, p. 150.

Patre et Spiritu Sancto Deum esse confiteor, dignumque est, ut illi [*scil. Christo*] *animam meam refundam, qui mihi et creator est et redemptor* — I confess Christ to be God, with the Father and the Holy Ghost, and it is meet that I should give back my soul to Him [*i. e.*, Christ], Who is my Creator and Redeemer." [16] The holy deacon Vincent, who died a martyr's death, A. D. 304, is reported to have professed his faith in these words: "*Dominum Christum confiteor, Filium altissimi Patris, unici unicum, ipsum cum Patre et Spiritu Sancto unum solum Deum esse profiteor* — I confess the Lord Jesus Christ, Son of the most high Father, the Only One of the Only One, I confess Him with the Father and the Holy Ghost to be the one sole God." [17] To St. Euplus of Catania (+ 304) we owe one of the most beautiful confessions of faith in the Trinity that has come down to us from the early days. It is as follows: "*Patrem et Filium et Spiritum Sanctum adoro; sanctam Trinitatem adoro, praeter quam non est Deus. . . . Sacrifico modo Christo Deo meipsum. . . . Ego sacrifico et immolo meipsum Patri et Filio et Spiritui Sancto* — I adore the Father and the Son and the Holy Ghost; I adore the holy Trinity, besides which there is no God. . . . I now sacrifice my-

16 Ruinart, *Acta Martyr.*, p. 65, Veronae 1731.
17 Ruinart, *l. c.*, p. 325.

self to Christ, [who is] God; . . . I sacrifice and immolate myself to the Father, and to the Son, and to the Holy Ghost." [18]

READINGS: — On the worship of the Blessed Trinity by the early Christians, see Zaccaria, *Bibliotheca Ritual.*, t. I, diss. 2, c. 5.

On the acts of the martyrs, see *Ad. Harnack, *Geschichte der altchristlichen Literatur bis Eusebius,* Vol. I, Part 2, pp. 816 sqq., Leipzig 1893; Semeria, *Dogma, Gerarchia e Culto nella Chiesa Primitiva,* Roma 1902; cfr. also James Bridge in the *Catholic Encyclopedia,* Vol. IX, pp. 742 sqq.; H. Delehaye, S. J., *The Legends of the Saints,* London 1897.

ARTICLE 2

THE ANTE-NICENE FATHERS

1. THEIR CLEAR AND DEFINITE PROFESSION OF FAITH IN THE BLESSED TRINITY.—The Ante-Nicene Fathers acknowledged in the One Godhead three real Persons of coequal power, that is to say, not essentially subordinated one to the other. Hence it requires no special argument to prove that these Fathers professed the Catholic dogma of the Trinity. Of course any explicit and emphatic assertion, in their writings, of the Divinity of Jesus Christ must be of special weight. We shall have to confine ourselves to a few salient quotations.

a) Eminent among the "Apostolic Fathers" is St.

18 For further testimonies, see Franzelin, *De Deo Trino,* thes. 10; cfr. also Von Gebhardt, *Ausgewählte Märtyrerakten und andere Urkunden aus der Verfolgungszeit der christlichen Kirche,* Berlin 1902.

Ignatius of Antioch, who was exposed to wild beasts at Rome under Trajan, some time between A. D. 98 and 117.[19] In his much-discussed Epistles,[20] Ignatius frequently avers his faith in the Divinity of Jesus Christ, whom he calls "our God." In combating the absurd heresy of the Docetae,[21] he insists particularly on Christ's twofold nature, the divine and the human. "There is one physician," writes St. Ignatius, "fleshly and spiritual, generate and ingenerate, God and come in flesh, eternal life in death, from Mary and from God, first passible and then impassible." [22]

The truth that there are three Persons in the Godhead is clearly professed also by Athenagoras (about 170), who is called "the Christian Philosopher of Athens." [23] He says: "Who would not be astonished to hear those called atheists, who speak of the Father as God, and the Son as God, and the Holy Ghost; showing both their power in unity (τὴν ἐν ἑνώσει δύναμιν) and their distinction in order (τὴν ἐν τάξει διαίρεσιν)?" [24]

St. Irenæus of Lyons [25] deserves special mention, because he not infrequently refers to the Holy Ghost

19 Cfr. Bardenhewer-Shahan, *Patrology*, pp. 30 sqq.; J. Tixeront, *History of Dogmas*, Vol. I, pp. 121 sqq.; E. Bruston, *Ignace d'Antioche, ses Épîtres, sa Vie, sa Théologie*, Paris 1897.

20 Cfr. Newman, *Tracts Theol. and Eccles.*, pp. 95–135.

21 For an account of Docetism, see the dogmatic treatise on Christology. Properly speaking it is not a Christian heresy at all, but "rather came from without." Cfr. Arendzen in the *Catholic Encyclopedia*, Vol. V, *s. v.* "Docetae."

22 *Epist. ad Eph.*, VII, 2. Newman's translation, *Tracts Theol. and Eccles.*, p. 108. On St. Ignatius's refutation of Docetism see particularly Tixeront, *op. cit.*, p. 124.

23 The manuscript tradition of his *Apology* can be traced to the year 914. Cfr. Bardenhewer-Shahan, *Patrology*, pp. 64 sqq., and Peterson in the *Catholic Encyclopedia*, II, 42 sq. An English translation of his works in the *Ante-Nicene Fathers*, American Reprint, Vol. II, pp. 129 sqq., New York 1903.

24 *Legat.* 10, Migne, *P. G.*, VI, 909. Newman's translation, *Tracts Theol. and Eccles.*, p. 151.

25 Cfr. Bardenhewer-Shahan, *Patrology*, pp. 118 sqq.

as "Wisdom." Take, for instance, this passage:[26] "*Adest ei* [*scil. Deo Patri*] *semper Verbum et Sapientia, Filius et Spiritus, per quos et in quibus omnia libere et sponte fecit*—There is present to Him [*i. e.*, God the Father] always the Word and the Wisdom, the Son and the Spirit, through whom and in whom He has made all things freely and of His own accord."[27]

Of the many dicta of Clement of Alexandria, which could be quoted in support of our thesis, we select but one. "The Lord," he says, "apparently despised, but in reality adored, the Reconciler, the Saviour, the Meek, the Divine Logos, unquestionably true God, measuring Himself with the Lord of the Universe [*i. e.*, God the Father], because He was His Son, and the Logos was in God."[28]

b) Of occidental witnesses, let us adduce at least a few besides Irenæus. Tertullian (born about 160) in his usual rugged style writes: "*Custodiatur oeconomiae sacramentum, quae unitatem in trinitatem disponit, tres dirigens: Patrem et Filium et Spiritum Sanctum. Tres autem non statu, sed gradu; nec substantia, sed forma; non potestate, sed specie. Unius autem substantiae et unius status et unius potestatis, quia unus Deus, ex quo et gradus isti et formae et species, in nomine Patris et Filii et Spiritus Sancti deputantur*—Let the mystery of the dispensation be guarded, which distributes the unity into a Trinity, placing in their order the Three, *viz.*, the Father, the Son, and the Holy Ghost; Three not in condition, but in degree, not in substance, but in form, not in power, but in aspect; but of one substance, and of one condition, and of one power, because God is one,

26 *Adv. Haer.*, IV, 20, 1.

27 On a recent controversy apropos of St. Irenæus' Trinitarian teaching, see Appendix, *infra*, pp. 291 sq.

28 *Cohort. ad Gent.*, c. 10.

from whom these degrees, and forms, and aspects derive."[29]

The dogmatic encyclical of Pope Dionysius, which we have already mentioned above,[30] rejects both extremes, Sabellianism as well as Tritheism. "*Sabellii impietas,*" says this holy Pope, "*in eo consistit, quod dicat Filium esse Patrem et vicissim; hi vero* [*tritheitae*] *tres deos aliquomodo praedicant, cum in tres hypostases invicem alienas, omnino separatas, dividunt sanctam unitatem* (μονάδα). *Necesse est enim divinum Verbum Deo universorum esse unitum et Spiritum Sanctum in Deo manere ac vivere. . . . Credendum est in Deum Patrem omnipotentem et in Iesum Christum Filium eius et in Spiritum Sanctum* — The impiety of Sabellius consists in this, that he says that the Son is the Father and the Father the Son, but they [the Tritheists] in some sort preach three Gods, as dividing the Holy Monad into three subsistences foreign to each other and utterly separate. For it must needs be that with the God of the universe the Divine Word is united, and the Holy Ghost must repose and live in God. . . . We must believe in God the Father Almighty, and in Jesus Christ His Son, and in the Holy Ghost."[31]

2. VAGUE EXPRESSIONS.—The very confidence with which the Fathers of the fourth century defended the faith against Arius, is sufficient warrant for the orthodoxy of the Ante-Nicene period.

29 *Contr. Prax.*, c. 2.

30 *Supra*, p. 122. Cfr. also Bardenhewer-Shahan, *Patrology*, p. 224.

31 Quoted by St. Athanasius, *De Decr. Nicaen. Syn.*, n. 26. Cfr. Sprinzl, *Die Theologie der apostolischen Väter*, Wien 1880; Nirschl, *Die Theologie des hl. Ignatius*, Mainz 1880; Peterson, article "Apostolic Fathers" in the *Catholic Encyclopedia*, Vol. I, pp. 637–640.

It has been asserted that Subordinationist, *i. e.*, Arianizing views with regard to the relations of the Three Divine Persons were current "among the apologists and most of the Ante-Nicene Fathers."[32] Petavius even ventured to affirm that the majority of the Ante-Nicene Fathers were not in full accord with the Nicene Creed.[33] But before the first edition of his work on the Trinity (1644–1650) was completed, the great dogmatist found himself constrained to moderate this harsh judgment. In his "*Praefatio ad Libros de Trinitate*" he explains the apparent dissent of many of the Ante-Nicene Fathers as a mere "*modus loquendi.*" A number of learned theologians[34] subsequently undertook the defense of these Fathers against so grievous an accusation, and they may be said to have acquitted themselves on the whole victoriously. It must be admitted, however, that the writings of the Ante-Nicene Fathers, composed at a time when dogmatic terminology still lacked that precision which was imparted to it by the Nicene Creed, expressed themselves "with an unsuspicious yet reverent explicitness,"[35] which is apt to arouse the suspicion of heresy. But whenever such ambiguous terms and phrases admit of a Catholic interpretation, the rules of Patristic hermeneutics compel us to prefer the orthodox to the heretical sense, so long as the latter is not positively established. It is almost impossible to imagine that such a brilliant phalanx of theologians as Justin, Irenæus, Clement of Alexandria, Tertullian, etc., should have lapsed into material heresy in regard to a fundamental dogma of the Christian faith. "In such a

32 Cfr. Kuhn, *Christl. Lehre von der hl. Dreieinigkeit*, pp. 107 sqq., Tübingen 1857.

33 Cfr. *De Trinitate*, I, 3-5. (Petavius died in 1652.)

34 *E. g.*, Thomassin, Bossuet, Maranus, Lumper, Möhler, Franzelin, Schwane, Régnon, etc.

35 Newman, *The Arians of the Fourth Century*, p. 166.

fundamental dogma, such an error in such quarters would be incompatible with the infallibility of the Church." [36] As a matter of fact, upon closer scrutiny most of the "incorrect and unadvisable terms and statements in some of the early Fathers," [37] can be offset by parallel texts from the same Fathers which are clearly and unmistakably orthodox. It must be admitted, however, that prior to the Nicene Council the dogmatic formulation of the mystery of the Blessed Trinity was still in process of development, and theological speculation on the subject of the Logos, influenced by Platonism and Stoicism, frequently went astray and unconsciously scattered the seeds of future heresies.

Cardinal Franzelin reduces the incorrect and unadvisable terms and statements found in the early Fathers on the subject of the Blessed Trinity to four categories, which we will briefly review.

a) By insisting too strongly on the character of the Father as the source and principle of the two other Persons, some Ante-Nicene writers created the impression that they held the Son to be God in a less strict sense than the Father,—as it were "God in the second place"; and the Holy Ghost, "God in the third place." Thus St. Justin writes that the Son is "in the second

36 Wilhelm-Scannell, *Manual of Dogmatic Theology*, I, 288.

37 Newman, "Causes of the Rise and Success of Arianism," in *Tracts Theological and Ecclesiastical*, p. 208.— In *The Arians of the Fourth Century* (p. 164) Newman says of "the Ante-Nicene language" that it "was spoken from the heart" and must not be "measured . . . by the necessities of controversies of a later date. . . . Those early teachers have been made to appear technical, when in fact they have only been reduced to a system; just as in literature what is composed freely, is afterwards subjected to the rules of grammarians and critics." (See also *op. cit.*, pp. 179 sqq.)

place (ἐν δευτέρᾳ χώρᾳ)" and the Holy Ghost "in the third order (ἐν τρίτῃ τάξει)."[38] Tertullian, on the other hand, upon whom fell the task of coining a Latin terminology, which he accomplished with rare ability, calls the Father "the totality of substance (*tota substantia*)," while he refers to the Son as "derived from the whole substance (*derivatio totius et portio*)."[39]

In connection herewith a few of the Fathers reserve the name "*Deus super omnia*" (God above all things), or "Very God"[40] to the Father, while they speak of the Son as Θεὸς ἐκ Θεοῦ, or simply Θεός without the article.[41] Novatian (A. D. 250), who in his otherwise excellent work on the Trinity endeavored to harmonize the doctrine of the Divinity of the Son with that of the unity of the Godhead, misconceives the Consubstantiality of Father and Son.[42]

It is plain that all these utterances, and a number of others which could be cited from Ante-Nicene writings, *can* be interpreted in an Arian sense; but it is equally certain that they *must* not be thus interpreted. So long as the general teaching of any writer is such that the true Catholic doctrine may be reasonably presumed to underly an occasional incorrect expression, we have no right to accuse him of favoring heretical tenets. Now, it is an article of faith that the Father, as the First Person of the Blessed Trinity, has His Divine Nature from Himself,[43] whereas the Logos-Son and the Holy Ghost have the same numerical Divine Nature by immanent procession from the Father. It is this idea the

38 *Apol.*, I, c. 13.

39 *Contr. Prax.*, 9.

40 Ὁ Θεός = αὐτόθεος.

41 Cfr. Newman, *The Arians of the Fourth Century*, pp. 163 sqq.

42 Cfr. Bardenhewer, *Geschichte der altk. Lit.*, II, 565; Duchesne, *Early History of the Christian Church*, Vol. I, pp. 235 sq.; A. d'Alès, *Novatien*, Paris, 1927.

43 Ἄναρχος, αὐτόθεος, ἀρχὴ τῆς ἀρχῆς.

Fathers in their crude language wished to express.[44]

b) There are certain other Patristic texts which seem to represent active generation on the part of the Father as "voluntary," as if the Father could be conceived without the Son. This might easily suggest the heretical conclusion that the Son is a mere creature of the Father, or at most a God of inferior rank. But all such utterances must be read in the light of the thesis which their respective authors were then and there defending against their heterodox opponents. When the exigencies of the conflict made it necessary to refute the error that the process of divine Generation implied external compulsion, or blind necessity, or corporeal division, the Fathers rightly insisted that "*Pater voluntate seu voluntarie genuit Filium* — The Father begot the Son voluntarily." But they did not employ "*voluntarie*" in the sense of "*libere.*" What they meant was that the Father begot His Divine Son as "willingly" as He is the infinite God. Later on, when the Arians and Eunomians began to propagate the heretical error that the Son is a creature, the product of a free act of creation on the part of the Father,[45] the Patristic

44 On the orthodoxy of Tertullian, see Scheeben, *Dogmatik*, Vol. I, § 111, n. 835 sqq., and Bardenhewer, *Geschichte der altkirchlichen Literatur*, II, 387 sq. Bardenhewer's opinion on this head is thus summarized in his *Patrology* (English edition by Shahan, p. 185): "In his defence of the personal distinction between the Father and the Son he [Tertullian] does not, apparently, avoid a certain Subordinationism. Nevertheless in many very clear expressions and turns of thought he almost forestalls the Nicene Creed." Cfr. also A. d'Alès, *La Théologie de Tertullien*, Paris 1905 and J. Tixeront, *History of Dogmas*, Vol. I, pp. 310 sqq. On the Trinitarian teaching of St. Justin Martyr, see A. L. Feder, S. J., *Justins des Märtyrers Lehre von Jesus Christus dem Messias*, Freiburg 1906.

45 "It was one of the first and principal interrogations put to the Catholics by their Arian opponents, whether the Generation of the Son was voluntary or not on the part of the Father; their dilemma being, that Almighty God was subject to laws external to Himself, if it were not voluntary, and that, if on the other hand it was voluntary, the

writers met the new difficulty by the declaration that the Procession of the Son from the Father is as necessary as the vital process in the bosom of the Godhead.

c) A further source of misunderstanding is the Patristic teaching that the Logos was begotten for a very definite purpose, namely, to serve as the instrument of creation. This seems to place the Son on a plane of undue subordination to the Father. Those who held this view accentuated it by making a distinction between the λόγος ἐνδιάθετος and the λόγος προφορικός. "The view of the Logos as Endiathetic and as Prophoric,— as the Word conceived and the Word uttered, the Word mental and the Word active and effectual . . . came from the Stoics, and is found in Philo."[46] With certain restrictions it admits of an orthodox interpretation, provided that those who employ the words do not dispute that the ministerial relation of the Logos, though subordinate with regard to origin, is truly divine, and that the Prophoric Word does not lose His Divine Nature and Sonship in consequence of the Creation and the Incarnation, but retains both in unaltered identity

Son was in the number of things created." Newman, *The Arians of the Fourth Century*, p. 196.

46 Newman, *Select Treatises of St. Athanasius*, II, 340. "Philo," he says in another place, "associating it [the doctrine of the Trinity] with Platonic notions as well as words, developed its lineaments with so rude and hasty a hand, as to separate the idea of the Divine Word from that of the Eternal God; and so perhaps to prepare the way for Arianism." And in a foot-note he illustrates this observation "by the theological language of the 'Paradise Lost,' which, as far as the very words go, is conformable both to Scripture and the writings of the early Fathers, but becomes offensive as being dwelt upon as if it were literal, not figurative. It is scriptural to say that the Son went forth from the Father to create the worlds; but when this is made the basis of a scene or pageant, it borders on Arianism. Milton has made Allegory, or the Economy, *real*." (*The Arians of the Fourth Century*, p. 93. Cfr. also pp. 199 sq. of the same work.)

with the Endiathetic Word. St. Irenæus, in demonstrating against the Gnostics that God did not need to employ angels in creating the universe, extols the "ministry of the Son and of the Holy Ghost" as a divine ministry to which "all angels are subject," and significantly adds: *"Hic Pater . . . fecit ea per semetipsum, hoc est per Verbum et Sapientiam suam*—The Father made these things by Himself, that is, by His Word and Wisdom."[47] St. Theophilus of Antioch (about 180), was, so far as we know, the first Christian theologian who did not hesitate to use the terms λόγος ἐνδιάθετος and προφορικός.[48] But his use of them, though incautious, is quite orthodox, as appears from the subjoined passage in the second of his three books *Ad Autolycum: "Cum voluit Deus ea facere, quae statuerat, hoc Verbum genuit prolatitium* (προφορικόν), *primogenitum omnis creaturae, non ita tamen, ut Verbo vacuus fieret, sed ut Verbum gigneret et cum suo Verbo semper versaretur*—When God purposed to make all that He had deliberated on, He begat this Word as external to Him, being the First-born antecedent to the whole creation; not, however, Himself losing the Word [that is, the Internal], but begetting it, and yet everlastingly communing with it."[49] Two other representatives of the Ante-Nicene period, Hippolytus and Tertullian, boldly venture a step farther and describe the intra-divine γέννησις as a mere conception, and the temporal γένησις, which manifests itself *ad extra,* as the birth of the Logos, claiming that the full Sonship of the Logos did not begin until after His temporal birth. This is

47 *Adv. Haeres.*, II, 30.

48 The use of the word "Wisdom" for "Holy Ghost" is also peculiar to Theophilus and to St. Irenæus (cfr. John XV, 26: "*Spiritus veritatis*").

49 *Ad Autol.* II, 22. Newman's translation; cfr. *The Arians of the Fourth Century*, p. 200.

no doubt speculation gone astray, but it does not trench on dogma, though Hippolytus, as we have already remarked, *did* incur a degree of blame for his ditheistic vagaries.

d) The fourth group of incautious Ante-Nicene expressions culminates in the teaching that the Father alone is by His very Nature,—*i. e.*, because of His immensity,— invisible, while the Son (and this is true of the Holy Ghost also) can manifest Himself visibly, and has in matter of fact so manifested Himself in the Old Testament theophanies and in the Incarnation. Petavius held that this theory necessarily entails the heretical inference that the Son is inferior to the Father. But we cannot share this view. It may be that the Fathers and ecclesiastical writers in question [50] did not distinguish sharply enough between "apparition" (*apparitio*) and "mission" (*missio*). But there can be no doubt that in speaking as they did they had in view only "mission." For while the First Person of the Divine Trinity, who proceeds from none, can be conceived only as "sending," and never as "sent," the distinctive personal character of the Logos-Son supplies a congruous reason why He should be "sent" into the world by the Father, from whom He proceeds by eternal generation. The writers with whom we are here concerned do not ascribe the attribute of immensity or immeasurableness exclusively to the First Person of the Trinity; they merely observe that the Logos in His visible manifestation (*i. e.*, according to His humanity), is not immense nor immeasurable.

3. Some Ante-Nicene Writers Whose Orthodoxy Remains Doubtful.—Though, as we

50 Justin, Irenæus, Clement of Alexandria, Tertullian, *et al.*

have seen, the evidence at hand does not warrant a summary indictment of the Ante-Nicene Fathers and ecclesiastical writers, all of them cannot be successfully cleared of the charge of heresy.

Some modern writers hold that even the *Didache*, or "Teaching of the Twelve Apostles," the oldest literary monument of Christian antiquity outside of the New Testament canon, must be the work of an Ebionitic or Monarchianistic writer, because it contains no formal profession of faith in the Divinity of Jesus Christ and the Atonement.[51] But Funk has conclusively shown in the "*Prolegomena*" to his edition of this much-discussed work,[52] that the *Didache* ranks Christ higher than a mere man.

It is somewhat more difficult to disprove the recent charge that Hermas, the author of *The Shepherd*, "the longest and for form and contents the most remarkable of the writings of the so-called Apostolic Fathers,"[53] constantly identifies the Person of the Son with that of the Holy Ghost.[54] Though various attempts have been made to save the orthodoxy of the "Shepherd,"[55] we can hardly escape the conclusion that he "bases the difference between the Son and the Holy Ghost on the fact of the Incarnation, the Son of God in His pre-existence being none other than the

51 See Krawutzky in the *Theologische Quartalschrift* of Tübingen, 1884, pp. 581 sqq.

52 P. XXXIX, Tubingae 1887.

53 Bardenhewer-Shahan, *Patrology*, p. 38. The *Shepherd* was composed about A. D. 150. On its dogmatic teaching cfr. Tixeront, *History of Dogmas*, Vol. I, pp. 114 sqq.

54 *E. g.*: "I [*i. e.*, the Shepherd] will show thee all things which the Holy Ghost (τὸ πνεῦμα τὸ ἅγιον) has shown thee, who spoke to thee in the figure of the Church; for that Spirit is the Son of God (ἐκεῖνο γὰρ τὸ πνεῦμα ὁ υἱὸς τοῦ Θεοῦ ἐστιν)." (*Pastor Hermae*, Sim. IX, I, 1.)

55 Among others by Brüll and R. Seeberg.

Holy Ghost."[56] There is some doubt as to whether Hermas is guilty of identifying the Holy Ghost, or the Son of God respectively, with the Archangel Michael, as charged by Funk. True, the "Shepherd" attributes identical functions to the Holy Ghost and the Archangel Michael, but he draws a distinction between them in regard to rank.[57]

St. Hippolytus of Rome, the rival of Pope St. Callistus (A. D. 217–222), and one of the first antipopes known to history, in his controversies with Noëtus and Sabellius championed Ditheistic views and even went so far as to refer to the Logos as θεὸς γενητός,[58] which caused Callistus to accuse him and his followers of being Ditheists: "Δίθεοί ἐστε."[59] Hippolytus retorted with the counter-charge of Modalism, saying that Callistus "falls sometimes into the error of Sabellius, and sometimes into that of Theodotus,"—which, says Bardenhewer, "can only mean that on the one hand Callistus maintained the equality and unity of nature in the Father and the Son, without denying, as did Sabellius, the distinction of Persons; and on the other maintained the perfect humanity of the Redeemer, without denying his divinity, as did Theodotus."[60]

Origen's Trinitarian teaching is rather enigmatic. In the mind of this learned writer the Hellene seems to wrestle with the Christian, the pagan philosopher with the

---

56 Bardenhewer, *Geschichte der altkirchlichen Literatur*, I, 577, Freiburg 1902.

57 Cfr. Bardenhewer, *op. cit.*

58 *Contr. Noët.*, c. 10; *Philos.*, X, 33. On the difference between γενητόν and γεννητόν, cfr. Newman, *Select Treatises of St. Athanasius*, II, 398 sq. Cfr. Pohle-Preuss, *God: His Knowability, Essence, and Attributes*, pp. 114 sq.

59 *Philos.*, IX, 12. Cfr. Duchesne, *Early History of the Christian Church*, Vol. I, pp. 212 sqq.

60 Bardenhewer-Shahan, *Patrology*, p. 210.

Catholic believer. St. Jerome [61] accuses him of Arianism, and the brilliant defense of Origen's orthodoxy by Pamphilus, Gregory Thaumaturgus, and Eusebius, and among modern writers by Vincenzi, has not fully dispelled this indictment. In his writings, Origen appears in a twofold rôle. Whenever he speaks as a simple witness to ecclesiastical Tradition, he voices the Catholic truth; [62] but when he speaks as a philosopher endeavoring to clear up the mysteries of the faith, he does not scruple to represent the Son of God as a κτίσμα Θεοῦ and as a "second God" (δεύτερος Θεός) — a name which Plato had applied to the world as fashioned by the Demiurge. To do full justice to Origen's position, it will be well to distinguish, as Athanasius does,[63] between what he states θετικῶς, as a witness to Tradition, and what he writes γυμναστικῶς, as a philosopher "inquiring and exercising himself," as Newman renders the term.[64] The *Tractatus Origenis de Libris SS. Scripturarum,* consisting of twenty homilies which have reached us in an Orleans manuscript of the tenth, and in another of St. Omer belonging to the twelfth century, discovered and edited by Batiffol in 1900, are not the work of Origen nor of Novatian. The well-developed Trinitarian terminology of these homilies clearly indicates a Post-Nicene composition. Weyman has shown that the Latin text is original, but the true author has not yet been ascertained.[65]

61 *Ep. 94 ad Avit.*

62 Cfr. *In Ioa.,* tr. 2, *apud* Migne, *P. G.,* XIV, 128: "*Didicimus credere (in Deo) esse tres hypostases: Patrem et Filium et Spiritum Sanctum.*" *In Ep. ad Rom.,* VII, 5, (*apud* Migne, *l. c.,* 1115) he says: "*Quomodo enim inferior dici potest, qui Filius est et omnia est, quae Pater?*"

63 *De Decret. Nicaen. Syn.,* 27.

64 *Select Treatises of St. Athanasius,* I, 48.

65 Cfr. Bardenhewer-Shahan, *Patrology,* p. 222; J. Tixeront, *History of Dogmas* (English tr.), Vol. I, pp. 261 sqq., St. Louis 1910.

READINGS: — On the Trinitarian teaching of the Ante-Nicene Fathers, see especially *Franzelin, *De Deo Trino,* thes. 10–11, Romae 1881; Heinrich, *Dogmatische Theologie,* Vol. IV, §§ 231–232, Mainz 1885; Kuhn, *Christliche Lehre von der hl. Dreieinigkeit,* §§ 12–18, Tübingen 1857; *Duchesne, *Les Témoins Anténicéens du Dogme de la Trinité,* Paris 1882; Petavius, *De Trinitate,* lib. I, c. 3–5, and the "*Praefatio*"; Thomassin, *De Trinitate,* c. 37–47; *Prud. Maranus, *De Divinitate Domini Nostri Jesu Christi,* ll. 2–4; B. Jungmann, *Dissertationes Selectae in Historiam Ecclesiasticam,* Vol. I, pp. 358 sqq., Ratisbonae 1880; B. Heurtier, *Le Dogme de la Trinité dans l'Épître de St. Clément de Rome et le Pasteur d'Hermas,* Lyon 1900; J. Tixeront, *History of Dogmas,* English tr., Vol. I, St. Louis 1910; E. Krebs, *Der Logos als Heiland im ersten Jahrhundert. Ein religions- und dogmengeschichtlicher Beitrag zur Erlösungslehre,* Freiburg 1910; F. Diekamp, *Über den Ursprung des Trinitätsbekenntnisses,* Münster 1910.

ARTICLE 3

THE NICENE AND POST-NICENE FATHERS

1. THE DOGMATIC TEACHING OF THE FATHERS AGAINST ARIUS AND MACEDONIUS. — a) The sensation caused throughout Christendom by the first appearance of the Arian heresy can be explained only on the assumption that the truth had been in quiet possession for three full centuries. The Bishop of Alexandria, Alexander, at a synod held in his episcopal city about the year 320, excommunicated Arius. He explained the motives for this step in a lengthy letter to Bishop Alexander of Constantinople. "*Quis unquam talia audivit?*" he said among other things, "*aut quis nunc audiens non obstupescat*

et aures obstruat, ut ne talium verborum sordes auditum contaminent? — Who ever yet heard such language? and who that hears it now, but is shocked and stops his ears, that its foulness should not enter into them?"[66] This utterance clearly proves that the heresy of Arius, which attacked the very foundations of the dogma of the Divine Trinity, by asserting that the Logos-Son (Christ) is a mere creature, was at the beginning of the fourth century regarded as an intolerable innovation. St. Athanasius himself took a leading part in the Arian controversies which for many years shook the entire Orient and even made their evil effects felt among the Germanic nations of the Western world, especially among the Vandals in Africa. Athanasius was Bishop of Alexandria and is deservedly called "the Great." He was ready to give up his life in defense of the Catholic truth that the Son is eternally begotten from the substance of the Father, and is consubstantial with Him, as defined by the Council of Nicaea.

b) When (about 360) Macedonius began to undermine that other pillar of the dogma of the Blessed Trinity, *viz.:* the Divinity and Consubstantiality of the Holy Ghost, Athanasius again appeared in the arena and denounced his teach-

[66] *Opera Athanas.*, tom. I, p. 398, Paris 1689; Newman, *Select Treatises of St. Athanasius*, Vol. I, p. 5, 9th ed., London 1903.

ing as "impious" and "unscriptural."[67] "It is impious," he said, "to call the Holy Ghost created or made (κτιστὸν ἢ ποιητόν), seeing that both the Old and the New Testament connumerate and glorify Him with the Father and the Son, because He is of the same Divinity (συναριθμεῖ καὶ δοξάζει, διότι τῆς αὐτῆς θεότητός ἐστιν)." St. Athanasius found powerful allies in the "three Cappadocians," Gregory of Nazianzus, Gregory of Nyssa, and particularly St. Basil, who in his work *On the Holy Spirit*[68] quotes a number of older writers in confirmation of the ecclesiastical Tradition.[69]

Honorable mention must also be accorded to St. Amphilochius, who was consecrated Bishop of Iconium, A. D. 374, and later became metropolitan of Lycaonia, (+ after 394). In the name of a synod of his Lycaonian suffragans he published a magnificent letter on the Divinity of the Holy Ghost.[70]

To Didymus the Blind, of Alexandria, "one

67 Cfr. St. Athanasius, *De Incarnatione Dei Verbi*, reprinted in Migne, *P. G.*, XXVI, 998.

68 "It has always been the standard work on the subject" (Fortescue, *The Greek Fathers*, p. 81, London 1908), despite the reproach of "Economy" which attaches to it, because St. Basil avoided (as he himself admits) calling the Holy Ghost God.

69 A picturesque account of the lives of St. Gregory of Nazianzus and St. Basil will be found in A. Fortescue, *The Greek Fathers*, London 1908. For their works and an account of their teaching, as also of that of St. Gregory of Nyssa, cfr. Bardenhewer-Shahan, *Patrology*, pp. 286 sqq., pp. 295 sqq., and pp. 274 sqq. Note especially the passage from St. Gregory Nazianzen on the Trinity, *ibid.*, p. 291.

70 *Epistola Synod. contr. Pneumatomachos.*

of the most notable men of an age that abounded in great personalities," (+ about 395) we owe, besides an important work *On the Trinity* (περὶ τριάδος), a lucid treatise entitled *De Spiritu Sancto*, which has reached us only in the sixty-three brief chapters of St. Jerome's Latin translation,[71] and which is indeed, as Bardenhewer says, "one of the best of its kind in Christian antiquity."[72]

The most eminent defenders of the dogma in the West were St. Ambrose[73] and St. Augustine,[74] who was the first to attempt a systematic exposition of the mystery of the Divine Trinity. His famous work *On the Trinity* became the starting-point of the Trinitarian speculations of medieval Scholasticism. St. Anselm adopted Augustine's profound considerations in his *Monologium*, whence they found their way into the *Liber Sententiarum* of Peter Lombard, and through this channel into the numerous theological *Summae*, among which that of St. Thomas Aquinas has ever held the place of honor.[75]

2. Patristic Polemics.—The method which the Fathers chose to refute the Scriptural objections raised by the Arians and Semi-Arians furnishes a valuable argument for the purity and

71 Cfr. Bardenhewer-Shahan, *Patrology*, pp. 307 sqq.

72 *Ibid.*, p. 308. On Didymus the Blind cfr. Bardy, *Didyme l'Aveugle*, Paris 1910.

73 *De Spiritu Sancto ad Gratianum Augustum*, in three books.

74 *De Trinitate.*

75 Cfr. St. Thomas, *S. Theol.*, 1a, qu. 27 sqq.

imperishable freshness of the ecclesiastical Tradition touching the dogma of the Blessed Trinity.

a) Prov. VIII, 22 reads: "*Dominus possedit me in initio viarum suarum* — The Lord possessed me in the beginning of his ways." The Septuagint has: ἔκτισέ με ἀρχὴν ὁδῶν αὐτοῦ. This text was considered by the Arians as the weak spot in the Catholic armor. Catholics did not deny that the passage referred to the Logos, and the Arian contention that the Septuagint offered sufficient warrant for taking Christ to be κτίσμα Θεοῦ — a creature of God — seemed well founded. It was a Gordian knot, which the Fathers, each in his own way, tried hard to unravel. Some suggested that the Septuagint text had been practiced upon by the Arians. Others referred the difficult passage to our Lord's sacred Humanity, while others again thought it applied to His Divinity. On one point, however, all were unanimously agreed, *viz.*, in holding that Christ was God and the Second Person of the Divine Trinity. Those among the Fathers who (wrongly) believed that ἔκτισε was an Arian forgery for ἔκτησε = ἐκτήσατο (from κτάομαι = *acquiro, possideo*) were guided by the thought that, since Eve said after the birth of Cain: "*Possedi* (קָנִיתִי from קָנָה = *possedit*) *hominem per Deum* — I have gotten a man through God,"[76] the Hebrew text of Proverbs must have read, as our Latin Vulgate reads: "*Dominus possedit me* (קָנָנִי, *i. e., generatione habet me;* ἔκτησε or ἐκτήσατό με). This interpretation was favored by Epiphanius, Basil, Gregory of Nyssa, and Jerome. Most of the other Fathers, however, notably Athanasius and Nazianzen, in view of a parallel passage in Ecclesiasticus,[77]

76 Gen. IV, 1.

77 Ecclus. XXIV, 14: "*Ab initio et ante saecula creata* (ἔκτισε) *sum.*"

referred Prov. VIII, 22 to the Humanity of Christ and interpreted it thus: "The Lord created me in my human nature as the beginning [ἀρχή = principle] of his ways." [78] There was a third group of Fathers who did not hesitate to apply Prov. VIII, 22 to Christ's Divine Nature. They interpreted the verb κτίζειν generically as *producere* = *gignere*,[79] or looked upon it as a drastic term calculated to throw into relief the hypostatic self-existence of the Logos in contradistinction to the Father.[80] The dogma of the Divinity of Christ, and consequently that of the Blessed Trinity, was safeguarded in any event.[81]

The New Testament *pièce de resistance* of the Arian heretics was Christ's own declaration, recorded in John XIV, 28: "*Pater maior me est*—The Father is greater than I." Here, they alleged, Christ Himself attests His subordination to the Father. This objection, too, was met differently by different Fathers. While the Latins were inclined to limit John XIV, 28 to Christ's Humanity (in which hypothesis the Arian argument simply collapsed), most of the Greek Fathers, notably Athanasius and Nazianzen, preferred the somewhat strained assumption that Christ is subject to the Father even in His Divine Nature, *i. e.*, that the Father, by virtue of His being the First Person (αὐτόθεος = ἄναρχος), is at the same time the principle of the Son, who must therefore be conceived essentially as "*Deus de Deo*." According to this theory the expression "*maior me*" signifies Christ's immanent succession with

78 For further details, see Petavius, *De Trinitate*, II, 1, 3.

79 Thus St. Ephrem.

80 This was the opinion of St. Hilary.

81 On these various interpretations, cfr. especially Ruiz, *De Trinitate*, disp. 96; also St. Thomas, *S. Theol.*, 1a, qu. 41, art. 3.

regard to origin in the Godhead, not a difference in rank or power.

The difficulty based on Christ's primogeniture was tersely and effectively refuted by St. Ambrose: "*Legimus primogenitum, legimus unigenitum: primogenitus, quia nemo ante ipsum; unigenitus, quia nemo post ipsum* — We read 'the First-born,' and we read 'the Only-begotten': He is the First-born, because there was no one before Him; He is the Only-begotten, because there is no one after Him." [82]

b) Besides a large number of philosophical fallacies, the Macedonians marshalled against the dogma of the Divinity of the Holy Ghost a series of Scriptural texts, which were loyally and learnedly restored to their true meaning by the Fathers. From Rom. VIII, 26: "*Ipse Spiritus postulat pro nobis gemitibus inenarrabilibus* — The Spirit himself asketh for us with unspeakable groanings," these heretics concluded: One who prays to God with unspeakable groanings cannot be Himself God; therefore the Holy Ghost is a mere creature. Without pointing to the evident anthropomorphism in this text, St. Augustine refutes the false interpretation of the Macedonians by the simple remark: "*Dictum est 'interpellat,' quia interpellare nos facit nobisque interpellandi et gemendi inspirat affectum* — The Bible says, the Spirit intercedes for us, because He makes us intercede and puts it into our hearts to intercede and groan." [83] 1 Cor. VIII, 6, where, strangely enough, the name of the Holy Ghost does not occur at all, was cited by the Pneumatomachians in favor of their

82 Ambros., *De Fide*, I, 7. Cfr. Newman, *Tracts Theological and Ecclesiastical*, pp. 199 sqq., new ed., London 1895. Other Arian difficulties of less importance are canvassed by Kleutgen, *De Ipso Deo*, pp. 458 sqq., Ratisbonae 1881; cfr. also Schwane, *Dogmengeschichte*, 2nd ed., Vol. II, § 12, Freiburg 1895.

83 Aug., *Ep.*, 194 (al. 105), n. 6.

heretical tenet that the Third Person is a creature and therefore cannot be God. But, as St. Athanasius effectively retorted: "The Holy and Blessed Trinity is so indivisibly united with itself, that when the Father is named, His Logos is included, and in the Logos also the Spirit. And when the Son is named, the Father is in the Son, nor is the Spirit outside the Logos, inasmuch as there is but one grace, which is perfected out of the Father, through the Son, in the Holy Ghost."[84]

Readings: — Petavius, *De Trinitate,* I, 7 sqq.; George Bull, *Defensio Fidei Nicaenae* (against Petavius, I, 3 sqq.), Oxon. 1685 (On Bull's work and its unmerited reputation, cfr. Hunter. *Outlines of Dogmatic Theology,* Vol. II, pp. 206 sq.); *Möhler, *Athanasius der Grosse,* 2nd ed., Vol. I, pp. 1–116, Mainz 1844; Hergenröther, *Die Lehre von der göttlichen Dreieinigkeit nach Gregor von Nazianz,* Ratisbon 1850; Atzberger, *Die Logoslehre des hl. Athanasius,* Freiburg 1880; A. Beck, *Die Trinitätslehre des hl. Hilarius von Poitiers,* Mainz 1903; J. Bilz, *Die Trinitätslehre des hl. Johannes von Damaskus,* Paderborn 1909.

On the apologetical aspects of the subject, see Hettinger, *Apologie des Christentums,* 9th ed., Vol. III, Freiburg 1907.

84 *Ep. 1 ad Serap.* 14. For further information on this aspect of the matter, see Kleutgen, *De Ipso Deo,* pp. 490 sqq., and Th. Schermann, *Die Gottheit des Hl. Geistes nach den griechischen Vätern des vierten Jahrhunderts,* Freiburg 1901.

CHAPTER III

THE PRINCIPLE OF THE BLESSED TRINITY, OR THE DOCTRINE OF THE IMMANENT PROCESSIONS IN THE GODHEAD

Divine Revelation tells us that there are Three Persons in the Godhead. It also points out the cause of this difference, *viz.*: the fact of the Divine Processions.

It is these Processions that properly constitute the mystery of the Blessed Trinity and furnish the basis for the distinction of three real Hypostases,—Father, Son, and Holy Ghost.

By "Procession" we understand "the origination of one Divine Person from another."

There are two such Processions, *viz.*, Generation (*generatio*, γέννησις) and Spiration (*spiratio*, πνεῦσις).

We shall treat them separately.

SECTION 1

THE PROCESSION OF THE SON FROM THE FATHER BY GENERATION

1. The Scriptural Argument.—The Nicene Council having incorporated the notion of γέννησις into the dogmatic definition of the Blessed Trinity, there can be no doubt that Christ's generation by the Father is as much an article of faith as His Divine Sonship. This can be demonstrated from Holy Scripture in a twofold manner.

a) Indirectly, by arguing from the fact of the Divine Paternity and Sonship, which we have already proved from Holy Scripture. The relation of Father and Son is conceivable only on the assumption of a real and true γέννησις in the proper sense of the term.[1] Consequently there is in the bosom of the Godhead a first Procession, which is true Generation. If, as St. Paul tells us,[2] all paternity in heaven and on earth is a weak imitation of the paternity of "the Father of our Lord Jesus Christ," and if the supernatural adoption of the just is but an analogue of Christ's true Sonship,[3] it follows, not indeed that the divine *gen-*

1 On the term γέννησις, cfr. Newman, *Select Treatises of St. Athanasius*, II, 352 sq.

2 Eph. III, 14 sq.

3 Cfr. John, I, 12; Gal. IV, 4 sq.

nesis must be conceived figuratively after the manner of creatural generation, but, contrariwise, that the latter is merely an imperfect representation of the former. The only true generation, in the highest sense, therefore, is the divine γέννησις, as the Godhead alone is Being in its truest and highest sense. Holy Scripture frequently intimates the genuineness of the divine γέννησις by applying to Christ such epithets as "the Only-begotten of the Father,"[4] and "the Only-begotten Son of the Father."[5]

b) Holy Scripture, moreover, distinctly teaches that the Son proceeds from the Father by eternal generation. Heb. I, 5: *"Cui enim dixit aliquando angelorum: Filius meus es tu, ego hodie genui te* (γεγέννηκά σε)? — For to which of the angels hath he said at any time: Thou art my Son, to-day have I begotten thee?"

Most clearly perhaps this divine Procession is taught in Psalm CIX, verse 3. *"Tecum principium in die virtutis tuae in splendoribus sanctorum: ex utero ante luciferum [= ab aeterno] genui te* — With thee is the principality in the day of thy strength: in the brightness of the saints: from the womb before the day star I begot thee." It is true, the Masoretic text, as we have it, renders this passage differently. Inasmuch, however, as (aside from the Itala and the Vulgate) the Septuagint[6] and the Syriac

[4] John III, 16, *et passim.*

[5] John I, 14, *et passim.*

[6] The Septuagint translates: 'Εκ γαστρὸς πρὸ ἑωσφόρου ἐγέννησά σε.

Peshitta, which were both made directly from the original Hebrew, give the passage as above quoted, the Masoretic variation can safely be attributed to a mistake made by the Jewish writers who some time previous to the tenth century drew up that collection of criticisms and marginal notes which forms the basis of our present Hebrew Old Testament. This theory is all the more plausible in view of the fact that the elimination of two small words, מִי and לְךָ, and a change in the punctuation of the remainder of the text, would make the seemingly corrupt passage conform with the Vulgate. Another important consideration in clearing up this difficulty is that for several centuries the Fathers employed this particular text to prove the Consubstantiality of the Logos with the Father by virtue of His eternal Generation.[7] Thus St. Basil, or rather the author of the fifth Book against Eunomius found among St. Basil's works, writes: "*Propterea habere se in generando uterum dixit Deus ad confusionem impiorum, ut vel sua ipsorum natura considerata discant, Filium fructum esse Patris genuinum, utpote ex eius utero emergentem* — God speaks of His womb for the purpose of confounding the impious, that they may learn by a consideration of their own nature that the Son is the genuine

7 Cfr. Ruiz, *De Trinit.*, disp. 4, sect. 1.

product of the Father, as if He had emerged from His womb." [8]

A parallel passage to Ps. CIX, 3, is John I, 18: *"Unigenitus Filius, qui est in sinu Patris* (ὁ μονογενὴς υἱὸς ὁ ὢν εἰς τὸν κόλπον τοῦ πατρός) — The only begotten Son, who is in the bosom of the Father." Taken in connexion with certain pregnant terms found in the Sapiential Books, such as *"parturiebar"* and *"concepta eram"* [9] and passages like Ecclus. XXIV, 5,[10] these texts seem to remove all doubt as to the scripturality of the doctrine of the divine γέννησις.

2. THE ARGUMENT FROM TRADITION.—The dogma of the Son's generation was brought prominently forward by all the Fathers and ecclesiastical synods of the fourth century, because it is the foundation and logical antecedent of the dogma of the Consubstantiality of Son and Father.

a) St. Hilary tersely declares: *"Ignorat Deum Christum, qui ignorat Deum natum; Deum autem nasci non est aliud quam in ea natura esse, qua Deus est* — He knows not the God-Christ, who knows not that God is begotten; but to say that God is begotten, is tantamount to saying that He is of the same nature

8 *Contr. Eunom.*, l. 5; Migne, *P. G.*, XXIX, 715.

9 Prov. VIII, 24.

10 *"Ego ex ore Altissimi prodivi, primogenita ante omnem creaturam* — I came out of the mouth of the most High, the firstborn before all creatures." (On "The Doctrine of the Primogenitus," see Newman, *Tracts Theological and Ecclesiastical*, pp. 199 sqq.)

as God."[11] And St. Augustine: "*Ideo quippe Filius, quia genitus, et quia Filius, utique genitus*—For He is therefore a son, because begotten, and because a son, therefore certainly begotten."[12] This unanimous teaching of the Fathers faithfully echoes all the ancient creeds, from the Apostles' to the Athanasian,—which latter sharply emphasizes the fact that "*Pater a nullo est factus nec creatus nec genitus; Filius a patre solo est, non factus nec creatus, sed genitus*—The Father is made of none, neither created, nor begotten. The Son is of the Father alone; not made, nor created, but begotten."[13] We must also mention in this connection the eleventh of the "*Anathematismi*" of Pope St. Damasus I (A. D. 380). It reads as follows: "*Si quis non dixerit Filium natum de Patre, id est de divina substantia ipsius, anathema sit*—If any one will not profess that the Son is begotten by the Father, that is to say, from the Divine Substance of the Father, let him be anathema."[14]

b) The Fathers and Catholic theologians generally are one in teaching that the process of divine Generation is a relation involving only the Father and the Son. Various attempts at positing in the Godhead other such relations, as, *e. g.*, maternity, were indignantly re-

11 *De Trinitate*, l. 11. Petavius (*De Trinit.*, II, 5, n. 7), quotes the following passage from Theodorus Abucara: "Since the Son's generation does but signify His having His existence from the Father, which He has ever, therefore He is ever begotten. For it became Him who is properly (κυρίως) the Son, ever to be deriving His existence from the Father, and not as we who derive its commencement only. In us generation is a way to existence; in the Son of God it denotes the existence itself; in Him it has not existence for its end, but it is itself an end (τέλος), and is perfect (τέλειον)." Cfr. Newman, *Select Treatises of St. Athanasius*, II, 353. (On Theodorus Abucara, cfr. Herder's *Kirchenlexikon*, XI, 1508 sq.)

12 *De Trinitate*, V, 6, 7 (Haddan's translation, p. 151).

13 Denzinger-Bannwart, *Enchiridion*, n. 39.

14 Denzinger-Bannwart, *Enchiridion*, n. 69.

jected by the Fathers as blasphemous.[15] Since the divine γέννησις must be conceived as a purely intellectual process, there is no need of postulating in the Godhead a special principle of conception and parturition. The Father generates His Divine Son by way of understanding, as the adequate likeness of His Essence. When the Patristic writers speak of the "conception" and "birth" of the Son of God, or advert to the "bosom" of the Father, they merely mean to emphasize the truth of the divine Generation as such.

The Sapiential Books of the Old Testament sometimes refer to Hypostatic Wisdom as the "First-born" or as "Mother of fair love." But these phrases offer no serious difficulty. The epithet "Mother of fair love" is merely meant to intimate the maternal tenderness of God's affection for us, and the feminine form "*primogenita*" (instead of "*primogenitus*") is due to the grammatical accident that in Hebrew חָכְמָה (*i. e., sapientia*), like σοφία in the Greek Septuagint, is of feminine gender.

READINGS: — St. Anselm, *Monologium,* c. 39–43; Ruiz, *De Trinitate,* disp. 4 sqq.; Hurter, *Compendium Theol. Dogmat.,* tom. I, thes. 107 (Hunter, *Outlines of Dogmatic Theology,* II, pp. 176 sqq., 2nd ed.); *Kleutgen, *De Ipso Deo,* l. II, qu. 4, c. 1 sqq.; Franzelin, *De Deo Trino,* thes. 30; Heinrich, *Dogmatische Theologie,* Vol. IV, § 241; G. B. Tepe, *Instit. Theol.,* Vol. II, pp. 293–325, Paris 1895; Newman, *The Arians of the Fourth Century,* pp. 158 sqq., New Impression, London 1901; IDEM, *Select Treatises of St. Athanasius,* Vol. II, pp. 287 sqq., 337 sqq.; 9th ed., London 1903; A Stüdle, *De Processionibus Divinis,* Frib. Helv. 1895.—Jos. Grendel, S. V. D., "Die persönlichen Ausgänge in Gott nach der Auffassung des Morgen- und Abendlandes" in *Jahrbuch des Missionhauses St. Gabriel,* Vol. I, pp. 120–161, Vienna 1922.

15 Cfr. Epiphanius, *Haer.,* 62.

SECTION 2

THE PROCESSION OF THE HOLY GHOST FROM THE FATHER AND THE SON

The second Procession in the Godhead is qualitatively distinct from Generation. Though often designated by the generic term *processio* (ἐκπόρευσις), it is by most theologians and several councils called Spiration (*spiratio,* πνεῦσις). Revelation leaves no room for doubt as to the Procession of the Holy Ghost from the *Father.* But the Greeks, since the schism of Photius, heretically assert that He proceeds *from the Father alone,* and not from the Son. To this heretical assertion, which has been expressly rejected by the Church, we oppose the Catholic doctrine that the Holy Ghost proceeds *from the Father and the Son.*

ARTICLE 1

THE HERESY OF THE GREEK SCHISM AND ITS CONDEMNATION BY THE CHURCH

1. The Heresy of the Schism.—It is impossible to ascertain just when the heresy asserting the Procession of the Holy Ghost from

the Father alone originated. When the Macedonians declared the Holy Ghost to be a creature of the Logos-Son, the Second Ecumenical Council (A. D. 381), to safeguard the dogma of His Divinity, thought it sufficient to affirm His Consubstantiality with the Father in the phrase: "*Qui ex Patre procedit* — Who proceeds from the Father."

Petavius and Bellarmine assume, but without sufficient warrant, that Theodore of Mopsuestia and Theodoret were the original authors of the heresy with which we are dealing.[1] The more probable theory is that certain Nestorians, whose identity can no longer be ascertained, in course of time somehow came to believe that the Council of Constantinople by "*ex Patre*" meant "*ex solo Patre.*" This view was publicly defended for the first time in Jerusalem, A. D. 808, by some fanatic monks, who protested against the insertion of the word "*Filioque*" into the Nicene Creed, because, as they alleged, the Holy Ghost does not proceed from the Son. It was, however, reserved for Photius, the ambitious and crafty Patriarch of Constantinople, the most learned scholar of his age,[2] (+ 891), to accuse the Latins of heresy for adopting the "*Filioque*" and to raise the denial of the procession of the Holy Ghost from the Son to the rank of a palmary dogma of the Greek Church. At a great council held in Constantinople, A. D. 879, which was attended by 380 bishops, the

1 On Theodore of Mopsuestia, see Bardenhewer-Shahan, *Patrology*, pp. 318-322; on Theodoret, the same work, pp. 370-376.

2 For a fine character sketch of Photius, see A. Fortescue, *The Orthodox Eastern Church*, pp. 138 sqq. Cfr. also the same brilliant writer's C. T. S. brochure, *Rome and Constantinople*, pp. 12 sqq.

Greeks formally pronounced sentence of anathema against all who should add to, or take from, the Symbol of Nicaea. After Photius's death "peace was restored temporarily between the churches, although by this time there is already a strong anti-papal party at Constantinople. But the great mass of Christians on either side are reconciled, and have no idea of schism for one hundred and fifty more years."[3] In the eleventh century came the final rupture under Michael Cerularius. The Great Schism settled into permanency, and, after a brief reunion in the fifteenth century, still continues.[4]

2. THE TEACHING OF THE CHURCH ON THE PROCESSION OF THE HOLY GHOST.—The Church jealously guarded the Apostolic teaching that the Holy Ghost proceeds from both the Father and the Son. This appears clearly from the insertion of the word *"Filioque"* into the Constantinopolitan Creed.

Though the Council of Chalcedon (A. D. 451) had forbidden the reception into the Creed of any other faith[5] than that of Nicaea, there soon came a time when it was found necessary to enforce explicit profession of faith in the Procession of the Holy Ghost from the Son as well as from the Father. The "*Filioque*" first came into use in Spain. On the occasion of the conversion of the Arian Goths under King Reccared, the Third Council of Toledo (A. D. 589) decreed the insertion of the term into the Creed and ordered that the

[3] Fortescue, *The Orthodox Eastern Church*, p. 171.

[4] Fortescue, *The Orthodox Eastern Church*, pp. 201 sqq.

[5] Ἑτέρα πίστις (whereby it can have meant nothing else than heterodox additions).

words "*ex Patre Filioque*" should be sung "with raised voices" during the celebration of the Divine Mysteries. In course of time the "*Filioque*" spread to France and Germany, thence to England and Upper Italy, and finally to Rome, where, however, for disciplinary reasons, the Popes did not encourage its adoption, though from a purely dogmatic point of view the matter had long been ripe for a decision. As early as A. D. 410, a large number of bishops, assembled in synod at Seleucia, had solemnly professed their faith "*in Spiritum vivum et sanctum, Paraclitum vivum et sanctum, qui procedit ex Patre et Filio* — In the living and holy Ghost, the living and holy Paraclete, who proceeds from the Father and the Son."[6] The "Athanasian Creed" contains the clause: "*Spiritus Sanctus a Patre et Filio* — The Holy Ghost [is] of the Father and the Son;" and long before its composition (5th or 6th century) a synod believed to have been held at Toledo (A. D. 447), had defined that "the Holy Ghost proceeds from the Father and the Son."[7] Pope Hormisdas (+ 523), in a letter to the Emperor Justin I, employed the phrase: "*de Patre et Filio.*" Many provincial synods inculcated the same doctrine (Aix-la-Chapelle, A. D. 789; Friaul, A. D. 791; Worms, A. D. 868; etc.). The Emperor Charlemagne was particularly attached to the "*Filioque*" and it consequently became very popular among the Franks. But when a few Frankish zealots

6 Cfr. Lamy, *Concilium Seleuciae et Ctesiphonti Habitum a. 410*, Lovanii 1868; Idem, "Le Concile tenu à Seleucie-Ctésiphon," printed in the *Compte rendu du 3e Congrès Scientifique International des Catholiques, Bruxelles* 1895, Sect. II, pp. 267 sqq.

7 According to the recent researches of Morin and Künstle this synod was never held, and what were hitherto thought to be its decrees are the production of an individual Spanish bishop. Cfr. Bilz, *Die Trinitätslehre des hl. Johannes von Damaskus*, p. 157, Paderborn 1909.

undertook to censure as insufficient the Greek formula "*a Patre per Filium,*" Pope Hadrian I defended it and quoted the Greek Fathers in its support.

Long after the outbreak of the Great Schism the Fourth Lateran Council (A. D. 1215) again took up the matter and defined it as an article of faith that "*Pater a nullo, Filius a Patre solo, ac Spiritus Sanctus pariter ab utroque* — The Father [is] from no one; the Son [is] from the Father alone; and the Holy Ghost [is] equally from both the Father and the Son." Lastly there is the important definition of the Ecumenical Council of Lyons, A. D. 1274, that the Holy Ghost proceeds eternally from the Father and the Son as from one principle and in one Spiration: "*Spiritus Sanctus aeternaliter ex Patre et Filio, non tamquam ex duobus principiis, sed tamquam ex uno principio, non duabus spirationibus, sed unica spiratione procedit.*"[8] This teaching was solemnly confirmed in the decree by which the Council of Florence (1439) sealed the restored union:[9] "*Diffinimus, quod Spiritus Sanctus ex Patre et Filio aeternaliter est et essentiam suam suumque esse subsistens habet ex Patre simul et Filio, et ex utroque aeternaliter tamquam ab uno principio et unica spiratione procedit* — We define that the Holy Ghost is eternally from the Father and the Son, and has His essence and subsistence at once from the Father and the Son; and that He eternally proceeds from both as from one Principle and by one Spiration."[10]

In consequence of the machinations of the schismatical Bishop Mark of Ephesus, the re-

8 Cfr. Denzinger-Bannwart, *Enchiridion*, n. 460.

9 Published on July 6, 1439. Denzinger-Bannwart, n. 691.

10 Upon this definition is based the well-known theological axiom: "*Duo quidem spirantes, sed unus spirator.*"

union brought about at Florence came to as bad an end as that effected at Lyons two centuries earlier. It must have seemed to many like a manifestation of divine anger when, on Pentecost Sunday, A. D. 1453, the Turks broke down the walls of Constantinople, and its last Emperor, Constantine Dragases, fell in battle at the gate of St. Romanus.

Readings: — Werner, *Geschichte der apologet. und polem. Literatur der christl. Theologie,* Vol. III, Schaffhausen 1864; *Hergenröther, *Photius,* Freiburg 1867–69, I, 684 sqq.; III, 399 sqq.; Idem, *Kirchengeschichte,* 4th ed., Vol. II, pp. 234 sqq., Freiburg 1904; Langen, *Die trinitarische Lehrdifferenz zwischen der abendländischen und morgenländischen Kirche,* Bonn 1876; Hefele, *Conciliengeschichte,* Vol. IV, 2nd ed., Freiburg 1879; Fortescue, *The Orthodox Eastern Church,* pp. 134 sqq., London 1907; Duchesne-Mathew, *The Churches Separated From Rome,* pp. 109 sqq., London 1907; S. Vailhé, *s. v.* "Greek Church," in the *Catholic Encyclopedia,* Vol. VI, pp. 763 sqq.— Jos. Slipyj, *Trinitätslehre des Photios,* Innsbruck 1921.

ARTICLE 2

THE POSITIVE TEACHING OF REVELATION

1. Scriptural Argument.—Sacred Scripture expressly mentions only the Procession of the Holy Ghost from the *Father.*[11] But this does not argue that there is no Scriptural warrant for the dogma of His Procession from the Son.

11 John XV, 26: "The Paraclete . . . who proceedeth from the Father."

On the contrary, the Procession of the Holy Ghost from the Son can be proved by a threefold argument based on Biblical texts.

a) In the New Testament the Holy Ghost is represented not only as "the Spirit of the Father," but likewise as "the Spirit of the Son."[12] These phrases can have but one meaning, *viz.*, that He proceeds from the Son as well as from the Father. For *"Spiritus Filii,"* expressing as it does a relation (*spiritus alicuius*), can only mean *"spiramen Filii" or "spiratus a Filio;"* that is to say, the Holy Ghost is the spiration or breath of the Son. This conclusion cannot consistently be denied by those who, like the Greek schismatics, find themselves constrained to admit that the only reason why the Holy Ghost can be called *"Spiritus Patris,"*[13] is that He proceeds from the Father. If this be true, it must *a pari* be concluded that He can be called *"Spiritus Filii"* only for the reason that He proceeds also from the Son,—a conclusion which is fortified by the Scriptural phrase *Filius Patris* (or *Filius Dei*), which evidently expresses a procession of the one from the other. It was but natural, therefore, for the Greek[14] as well as for the Latin[15] Fathers to employ

12 "*Spiritus Filii*" (Gal. IV, 6); "*Spiritus Christi*" (Rom. VIII, 9; Phil. I, 19; 1 Pet. I, 11).

13 Matth. X, 20.

14 Athanasius, Gregory of Nyssa, Maximus, Cyril of Alexandria, and others.

15 *E. g.*, Augustine.

this text as an argument for the Procession of the Holy Ghost from the Son.

The schismatics object that the Scriptural term "*Spiritus Filii*" has its justification in the consubstantiality of the Son with the Father, from whom alone, they claim, the Holy Ghost proceeds. But this is a mere evasion. Is not the Holy Ghost, too, consubstantial with the Father, from whom alone proceeds the Son? Yet we could not without heresy call Christ "*Filius Spiritus Sancti,*" because the Son does *not* proceed from the Holy Ghost. Hence the inevitable conclusion that the Holy Ghost is "*Spiritus Filii*" only because He proceeds from the Son as well as from the Father.

b) A still stronger argument can be drawn from what is known as the "Mission" of the Holy Ghost. *Missio,* in its abstract sense, signifies "the procession of one from another by virtue of some principle and for the purpose of accomplishing some task."

The three essential notes of any mission, be it divine or human, are: (1) A real distinction between the sender and the person sent, for it is obvious that no being can send itself. (2) A certain dependency of the "sent" in regard to the "sender." (3) A relation on the part of the "sent" to some terminus (place or effect). It follows that every "*missus*" enters into a twofold relation: a relation to the sender (*mittens*) as his *terminus a quo,* and a relation to the goal of his mission, which constitutes his *terminus ad quem.* In applying the concept of "mission" to the Divine Persons we must first purge it of all human imperfections. In the Divinity any influence of the "Sender" on the "Sent," other than the relation of origin, would be repugnant to the Essence of the Triune God. The eternal Procession of one Divine Person from another may be called Internal Mission (*missio ad intra*). The Temporal Mission is external and merely reflects the internal.

We know as the result of a complete induction that Holy Scripture invariably represents the Father as "sending," never as "sent"; the Son both as "sending" and as "sent"; and the Holy Ghost always as "sent," but never as "sending." Inasmuch as the Father sends the Son as well as the Holy Ghost, it is a patent conclusion, admitted also by the schismatic Greeks, that the Son and the Holy Ghost proceed from the Father. But the Bible distinctly teaches that the Holy Ghost is sent not only by the Father, but also by the Son.[16] Consequently, the Holy Ghost proceeds not only from the Father, but also from the Son. This Scriptural argument is so simple and convincing that it was often employed by the Fathers and ecclesiastical writers, both Greek and Latin.[17] Thus St. Fulgentius teaches: *"Filius est a Patre missus,*

16 John XIV, 16: "And I will ask the Father, and He shall give you another Paraclete, that he may abide with you for ever." John XV, 26: "But when the Paraclete cometh, whom I will send you from the Father. . . ." John XVI, 7: "It is expedient to you that I go: for if I go not, the Paraclete will not come to you; but if I go, I will send him to you."

17 Cfr. Franzelin, *De Deo Trino*, thes. 33.

quia Filius est a Patre natus, non Pater a Filio; similiter etiam Spiritus Sanctus a Patre et Filio legitur missus, quia a Patre Filioque procedit — The Son is sent by the Father, because the Son is begotten by the Father, not the Father by the Son; similarly we read that the Holy Ghost is sent by the Father and the Son, because He proceeds from the Father and the Son." [18]

c) The principal Scriptural argument for our present thesis is based on John XVI, 13 sqq.: "*Cum autem venerit ille Spiritus veritatis, docebit vos omnem veritatem. Non enim loquetur a semetipso, sed, quaecumque audiet, loquetur et, quae ventura sunt, annuntiabit vobis. Ille me clarificabit, quia de meo accipiet et annuntiabit vobis. Omnia quaecumque habet Pater, mea sunt. Propterea dixi: quia de meo accipiet* [λήψεται, other codices have λαμβάνει] *et annuntiabit vobis* — But when he, the Spirit of truth, is come, he will teach you all truth, for he shall not speak of himself; but what things soever he shall hear, he shall speak; and the things that are to come, he shall shew you. He shall glorify me; because he shall receive of mine, and shall shew it to you. All things whatsoever the Father hath, are mine. Therefore, I said that he

18 *Contra Fabianum*, fragm. 29. We possess only thirty-nine fragments of this precious work. For an account of the life and writings of St. Fulgentius of Ruspe, cfr. Bardenhewer-Shahan, *Patrology*, pp. 616–618.

shall receive [receives] of mine, and shew it to you." The bearing of this precious dogmatic text will appear from the following considerations. In the first place it is said of the Holy Ghost that he "hears" and "receives" His knowledge of "the things that are to come," (*i. e.*, of the future), from Christ. Being in the future tense, *"audiet"* and *"accipiet"* cannot refer to the intrinsic, eternal essence of the Holy Ghost, but solely to His future temporal manifestation *ad extra.* Now, one Divine Person can "hear" and "receive" from another only in so far as He does not, like the Father, possess His knowledge, and consequently His essence, from Himself (*a semetipso,* ἀφ' ἑαυτοῦ), but receives it by way of essential communication. *"Ab illo audiet,"* says St. Augustine, elucidating the passage, *"a quo procedit. Audire illi scire est, scire vero esse. . . . A quo illi essentia, ab illo scientia* — He shall hear of Him from whom He proceedeth. To Him, to hear is to know; but to know is to be . . . from whom His Being is, from the same is His knowing." [19] Christ, too, derives His divine knowledge from the Father and "hears" and "learns" from the Father, by whom He is sent. "He that sent me, is true: and the things I have heard of him, these same I speak in the world. And they

19 *Tract. in Ioa.*, 99, 4. Browne's translation, II, 919.

understood not that he called God his Father." [20] And again: "I do nothing of myself, but as the Father hath taught me, these things I speak." [21] Hence, just as Christ "hears" and "learns" from His Father only in so far as His divine nature with all the attributes of omnipotence, omniscience, etc., are communicated to Him by His eternal Generation from the Father; so, too, the Holy Ghost "hears" and "receives" from the Son only in this sense that all His knowledge and His whole essence are derived through origination from Christ.[22] Consequently the Holy Ghost proceeds from the Son as well as from the Father.

In their anxiety to escape the force of this argument the adherents of Photius have not scrupled to explain the text by interpolation. For *ἐκ τοῦ ἐμοῦ λήψεται* they read *ἐκ τοῦ ἐμοῦ [πατρός] λήψεται*, *i. e.*, the Holy Ghost receives His knowledge, as He receives His essence, from the Father, and hence proceeds from Him. But, as Cardinal Bessarion has observed, this construction conflicts with the rules of Greek grammar. It is untenable also for this additional reason that the context does not mention the Father at all, but speaks

20 John VIII, 26 sq.: "*Qui me misit, verax est; et ego, quae audivi ab eo, haec loquor in mundo. Et non cognoverunt, quia Patrem eius dicebat Deum.*"

21 John VIII, 28: "*A meipso* (*ἀπ' ἐμαυτοῦ*) *facio nihil, sed sicut docuit me Pater, haec loquor.*"

22 *De meo accipiet* = *ex me procedit.* See J. E. Belser, *Das Evangelium des hl. Johannes übersetzt und erklärt*, pp. 440 sqq., Freiburg 1905. Cfr. Epiphanius, *Ancor.*, c. 8: "'*Qui a Patre procedit et de meo accipiet,' ut ne alienus a Patre et Filio crederetur, sed eiusdem substantiae ac divinitatis, . . . ex Patre et Filio tertius appellatione.*" (Migne, *P.G.*, XLIII, 30.)

solely of Christ and His relation to the "*Spiritus veritatis.*"[23] Hence ἐκ τοῦ ἐμοῦ is the genitive of the neuter noun τὸ ἐμόν, *i. e.*, that which is mine. This interpretation is absolutely irrefutable in the light of John XVI, 15: "*Omnia, quaecumque habet Pater, mea sunt;*[24] *propterea*[25] *dixi: quia de meo*[26] *accipiet.*" The context is so clear that not a single Greek Father can be adduced who took ἐκ τοῦ ἐμοῦ to be other than a neuter phrase, meaning: "He shall receive of [what is] mine."[27]

For the rest, Christ Himself tells us the precise reason why and in how far the Holy Ghost "receives" from Him. "All things whatsoever[28] the Father hath," he says, "are mine; therefore[29] I said that he shall receive of mine, and shew it to you."[30] Accordingly, the Son has whatsoever the Father has, with the sole exception of Paternity, which is incommunicable. If, therefore, as the schismatics admit, the Father has the power of Spiration, this power, being communicable, also belongs to the Son. Therefore the Son breathes the Holy Ghost together with the Father. Consequently the latter proceeds from the Son as well as from the Father. Anselm of Havelsburg has thrown this argument into the form of a pretty sorites: "*Unde illi*

23 John XVI, 13 sq.

24 ἐμά ἐστι.

25 διὰ τοῦτο.

26 ἐκ τοῦ ἐμοῦ.

27 On the Patristic exegesis of this passage, consult Petavius, *De Trinit.*, VII, 5; Ruiz, *De Trinit.*, disp. 67, sect. 2.

28 πάντα ὅσα.

29 διὰ τοῦτο.

30 John XVI, 15.

[*scil. Spiritui Sancto*] *essentia, inde illi audientia; et unde illi audientia, inde illi scientia; et unde illi scientia, inde illi processio* — Whence He [the Holy Ghost] has His essence, thence He has His hearing; and whence He has His hearing, thence He has His knowledge; and whence He has His knowledge, thence He has His Procession."[31] This interpretation coincides with that of the Greek Fathers, and the schismatics cannot disavow it without stultifying themselves.[32]

2. PATRISTIC ARGUMENT.—The Greek schismatics freely admit that the Latin Fathers unanimously teach the Procession of the Holy Ghost from the Father and the Son. Note that, in making this admission, they inadvertently condemn their own attitude; for it is absurd to imagine that the Latin Church, which for eight centuries together with the Greek formed the one true Church of Christ, should have harbored a disgraceful heresy during all that time. But even if we put this consideration aside, we can convict the Greeks out of the mouths of their own Fathers. We shall confine ourselves to establish this point here. The argument from Tradition, so far as it rests on conciliar decisions and the usage of the primitive Church, has al-

31 *Dial.*, II, 8. On Anselm of Havelsburg, Ord. Praem., and his *Dialogi*, consult Hurter, *Nomenclator Literarius Theologiae Catholicae*, ed. alt., Vol. II, 107 sqq., Oenip. 1906.

32 Cfr. Petavius, *De Trinitate*, VII, 6.

ready been developed in a previous Section of this treatise.[33]

a) One of the most authoritative of the Greek Fathers is St. Athanasius (+ 373). He expressly teaches that "the Holy Ghost holds the same relation to the Son as to the Father," and that consequently the total substance of the Father is communicated to the Holy Ghost "through the mediation of the Son."[34] Christ's breathing upon the Apostles he explains as a symbol of the "Procession" of the Holy Ghost from the Son. "The Son breathed the Holy Ghost into the Apostles' countenance and said: 'Receive ye the Holy Ghost,' in order that we might learn that the Spirit given to the Disciples is from the fulness of the Godhead; for in Christ, says the Apostle, the whole plenitude of the Godhead indwells corporeally."[35] For this reason he designates the Son as "the fountainhead (or source) of the Holy Ghost."[36] These and many similar phrases are merely equivalent terms signifying the "Procession" of the Holy Ghost from the Son.

b) St. Basil's attitude on the question of the "*Filioque*" may be gathered from his constant teaching that the Holy Ghost proceeds "from the Father through the Son."[37] He furthermore affirms that "the divine dignity comes to the Holy Ghost from the Father through

33 *Supra*, pp. 168 sqq.

34 S. Athanas., *Ad Serap.*, ep. 1, n. 19: "*Qualem scimus proprietatem* (ἰδιότητα) *esse Filii ad Patrem, eandem ad Filium habere Spiritum S. comperiemus. Et quemadmodum Filius dicit: Omnia, quaecunque habet Pater, mea sunt,' ita haec omnia per Filium in Spiritu Sancto esse deprehendemus.*"

35 *Ad Serap.*, ep. 3.

36 τὴν πηγὴν τοῦ ἁγίου πνεύματος. *De Incarnatione contra Arianos*, 9.

37 St. Basil, *De Spiritu Sancto*, XVIII, 45: "Ἓν δὲ καὶ τὸ ἅγιον πνεῦμα, . . . δι' ἑνὸς υἱοῦ τῷ ἑνὶ πατρὶ συναπτόμενον.

[His] Only-begotten Son." [38] In a famous passage, which gave rise to acrid disputes at Florence, in 1439, St. Basil says that the Spirit holds His place after the Son, "because He holds from Him His being, and receives from Him and communicates to us, and depends entirely on that principle (or cause)." [39] "*Dignitate [i. e., secundum originem] namque Spiritum secundum esse a Filio [cum habeat esse ab ipso atque ab ipso accipiat et annuntiet nobis, et omnino ab illa causa dependeat] tradit pietatis sermo.*" [40] The bracketed clause, which definitely asserts the Procession of the Holy Ghost from the Son,[41] was vigorously impugned by the Greeks, who claimed that it was spurious. But, as Dr. Bardenhewer points out, "that these are the genuine original words of Basil is proved by good arguments, extrinsic and intrinsic. But even were they the words of a forger, their meaning is true: and the entire argument of Basil presupposes it as something logical and indispensable." [42]

c) Of St. Gregory of Nazianzus (+ 389) Bardenhewer observes: "The *Filioque* is not found in the writings of St. Gregory as clearly and openly as in those of Basil. He takes it, however, for recognized and granted, that the Son also is principle or origin of the Holy Spirit. When he says [43] in his discourse delivered at the Second Ecumenical Council (381), that the Father

38 *L. c.*, n. 47: *ἐκ πατρὸς διὰ τοῦ μονογενοῦς ἐπὶ τὸ πνεῦμα.*

39 The Latin Fathers prefer the word *principle* for the Father and Son; the Greeks more frequently use *cause* (αἰτία).

40 *Contra Eunom.* III, 1 (*apud* Migne, *P. G.*, XXIX, 653 sqq.).

41 It runs as follows in the original Greek: Παρ' *αὐτοῦ τὸ εἶναι ἔχον καὶ παρ' αὐτοῦ λαμβάνον καὶ ἀναγγέλλον ἡμῖν καὶ ὅλως τῆς αἰτίας ἐκείνης ἐξημμένον.*

42 Bardenhewer-Shahan, *Patrology*, p. 282. For further information on this point, cfr. A Kranich, *Der hl. Basilius in seiner Stellung zum Filioque*, Augsburg 1882.

43 *Or.*, 42, n. 15.

is ἄναρχος,[44] the Son ἀρχή, and the Holy Spirit τὸ μετὰ τῆς ἀρχῆς, he implicitly affirms that the mutual relation between the Holy Spirit and the Son is that of one who proceeds to Him from whom He proceeds. Moreover, he expressly says that the Holy Spirit is τὸ ἐξ ἀμφοῖν συνημμένον,[45] *i. e.*, He proceeds equally from the Father and the Son. The poem entitled *Praecepta ad Virgines* ends with these words: 'One God from the Begetter through the Son, to the great Spirit (εἷς θεὸς ἐκ γενέταο δι' υἱέος ἐς μέγα πνεῦμα [this is the so-called κίνησις τῆς μονάδος εἰς τριάδα]), since the perfect Divinity subsists in perfect Persons.'"[46]

Gregory of Nyssa, a brother of Basil the Great (+ after 394), also teaches that "the Holy Ghost is considered a distinct Hypostasis, because He is from God (ἐκ τοῦ Θεοῦ), and is of Christ (τοῦ Χριστοῦ), so that He does not share either the property of not proceeding (τὸ ἀγέννητον) with the Father, or the property of being the Only-begotten with the Son."[47] There is another passage in the writings of Gregory, which, if its genuineness could be established, would be even more conclusive. Cardinal Bessarion cited it against those of his Greek countrymen who were opposed to the reunion, and at the same time protested against the perversion to which the passage had been subjected in an ancient manuscript codex of the works of St. Gregory at Florence, wherein some Greek forger had clumsily expunged the preposition ἐκ. The passage occurs in the third of Gregory's *Sermones in Orationem Dominicam,* and reads

44 On this term, in connection with ἀρχή, cfr. Newman, *Select Treatises of St. Athanasius,* II, 348 sq.

45 *Or.*, 31, n. 2.

46 Cfr. Bardenhewer-Shahan, *Patrology,* p. 292. See also Hergenröther, *Die Lehre von der göttlichen Dreieinigkeit nach dem hl. Gregor von Nazianz,* Ratisbon 1850.

47 *Sermo contr. Macedonianos,* n. 2.

thus: "*Spiritus Sanctus et ex Patre* (ἐκ τοῦ πατρός) *dicitur et ex Filio esse* (καὶ [ἐκ] τοῦ υἱοῦ) *perhibetur*— The Holy Ghost is said to be from the Father and is shown to be also from the Son." [48]

d) The "*Filioque*" was very clearly taught by St. Epiphanius, Bishop of Constantia (+ 403). In his *Ancoratus* [49] he employs the formula τὸ πνεῦμα ἐκ τοῦ πατρὸς καὶ τοῦ υἱοῦ at least three times.[50] And in his work "The Medicine-Chest," [51] usually cited as *Haereses,* because written against eighty heresies,[52] he says: "*Audi, quisquis es, quod Pater vere est Filii Pater, totus lux, et Filius vere Patris lumen de lumine, . . . et Spiritus Sanctus veritatis lumen tertium a Patre et Filio* (φῶς τρίτον παρὰ πατρὸς καὶ υἱοῦ)." [53]

To these authorities we may add Didymus the Blind (+ about 395), who, despite his Origenistic tendencies, according to the testimony of St. Jerome was certainly orthodox in his treatise on the Trinity.[54] Didymus paraphrases John XVI, 13 as follows: "*Non enim loquetur a semetipso, hoc est non sine me et Patris arbitrio, quia inseparabilis a mea et Patris voluntate; quia non ex se, sed ex Patre et me est: hoc enim ipsum, quod subsistit, a Patre et me illi est*—[St. John XVI, 13, says: But when he, the Spirit of truth, is come, he will teach you all truth. For he shall not speak of himself; but what things soever he shall hear, he shall speak; and the things that are to come, he shall shew you.] He will not speak of himself, that is to say, not

48 On the Trinitarian doctrine of St. Gregory of Nyssa, cfr. Bardenhewer-Shahan, *Patrology,* pp. 300–302.

49 Ἀγκυρωτός, *i. e.,* the firmly-anchored man.

50 *Ancor.,* nn. 8, 9, 11.

51 Πανάριον or Πανάρια.

52 Migne, *P. G.,* XLI sq. Cfr. Bardenhewer-Shahan, *Patrology,* pp. 310 sqq.

53 *Haereses,* 74, 8.

54 Hieron., *Contra Rufin.,* II, 16: "*Certe in Trinitate catholicus est.*"

without Me and the judgment of the Father, because He is inseparable from Mine and the Father's will; because He is not from Himself, but from the Father and Me; for He has His very subsistence from the Father and Me." [55]

Lastly we will mention St. Cyril of Alexandria (+444), whose writings fairly swarm with texts in support of the "*Filioque.*" Not only does he employ the formula "Ἐκ πατρὸς δι' υἱοῦ προχεόμενον πνεῦμα — The Holy Ghost flows forth from the Father through the Son," [56] but he distinctly asserts: "*Spiritus Sanctus procedit ex Patre et Filio* (πρόεισι δὲ καὶ ἐκ πατρὸς καὶ υἱοῦ) — The Holy Ghost proceeds from the Father and the Son." [57]

e) Cardinal Bessarion, in his famous dogmatic discourse at the Council of Florence, A. D. 1439, summarized the teaching of the entire Patristic period on the dogma of the Blessed Trinity in these words: "*Latini Patres clarissime et dissertissime docent, Spiritum Sanctum procedere ex Filio et Filium, sicut Patrem, esse eius principium. Deinde Orientales quoque, non secus ac Occidentales, hoc ipsum dicere demonstravimus, cum alii Spiritum ex Patre per Filium procedere, alii ex Patre et Filio atque ex ambobus esse aiunt, sicque aperte docent, esse etiam ex Filio* — The Latin Fathers teach most clearly and eloquently that the Holy Ghost proceeds

[55] Didymus, *De Spiritu Sancto*, 2. Another, larger extract from the writings of Didymus on the Trinity is quoted by Petavius, *De Trinitate*, VII, 3, 6.

[56] *De Adorat. in Spiritu et Veritate*, *apud* Migne, *P. G.* LXVIII, 147.

[57] *Thesaurus Assert.*, 34. Migne, *P. G.* LXXV, 586.

from the Son, and that the Son, like the Father, is His principle. We have also demonstrated that the Greek Fathers, too, agree in this teaching of the Latins; some of them saying that the Spirit proceeds from the Father through the Son, while others declare that He proceeds from the Father and the Son, or from both, which manifestly means that He proceeds also from the Son."[58] In matter of fact it is only by harmoniously blending the Latin *"ex Patre Filioque"* with the Greek *"ex Patre per Filium"* that we arrive at the whole truth. Nor was the Latin formula limited to the Latins, or the Greek formula to the Greeks. The Greek formula, which Scheeben calls "the organic conception," occurs *e. g.* in the writings of Tertullian,[59] Novatian, and Hilary;[60] while, conversely, the Latin conception, which has been styled the "personal," is familiarly employed by several of the Greek Fathers, as we have seen in a previous paragraph. In the "organic" formula the preposition διά has a causal meaning, indicating that the Son is not merely the passage or "channel," as it were, of the paternal Spiration of the Holy Ghost, but Himself positively coöperates in the act of Spiration; for the Father and the Son together constitute one undivided principle of Spiration, and

58 Cfr. Hardouin, *Concil.*, t. IX, p. 367.

59 *Contr. Prax.*, c. 4.

60 *De Trinit.*, XII, n. 57.

Spiration itself is one single (notional) act consummated by both Divine Persons in consort. The coördinating conception of the Latins brings this out very clearly, but it rather neglects another equally important truth, *viz.*, that, despite the identity of the act of Spiration, the Father is its original principle (ἄναρχος), whereas the Son is the *"principiatum"* (Θεὸς ἐκ Θεοῦ), who receives the *"virtus spirandi"* from the Father. This truth is more sharply emphasized in the Greek formula.[61]

It is in the light of considerations such as these that we must interpret certain utterances of St. John of Damascus, of which the schismatics make much, and which St. Thomas thought it his duty to censure. In matter of fact the Damascene does not deny the procession of the Holy Ghost from the Son. He merely says: "Καὶ υἱοῦ δὲ πνεῦμα, οὐχ' ὡς ἐξ αὐτοῦ, ἀλλ' ὡς δι' αὐτοῦ ἐκ τοῦ πατρὸς ἐκπορευόμενον· μόνος γὰρ αἴτιος (= ἀρχὴ ἄναρχος) ὁ πατήρ."[62] This view is fully shared by the Latin Fathers. St. Augustine, *e. g.*, says: "*Spiritus Sanctus principaliter procedit de Patre . . . qui, quidquid unigenito Verbo dedit, gignendo dedit*—The Holy Ghost proceeds principally from the Father. . . . who, whatever He gave to the Only-begotten Word, He gave by begetting Him."[63] Similarly St. John Chrysostom: "The phrase *through Him* (δι' αὐτοῦ), is employed for no other rea-

61 Cfr. St. Thomas, *S. Theol.*, 1a, qu. 36, art. 3.

62 *De Fide Orthodoxa*, I, 12, Migne, *P. G.*, XCIV, 849. On the analogous teaching of St. Maximus the Confessor († 662), whom the Greek schismatics cite as an authority second only to St. John Damascene, cfr. Franzelin, *De Deo Trino*, thes. 36, n. 2.

63 St. August., *De Trinitate*, XV, 17.

son than to exclude the suspicion that the Son is ingenerate."[64] The Council of Florence (A. D. 1439), following that of Lyons (A. D. 1274), confirmed this view in its famous decree of reunion,[65] and formally defined both the "*ex Patre et Filio*" and the "*unica spiratio amborum*" as articles of faith.

3. THEOLOGICAL ARGUMENT.—In their debates with the anti-unionist Greeks at the Council of Florence, the Latin theologians rightly insisted that, if the Son were excluded from coöperation in the act of Spiration, there would be no ground for distinguishing Him hypostatically from the Holy Ghost; because the Son is hypostatically distinct from the Holy Ghost only by virtue of the relative opposition involved in breathing (*spirare*) and being breathed (*spirari*).

a) St. Thomas[66] and his school adopted and developed this theological argument, whereas Duns Scotus,[67] with a few of his followers, denied its cogency,[68]— an attitude for which they have been more or less severely blamed by the "*sententia communis.*"[69] In matter of fact the argument stands unshaken to the present day. It is a theological axiom that "All is indistinctly one in the Godhead, except where a relative opposition of Person to Person furnishes the basis for a real distinction." If this be true, as we shall demonstrate later on in treat-

64 *Hom. in Ioa., V,* n. 2.

65 Denzinger-Bannwart, *Enchiridion,* n. 691.

66 *S. Theol.,* 1a, qu. 36, art. 2.

67 *Comment. in Quatuor Libros Sent.,* I, Dist. 11, qu. 2.

68 Cfr. De Rada, *Controv. Theol. inter S. Thomam et Scotum,* lib. I, controv. 15, Coloniae 1620.

69 Cfr. Ruiz, *De Trinit.,* disp. 68, sect. 5.

ing of the divine Relations, no personal distinction can be posited between the Son and the Holy Ghost outside of that of a relative opposition between two Divine Persons. Now, no such relative opposition is conceivable between them unless One proceeds from the Other. Consequently the Holy Ghost proceeds also from the Son, else both would coincide in an indistinguishable unity and lose their independence as distinct Hypostases.

b) Scotus's objections against this theological argument will not bear scrutiny. If, he says, the Son alone without the Father breathed the Spirit, the personal distinction between the Father and the Holy Ghost would still remain; consequently, Procession as such cannot be a *conditio sine qua non* of the relative opposition and the hypostatic differences existing in the Godhead. We answer that in the hypothesis of Scotus the Holy Ghost would still proceed from the Father. True, His Procession would be a mediate one through the Son; but even such a mediate Procession would suffice to establish relative opposition, and therefore a hypostatic difference. If, conversely, we assumed with the schismatics that the Father alone breathes, without the Son, the Son would differ hypostatically from the Father by virtue of His Filiation, but He would not differ hypostatically from the Holy Ghost, nor could any personal difference arise unless the Son were placed in relative opposition to the Holy Ghost, which is conceivable only on the basis of a *processio*. All of which proves that it is a postulate of theological consistency that the Holy Ghost proceeds from the Son.

Readings: — Van der Moeren, *De Processione Spiritus Sancti ex Patre Filioque,* Lovanii 1864; *Kleutgen, *Theologie der Vorzeit,* 2nd ed., Vol. I, Münster 1867; A. Vincenzi, *De Processione Spiritus Sancti,* Romae 1878; *Franzelin, *De Deo Trino,* thes. 32–

41, Romae 1881 (a very exhaustive treatise); IDEM, *Examen Doctrinae Macarii Bulgakow . . . de Processione Spiritus Sancti*, Romae 1876; A. Kranich, *Der hl. Basilius und seine Stellung zum Filioque*, Braunsberg 1882; B. J. Otten, S. J., *A Manual of the History of Dogmas*, Vol. I, St. Louis 1917, pp. 490 sqq.

Of the Scholastics, cfr. St. Thomas, *Contr. Gent.*, IV, 24 sqq. (Rickaby, *Of God and His Creatures*, pp. 356 sqq., London 1905); *St. Anselm, *De Processione Spiritus Sancti contra Graecos;* Suarez, *De Trinit.*, l. X; Ruiz, *De Trinit.*, disp. 67; Petavius, *De Trinit.*, l. VII. Cfr. also Petr. Arcudius, *Opuscula Aurea Theologica*, Romae 1670 and Hugo Laemmer, *Scriptor. Graeciae Orthodox. Bibliotheca Selecta*, Friburgi 1864 sq.

CHAPTER IV

THE SPECULATIVE THEOLOGICAL DEVELOPMENT OF THE DOGMA OF THE TRINITY

That there are Three Persons in one God is and must ever remain a sacrosanct mystery which human reason cannot fathom. It is only through Divine Revelation that we know of the existence of that immanent process of Generation and Spiration which underlies the real distinction of three Persons in the Godhead.

Enlightened and guided by faith, however, reason is able, by means of syllogistic deductions, analogies, etc., and by skilfully synthesizing the various scattered data furnished by Revelation, to attain to a progressive theological understanding of the dogma, nay even to a degree of certainty concerning some of its more abstruse features. Speculative discussion, which for safety's sake must always keep itself solidly planted on the teaching of Revelation, as defined by the infallible Church, is concerned chiefly with two classes of problems, *viz.:* (1) the precise character of the two Processions *per intellectum et voluntatem;* and (2) the corollaries which flow therefrom with regard to the divine Relations, Properties, and Notions. To these two categories must be added the theory of the divine Appropriations and Missions. As for the degree of certitude enjoyed by these doctrines, Glossner justly observes that they "represent merely the immediate consequences of the dogma" and "are, as it were, a hedge surrounding the law, which no theologian may with impunity ignore."[1]

Readings: — B. J. Otten, S. J., *A Manual of the History of Dogmas,* Vol. II, St. Louis 1918, pp. 842 sqq.— Wm. Moran, "The Dogma of the Trinity and Its Development by Theologians" in the *Irish Ecclesiastical Record,* 5th Series, Vol. XXVII, No. 697 (Jan., 1926), pp. 1–22.

1 *Lehrbuch der kath. Dogmatik,* I, 2, pp. 128 sq., Ratisbon 1874. Cfr. S. Thom., *S. Theol.,* 1a, qu. 32, art. 4 (summarized in Bonjohannes's *Compendium,* Eng. ed. by W. Lescher, O. P., pp. 81–83, London 1906).

SECTION 1

THE DOGMA IN ITS RELATION TO REASON

1. The Blessed Trinity a Mystery.—That there are three Persons in one God is a mystery which human reason, left to its own resources, can neither discover nor demonstrate. Even after its actual revelation, theistic philosophy is unable stringently to prove the possibility, much less the existence and intrinsic necessity, of the Divine Trinity, which must therefore be counted among the mysteries called absolute or transcendental. St. Thomas Aquinas observes with perfect justice that whosoever ventures to demonstrate the Trinity by unaided reason, derogates from the faith.[2] This indemonstrability of the mystery of the Divine Trinity is due to the fact that, while here on earth, the human intellect, in spite of its being illumined by the light of Revelation, has no intuitive vision of the Divine Essence, but arrives at its knowledge of it by a contemplation of the physical universe,[3] which

2 *S. Theol.*, 1a, qu. 32, art. 1: "*Qui probare nititur trinitatem personarum naturali ratione, fidei derogat.*"

3 Cfr. Pohle-Preuss, *God: His Knowability, Essence, and Attributes*, pp. 17 sqq.

is the work, not of the Blessed Trinity as such, but of the One God who summoned the world out of nothingness. From the consideration of created things the human mind ascends to a knowledge of the Divine Nature as the creative principle of the cosmos. But it cannot arrive at a knowledge of the Divine Persons, except in so far as it is able to infer that the infinite Creator of spiritual beings must needs possess the simple perfection of personality. How this personality is constituted we have no means of determining. "*De mysterio Trinitatis,*" says St. Jerome, "*recta confessio est ignoratio scientiae.*" [4]

This absolute inscrutability is plainly intimated in Matth. XI, 27: "*Nemo novit Filium nisi Pater; neque Patrem quis novit nisi Filius et cui voluerit Filius revelare* — No one knoweth the Son, but the Father: neither doth any one know the Father, but the Son, and he to whom it shall please the Son to reveal him." Cfr. 1 Cor. II, 11: "*Quae Dei sunt, nemo cognovit nisi Spiritus Dei* — The things that are of God no man knoweth, but the Spirit of God." Though there exists no formal definition on the subject, the absolute incomprehensibility of this mystery is a certain theological conclusion, flowing from the declaration of the Vatican Council that there are absolute mysteries of the faith.[5]

4 *In Is., Prooem. ad l. 18.*

5 *Sess. III, De Fide et Ratione, can. 1.* Denzinger-Bannwart, n. 1816: "*Si quis dixerit, in revelatione divina nulla vera et propria dicta mysteria contineri, sed universa fidei dogmata posse per rationem rite excultam e naturalibus principiis intelligi et demonstrari: anathema sit* — If any one shall say that in divine Revelation there are no mysteries, truly and properly so called, but that all the doctrines of faith can be understood and demon-

Believing Christians have always looked upon the dogma of the Trinity as the most important and fundamental, as well as the highest and most profound of all revealed mysteries.

2. THE INDEMONSTRABILITY OF THE BLESSED TRINITY.—The foregoing truths afford us a safe criterion for properly estimating the manifold philosophical considerations which Scholastic theology employs to clear up the mystery, and especially for judging at their true worth the extremely audacious attempts at demonstration which have from time to time been made by non-Scholastic theologians.

a) The Schoolmen employed various analogues from both nature and reason to show forth the vestiges (*vestigia*) and the likeness (*imago*) of the Holy Trinity in the created universe. In doing this they did not mean to construct a cogent argument, but merely to supply supernaturally enlightened reason with some auxiliary conceptions, whereby it might attain to a deeper understanding of the revealed mystery.[6] It is in this sense that the Provincial Council of Cologne (A.D. 1860) teaches: "*Argumentis etiam quibusdam, non quidem necessariis et evidentibus demonstrare, sed congruis tantum et quasi similitudinibus illustrare et aliquatenus manifestare mysteria ratio potest, quemadmodum Patres et S. Augustinum prae ceteris circa SS. Trinitatis myste-*

strated from natural principles, by properly cultivated reason; let him be anathema." Cfr. St. Hilary, *De Trinit.*, II, 5: "*Posuit naturae nomina Patrem, Filium, Spiritum Sanctum; . . . quidquid ultra quaeritur, non enuntiatur, non attingitur, non tenetur.*"

6 Cfr. St. Thomas, *S. Theol.*, 1a, qu. 45, art. 7; qu. 93, art. 8.

rium versatos esse videmus—Reason cannot indeed demonstrate the mysteries [of faith] by necessary and evident arguments; but it can illustrate, and in a measure manifest them by congruous arguments and, as it were, by similitudes, after the manner in which the Fathers, and especially St. Augustine, treated of the mystery of the Blessed Trinity."[7] Following the lead of St. Augustine, Scholastic theology enlisted philosophy in the service of the dogma, not indeed with a view to demonstrating what is in itself incomprehensible, but in order to enable the human mind to perceive the precise nature of the mystery which it is asked to believe. St. Augustine's comparison of the two divine Processions with human self-knowledge and self-love stands as a perpetual monument to the speculative genius of the great Bishop of Hippo. "*Et est quaedam imago Trinitatis, ipsa mens et notitia eius, quod est proles eius ac de se ipsa verbum eius et amor tertius; et haec tria unum atque una substantia. Nec minor proles, dum tantam se novit mens, quanta est; nec minor amor, dum tantum se diligit, quantum novit et quantus est*—And so there is a kind of image of the Trinity in the mind itself, and the knowledge of it, which is its offspring and its word concerning itself, and love as a third, and these three are one and one substance. Neither is the offspring less, since the mind knows itself according to the measure of its own being; nor is the love less, since it loves itself according to the measure both of its own knowledge and of its own being."[8] Like Augustine, the orthodox Scholastics always subordinated their Trinitarian speculations to the revealed teaching as defined by the Church, never once trenching on the

[7] Tit. 1, cap. 6. *Collect. Lacensis*, t. V, p. 280.

[8] S. August., *De Trinit.*, IX, 12, 18. (Haddan's translation, p. 240.)

mystery embodied in the dogma. From this statement we need not even except Richard of St. Victor, who plumed himself upon having found "*rationes necessarias*" for the Blessed Trinity. His "necessary reasons" are mere congruities, which can claim no value except on the assumption that the mystery is already revealed.[9]

b) There is, however, a class of divines who left the safe path blazed out by the Fathers and the Schoolmen, and presumed to demonstrate the mystery of the Trinity by arguments, more or less bold, drawn from unaided human reason. Beginning with Raymond Lully, down to Anton Günther, these audacious innovators invariably ended by counterfeiting the concept of the Blessed Trinity instead of clearing it up. Of Lully, Ruiz says that his demonstrations are the dreams of a feeble and delirious brain.[10] Marcus Mastrofini elaborated a "mathematical demonstration," which, based as it was upon a wrong conception of the infinite,[11] proved as derogatory to the dogma as the Tritheistic teaching of Günther, which Joseph Kleutgen, S. J., so effectively refuted in his immortal work *Die Theologie der Vorzeit.*[12] Lost in the mazes of Hegelian Pantheism Günther evolved the Trinity as "thesis, antithesis, and synthesis," or as "subject, object, and identity," from the "elements of self-consciousness,"— a theory which is plainly tritheistic, because it supposes "a triplicated existence of one and the same Divine Substance." Rosmini pantheistically identified the Three Divine Persons with

9 Cfr. S. Thom., *De Potent.*, qu. 9, art. 5; Rich. a S. Vict., *De Trinit.*, I, 4; III, 5; IX, 1.

10 *De Trinit.*, disp. 41, sect. 1: "*Demonstrationes* [*eius*] *ridiculae sunt, deliria somniantis et male sani capitis.*" See also Vasquez, *In S. Theol.*, 1a, disp. 133.

11 Refuted by Franzelin, *De Deo Trino*, thes. 18.

12 See especially Vol. I, 2nd ed., pp. 399 sqq., Münster 1867.

"the highest modes of being, *viz.:* subjectivity, objectivity, and sanctity," or "reality, ideality, and morality." Both systems have been condemned as un-Catholic, Günther's by Pius IX, Rosmini's by Leo XIII.[13]

c) Certain Rationalists have attempted to explain the Christian dogma of the Trinity as the product of purely natural reflection on the part of pre-Christian philosophers and religionists. Having emptied it of its supernatural content, they profess to find its germs and prototypes in the philosophy of Plato and the Neo-Platonists, in Philo's doctrine of the Logos, in the writings of the legendary Mercury Trismegistus, and, lastly, in the day-dreams of Kabbalistic theosophy. But all this is rank sophistry. As a matter of fact the Christian Trinity is diametrically opposed alike to the Platonic triad (God, ideas, and world), to the Hindoo triad (Brahma, Vishnu, and Siva), and to the Chinese Tao trinity of heaven, earth, and man. Indeed, none of the so-called ethnic trinities can be shown to possess more than a purely external resemblance to the revealed Trinity of the Christian dispensation.[14]

3. How Human Reason Can Defend the Dogma of the Blessed Trinity Against Infidel Objections.—Though it cannot explain the mystery, human reason is able to refute the objections of those who aver that it is impossible or absurd. To do this effectively it is not nec-

13 Cfr. Denzinger-Bannwart, *Enchiridion,* nn. 1655, 1915. On Rosminian Ontologism see Pohle-Preuss, *God,* pp. 119 sqq.; on Hegel's Pantheistic teaching, J. Hessen, *Hegels Trinitätslehre,* Freiburg 1922.

14 Cfr. G. van Noort, *De Deo Uno et Trino,* pp. 193 sqq.; E. Krebs, *Der Logos als Heiland im ersten Jahrhundert,* Freiburg 1910; J. Lebreton, *Les Origines du Dogme de la Trinité,* pp. 1–207, Paris 1910; B. Bartmann, *Dogma u. Religionsgeschichte,* Paderborn 1922, pp. 16–24.

essary to demonstrate that the Trinity is positively conceivable and therefore real. It will suffice to show the hollowness of the various objections that are urged against the dogma.

All the objections which heresy and infidelity have excogitated against the mystery of the Blessed Trinity, from the days of Celsus down to those of David Friedrich Strauss, Christian philosophy has triumphantly refuted as fallacious. We will mention only a few. Schopenhauer says that "Strictly speaking, a mystery is a dogma that is manifestly absurd."[15] This "*dictum ex cathedra*" is meaningless. Faith is not related to reason as absurdity is related to sound sense, but as truth is related to truth, and we know that all truths are derived from the same original source, *viz.:* God Himself. Strauss declares that "He who has sworn to uphold the '*Quicunque,*' has renounced the laws of human thought."[16] But where is the law of right thinking that contradicts the possibility of the Trinity? It would not, we fancy, be a difficult undertaking to show how those who deny the Trinity twist the rules of logic and rely on syllogisms that are one and all affected by the deadly malady of "*quaternio terminorum.*" It is equally wrong and absurd to allege that the dogma of the Blessed Trinity is based on an impossible mathematical formula, namely $3 = 1$. This would indeed be the case if the dogma spelled, "Three Gods are one God." But the concept of "Three Divine Persons in one Divine Nature" involves no such intrinsic contradiction. It leaves the fundamental metaphysical principles of identity, contradiction, and excluded mid-

15 *Parerga und Paralipomena*, II, p. 385, Leipzig 1874.

16 *Glaubenslehre*, Vol. I, p. 460, Tübingen 1840.

dle in full possession of the field, nay, it postulates them as a necessary logical condition of "*Trinitas in unitate,*" because without these fundamental laws the dogma could not stand. These considerations show how utterly groundless is the charge brought by Adolph Harnack when he says: "Arianism, too, seems to us moderns to bristle with contradictions; but it was reserved to Athanasius to achieve a complete *contradictio in adjecto.*" [17]

READINGS: — *Bañez, *Comment. in S. Theol.*, 1a, qu. 32, art. 1; Suarez, *De Trinit.*, I, c. 11–12; *Ruiz, *De Trinit.*, disp. 41–43; Franzelin, *De Deo Trino,* thes. 18–20, Romae 1881; Chr. Pesch, S. J., *Praelect. Dogmat.*, Vol. II, 2nd ed., pp. 262 sqq., Friburgi 1906; Heinrich, *Dogmatische Theologie,* Vol. IV, §§ 211–212, Mainz 1885; Rüttimann, *Das Geheimnis der hl. Dreieinigkeit,* Lindau 1887; Scheeben, *Die Mysterien des Christentums,* 2nd ed. (by Küpper), pp. 17 sqq., Freiburg 1898; Bayle, *Dictionnaire, s. v.* "Pyrrhonisme"; Faust. Socinus, *Christ. Religionis Brevissima Institutio,* in the *Bibliotheca Fratrum Polonorum,* tom. I, pp. 652 sqq., Irenopoli 1656; Anton Günther, *Januskӧpfe, Euristheus und Herakles, Lydia, Vorschule;* against him Kleutgen, *Theologie der Vorzeit,* Vol. I, 2nd ed., pp. 399 sqq., Münster 1867; J. Döderlein, *Philosophia Divina: Gottes Dreieinigkeit bewiesen an Kraft, Raum und Zeit,* Erlangen 1889; J. Lebreton, *Les Origines du Dogme de la Trinité,* Paris 1910; F. J. Hall, *The Trinity,* pp. 31 sqq., 156 sqq., New York 1910; J. H. Newman, *An Essay in Aid of a Grammar of Assent,* Ch. v, § 2.— J. S. Vaughan, "The Bl. Trinity Reflected in Man" and "Vestiges of the Blessed Trinity in Irrational Creatures," in *Thoughts for All Times,* 23rd Am. ed., Springfield, Mass., 1916, pp. 84–116.— Garrett Pierse, "Some Modern Sidelights on the Doctrine of the Trinity," in the *Irish Theol. Quarterly,* Vol. XIV (1919), No. 55, pp. 201 sqq.

17 *Dogmengeschichte,* Vol. II, 3rd ed., p. 219, Freiburg 1894. Cfr. H. Schell, *Das Problem des Geistes mit besonderer Berücksichtigung des dreieinigen Gottes und der biblischen Schöpfungsidee,* 2nd ed., Würzburg 1898; J. Uhlmann, *Die Persönlichkeit Gottes und ihre modernen Gegner,* Freiburg 1906.

SECTION 2

GENERATION BY MODE OF UNDERSTANDING AND SPIRATION BY MODE OF WILL

1. The Generation of the Son by Mode of Understanding.—According to the unanimous teaching of Fathers and theologians the proposition that the Father generates His Divine Son by mode of understanding, while not an article of faith, is a sure theological conclusion which is firmly rooted in Sacred Scripture, and cannot be denied without temerity.[1]

a) The Bible reveals the Second Person of the Divine Trinity not only as "*Filius unigenitus,*" (*i. e.,* the Only-begotten Son), but likewise as "*Verbum*" or "*Logos*" (*i. e.,* the Word of God). The only meaning we can attach to the term "*Verbum Dei*" is: Immanent terminus of the knowledge of the Father. Consequently divine Generation must signify the knowledge of the Father bringing forth His Son by an act of the understanding. The purely intellectual character of the act of divine Generation may also be inferred from those Scriptural texts which represent the Son of God as the "image[2] of the Father," or as "begotten Wisdom." Like "Logos," these terms define the mode of generation

1 Prominent among those who denied it were Durandus and Hirscher.

2 *Imago,* εἰκών.

as purely spiritual, or, more specifically, as intellectual. It is in this sense that the Fathers, so far as they touch upon the subject at all, interpret the Scriptural teaching concerning the "Logos." Thus St. Gregory of Nazianzus tersely declares: "The Son is called Logos, because His relation to the Father is the same as that of the [immanent] word to the intellect."[3] And St. Basil: "Why Word? In order that it may become manifest that it proceedeth from the intellect. Why Word? Because it is the likeness of the Begetter, which in itself reflects the whole Begetter, even as our word [concept] reflects the likeness of our whole thought."[4] St. Augustine goes into the matter even more deeply. He says: "*Tamquam seipsum dicens Pater genuit Verbum sibi aequale per omnia; non enim seipsum integre perfecteque dixisset, si aliquid minus aut amplius esset in eius Verbo, quam in ipso* — Accordingly, as though uttering Himself, the Father begat the Word equal to Himself in all things; for He would not have uttered Himself wholly and perfectly, if there were in His Word anything more or less than in Himself."[5]

b) A theological reason may be found in the circumstance that the Processions in the Godhead are only conceivable as purely spiritual and immanent vital processes.[6] God is a pure Spirit, and there are but two known modes of purely spiritual operation, *i. e.*, understanding and willing. Our own mind, which is in itself infecund and derives its knowledge of generation altogether from the realm of organic life, can scarcely form an idea of the eminent fecundity of

3 *Or.* 30, *apud* Migne, *P. G.*, XXXVI, 129.

4 *Hom.*, 16, 3.

5 St. August., *De Trinitate*, XV, 14, 23. Haddan's translation, p. 407. Many additional Patristic texts in Petavius, *De Trinitate*, II, 11; VI, 5 sqq.

6 Cfr. S. Thom., *S. Theol.*, 1a, qu. 27, art. 1.

the Infinite Intellect, and is consequently inclined to conceive the operation of the divine understanding and will as something exclusively essential and absolute. But once assured by Revelation of the existence of two Processions within the Godhead (*generatio* and *spiratio*), we cannot but connect the one with the intellect and the other with the will. Now we know that divine Generation depends on the intellect rather than the will, because the Son of God has been revealed to us as "Logos."

This immanent process in the Godhead naturally points to the most perfect analogue which the Blessed Trinity has in the intellectual life of man. According to the teaching of St. Augustine,[7] man's self-knowledge corresponds to the process of divine Generation, his self-love to the process of divine Spiration. The human Ego unfolds itself, as it were, in three directions. First it duplicates itself in its self-consciousness and, without destroying the identity of the Ego-substance, opposes the thinking Ego to the Ego thought. The thinking Ego, as the *terminus a quo,* represents the begetting Father, while the thought Ego, as the *terminus ad quem,* illustrates the Son. Out of the reciprocal comprehension and interpenetration of both — despite the opposition existing between them, they are not really distinct — there spontaneously burgeons forth self-love, which, as the fundamental law of the human will, completes the immanent spiritual process and furnishes a faint image of the Holy Ghost. In thus trying to bring the mystery nearer to our understanding, we must not, however, lose sight of the fact that no real trinity is possible in the spiritual life of the creature, for the obvious reason that

7 *Supra,* p. 197.

the two intrinsic termini of self-knowledge and self-love are not hypostases but mere accidents.[8]

2. The Spiration of the Holy Ghost by Mode of Will.—In arguing that the Spiration of the Holy Ghost takes place by way of volition, some theologians content themselves with the *argumentum exclusionis*. The Generation of the Son having been assigned to the intellect, they say, there remains only the will to account for the origination of the Holy Ghost. These writers seem to overlook the fact that Revelation furnishes positive as well as negative proofs in support of this doctrine.

a) Under the so-called Law of Appropriations, no external operations can be predicated of any Divine Person except such as are intrinsically related to that particular Person's hypostatic character. This constitutes the Appropriations a sure criterion for determining the personal character of each of the Divine Persons. The attributes of omnipotence and creation are appropriated to the Father, for the reason that, in regard to productions *ad intra*, He is at the same time ἀρχὴ ἄναρχος and ἀρχὴ τῆς ἀρχῆς. In the same way the works of wisdom are appropriated to the Son, because He is Hypostatic Wisdom. If, then, the works of love are attributed to the Holy Ghost, it must be because He *is* love, because He proceeds from love as His principle or source; — not, it is true, from that essential Love which is common to all three Divine Persons,[9] but from the

8 Cfr. S. Thom., *Contr. Gent.*, IV, 11.

9 Cfr. 1 John IV, 8: "He that loveth not, knoweth not God: for God is charity."

reciprocal notional love of Father and Son, of which the immanent product is Hypostatic Charity, *i. e.*, the Person of the Holy Ghost. Love being the fundamental affection of the will,[10] the Holy Ghost must proceed from the Father and the Son by mode of will (*per modum voluntatis*).

b) The fact that Holy Scripture attributes the proper name "*Spiritus*" and the epithet "*Sanctus*" to the Holy Ghost, will serve to confirm this conclusion. As a personal appellation the term "Holy Spirit," like "Father" and "Son," must be taken in a relative sense, as "*spiratus*" or "*spiratione productus.*" In its absolute sense "Spirit" is predicable of the Godhead as such. Cfr. John IV, 24: "God is a spirit." But in a nature which, like God's, is purely spiritual, Spiration, as opposed to intellectual Generation, can signify nothing else than an act of the will. This becomes still clearer when we consider that Spiration is an analogous term derived from the realm of nature, in which breath or wind is indued with motive power, which in the spiritual realm has its counterpart in the operation of the will. If, therefore, the Holy Ghost is called "breath of God" (*halitus Dei*), the reason is that Father and Son breathe the Holy Ghost *per modum voluntatis*. Since "the emission of the breath from the heart, notably in the act of kissing, gives a most real expression to the tendency of love towards intimate and real communion of life and an outpouring of soul into soul,"[11] we can well understand why St. Ambrose, St. Jerome, and St. Bernard of Clairvaux ventured to refer to the Holy Ghost as "*osculum Patris et Filii.*"[12]

10 Cfr. S. Thom., *Contr. Gent.*, IV, 19.

11 Scheeben. Cfr. Wilhelm-Scannell's *Manual*, I, 331–332.

12 Cfr. also St. Bonaventure: "*Spirare in spiritualibus solius est amoris; et quoniam amor potest spirari recte et ordinate, et sic est*

Analyzing the epithet "*Sanctus*," we find that it does not designate the absolute sanctity of the Blessed Trinity as such, but, relatively, the personal character of the Third Person; in other words it is synonymous with "*procedens ex principio sancto.*" Now, sanctity is an attribute of the will, as wisdom is an attribute of the intellect. Divine sanctity formally consists in "God's love for Himself."[13] Hence "Holy Ghost" is synonymous with "Hypostatic Love." The Eleventh Synod of Toledo (A. D. 675) formally identifies sanctity with love when it says: "*Spiritus Sanctus . . . simul ab utrisque processisse monstratur, quia caritas sive sanctitas amborum esse agnoscitur* — The Holy Ghost is shown to proceed from both, as He is acknowledged to be the love or sanctity of both."[14] The Fathers express themselves in a similar manner. Thus St. Augustine says: "*Cum Pater sit spiritus et Filius spiritus, et Pater sanctus et Filius sanctus, proprie tamen ipse vocatur Spiritus Sanctus, tamquam sanctitas substantialis et consubstantialis amborum* — Though the Father is a spirit and the Son is a spirit, and though the Father is holy and the Son is holy, yet He [the Third Person] is properly called Holy Spirit, because He is the substantial and consubstantial holiness of both [the Father and the Son]."[15]

The Greek Fathers compare the act of divine Spiration to "a special form of substantial emanation, analogous to

purus, ideo persona illa, quae est amor, non tantum dicitur Spiritus, sed Spiritus Sanctus — To breathe in matters spiritual belongs solely to love; and because love can be rightly and properly breathed, and thus is pure; therefore the Person who is Love, is not only called Spirit, but Holy Spirit." *Comment. in Quatuor Libros Sent.*, I, dist. 10, qu. 3.

13 Cfr. Pohle-Preuss, *God: His Knowability, Essence, and Attributes*, pp. 256 sqq.

14 Denzinger-Bannwart, *Enchiridion*, n. 277.

15 *De Civitate Dei*, XI, 24.

the emanation which takes place in plants side by side with generation, and is effected by the plants themselves and their products, *viz.*, the emission of the vital sap or spirit of life in the form of fluid oily substances in a liquid or ethereal state, such as balsam and incense, wine and oil, and especially the odor or perfume of the plant, which is at the same time an ethereal oil and the breath of the plant." [16]

c) The epithet "gift of God" (*donum Dei,* δωρεὰ Θεοῦ), which, following the lead of Sacred Scripture, many Fathers ascribe as a personal attribute to the Holy Ghost, also plainly indicates the mode of His procession. A gift supposes as its principle love of pure benevolence on the part of the giver, and consequently the Holy Ghost, considered in His personal attribute of "*donum Dei,*" cannot originate in the Intellect, but must spring from Love, that is, from the Divine Will. St. Thomas explains this luminously as follows: "*Donum proprie est datio irreddibilis, id est, quod non datur intentione retributionis et sic importat gratuitam donationem. Ratio autem gratuitae donationis est amor; ideo enim damus gratis alicui aliquid, quia volumus ei bonum. . . . Unde cum Spiritus Sanctus procedat ut amor, . . . procedit in ratione doni primi*—A gift, properly speaking, is something given without expectation of a quid pro quo; but the reason why one gives freely is love; for if we give something to some one without expecting an equivalent, it is because we wish him well. . . . Therefore, since the Holy Ghost proceeds by mode of love. . . . He proceeds after the man-

16 Scheeben, *Dogmatik,* Vol. I, p. 870 (Wilhelm-Scannell's *Manual,* Vol. I, p. 329). Cfr. Athanas., *Ad Serap.,* 3, n. 3: "This salve is the breath of the Son, the perfume and the figure of the Son."

ner of the first gift."[17] St. Augustine says: "*Non dicitur Verbum Dei nisi Filius, nec donum Dei nisi Spiritus Sanctus* — The Son and none other is called **the Word of God,** and the Holy Spirit and none other **the gift of God."**[18] He founds upon this distinction **the thesis that** the Holy Ghost cannot be identical with the Son: "*Exiit non quomodo natus, sed quomodo datus, et ideo non dicitur Filius* — For the Spirit came forth not as born, but as given; and so He is not called Son."[19]

3. **THE ESSENTIAL DIFFERENCE BETWEEN GENERATION AND SPIRATION.—There is between Generation and Spiration a marked distinction, similar to the one between intellect and will.**

a) To enable the human mind to penetrate as deeply as possible into the sublime mystery of the Blessed Trinity, the Schoolmen raised the question: In how far can the notional cognition of the Father be conceived as generation in the strict sense of the term? Can it be said that "knowing" is synonymous with "begetting"? Modern authorities on the philosophy of language have made the interesting discovery that, in the parent language from which the Indo-Germanic family derives its descent (*viz.:* Sanskrit), GEN is the root of two distinct word-groups, which denote "knowing" and "begetting." Compare, *e. g.*, in Greek, γίγνομαι and γεννάω with γιγνώσκω; in Latin, *gigno* with *cognosco*. "*Conceptus*" may signify either "concept" (idea) or "conception" in the physiological sense. Our English word

17 *S. Theol.*, 1a, qu. 38, art. 2.

18 *De Trinit.*, XV, 17, 29.

19 *De Trinit.*, V, 14, 15.

"conception," too, is used to describe both the act or process of forming an idea or notion of a thing, and the impregnation of an ovum. In the Semitic family of languages these two notions are also closely related and expressed by the same verb; cfr., *e. g.*, "*Adam vero cognovit* יָדַע *uxorem suam Hevam* — And Adam knew Eve his wife."[20] A still surer way of arriving at the point we are trying to make, is to analyze the concepts underlying these various terms. Generation is defined as "*origo viventis a principio vivente coniuncto in similitudinem naturae ex vi ipsius productionis,*"[21] which may be rendered into English as follows: Generation is the production of one living being by another living being, by communication of substance, resulting in a similarity of nature in progenitor and progeny *vi productionis, i. e.*, from the very mode of production.[22] The concept of generation, therefore, contains four essential marks: (1) The origin of one living being from another living being. Consequently the inanimate exudation of plants and animals, the growth of hair and nails in corpses, etc., cannot be called "generation." (2) The vital process of nature by which that which is generated proceeds from the substance of the generative principle. Hence such processes as the creation of the universe and the origin of Eve cannot be called "generation." (3) Similarity of nature in the being which is begotten and the being which begets. This eliminates spontaneous generation, so-called, or heterogeny. (4) An immanent tendency in the progeny to resemble its progenitor. Hence, *e. g.*, the likeness which a child bears to his

20 Gen. IV, 1.

21 Cfr. *S. Thom., S. Theol.*, 1a, qu. 27, art. 2.

22 Cfr. Wilhelm-Scannell, *Manual of Catholic Theology*, Vol. II, pp. 102 sq.

father is not accidental, but results from the act of generation itself.

b) The notional understanding of God the Father possesses all of these distinctive momenta. In the first place, the begetting Father and the begotten Son are both living persons, identical in nature with the absolute divine life. The communication of life takes place in the vital mode of nature, as the Divine Nature itself constitutes the "*principium quo*" and the Father the "*principium quod*" of generation. Thirdly, both Sacred Scripture and Tradition attest that the Son is the most perfect likeness of the Father and His most adequate utterance. And since this absolute essential likeness is rooted in the very mode of origination itself, *viz.:* an assimilative tendency in the notional understanding of the Father, the fourth condition, too, is verified. This last-mentioned note is by far the most important, for it alone ultimately differentiates divine Generation from Spiration. It is peculiar to the act of understanding, and to that act alone, that it tends to assimilate the object of knowledge with the knower, and thereby elevates even the lowest and basest object of cognition, (*e. g.* matter), to the spiritual plane of the cognizing principle. Thus the concept "tree," for example, is as spiritual as the conceiving intellect itself. Hence the well-known Scholastic axiom: "*Cognitum est in cognoscente non per modum cogniti, sed per modum cognoscentis* — Whatever is received by the intellect, is received in the manner, not of the thing known, but of the knowing intellect." Volition or love, on the other hand, is ecstatic in its effect, that is, it transports the lover as it were beyond himself and transforms him into the object of his affection. It is for this reason that the intrinsic value of love increases or diminishes in proportion to the value or dignity of its object; which explains the ennobling influence of the love of God as the supreme good, and the degrading effects of sinful love. St. Thomas describes the difference between understanding and willing with his usual clearness as follows: "There is this difference between the intellect and the will, that the intellect is actuated because the object known is in the intellect according to its likeness. The will, on the other hand, becomes actuated, not because it contains within itself any likeness of the object willed, but because it has a certain inclination towards that object." [23]

c) In respect of the second mode of procession, *i. e.*, Spiration, it must first of all be observed that the Holy Ghost, too, is a living Person, who derives His origin from a living Spirator; that He has His essence by a vital process from the Divine Substance itself; and, lastly, that by virtue of His consubstantiality (ὁμοουσία) He is a perfectly adequate likeness of the two Divine Persons by whom He is breathed. The fourth and discriminative mark of generation — namely an immanent essential tendency or inclination to produce a being of like nature — does not, however, apply to Spiration. For since Spiration is not understanding but love, it lacks that assimilative tendency which is the essential note of generation. Consequently Spiration is not Generation.[24]

23 "*Haec est differentia inter intellectum et voluntatem, quod intellectus sit in actu per hoc, quod res intellecta est in intellectu secundum suam similitudinem. Voluntas autem fit in actu, non per hoc quod aliqua similitudo voliti sit in voluntate, sed ex hoc quod voluntas habet quandam inclinationem in rem volitam.*" S. *Theol.*, 1a, qu. 27, art. 4.

24 Cfr. S. Thom., *De Pot.*, qu. 2, art. 4, ad 7: "*Cum Filius procedat per modum verbi, ex ipsa ratione suae processionis habet, ut procedat in similem speciem generantis, et sic quod sit Filius et eius processio generatio dicatur. Non autem Spiritus Sanctus hoc habet ratione suae processionis, sed magis ex proprietate divinae naturae: quia in Deo non potest esse aliquid, quod non sit Deus; et sic ipse amor divinus Deus*

d) From all of which it is plain that there can be in the Godhead but one Son and one Holy Ghost. The Logos-Son, as the adequately exhaustive Word of the Father, utters the Father's infinite substance so perfectly that the generative power of the Paternal Intellect completely exhausts itself, and there is no room left for a second, third, etc., Son or Logos. Similarly, Father and Son mutually love each other in a manner so absolutely perfect that the Holy Ghost represents the infinite, and therefore exhaustive, utterance of their mutual love. This cuts the ground from under the feet of the Macedonians, who sophistically charged the Catholic dogma of the Trinity with absurdity by alleging that it implies the existence of a divine grandfather, a divine grandchild, and so forth.[25]

4. Two Speculative Problems.—There is a subtle and purely speculative question as to what are the objects of notional, in contradistinction to essential, understanding and love. Is the Logos merely the utterance of the divine self-knowledge? or is He also the expression of God's knowledge of His creatures? And further: Is the Holy Ghost the personal expression of God's love for Himself only? or is He also the expression of God's love for the created universe?

a) The problem involved in the first question must be solved along these lines: If it is true that all essential knowledge, and hence the very nature of God, would cease to be if God had no divine self-comprehension

est, inquantum quidem divinus, non inquantum amor."

25 Cfr. S. Thom., *S. Theol.*, 1a, qu. 30, art. 2.

(*cognitio comprehensiva sui*) embracing His Essence and attributes, or no knowledge of all the possibles (*scientia simplicis intelligentiae*),[26] among which must be reckoned all created things before their realization; then the notional cognition of the Father must have its essential and necessary object chiefly in these two kinds of divine knowledge. For whatever is essential and absolutely necessary to the very being of the Godhead, cannot play a purely subordinate and unessential part in the generation of the Logos. Theologians all admit this principle in the abstract; but in explaining and interpreting it there is no real agreement among the different schools beyond the proposition that the Logos proceeds from the notional cognition of the primary and formal object of the Divine Intellect, *viz.*: the Essence and attributes of God.[27]

Extreme views on the subject were held by Scotus and Gregory of Valentia. Scotus limits the notional understanding by which the Father begets the Logos, strictly to the absolute essence of God. According to Gregory of Valentia it includes as a necessarily co-operating factor the contingent universe with all its creatures. Both are wrong. Scotus forgets that one of the essential factors in the production of the Logos is a knowledge of all possibles as well as of the three Persons of the Blessed Trinity. Gregory of Valentia does not distinguish with sufficient clearness between God's necessary and His free knowledge. The contingent and accidental world of creatures, which undoubtedly forms one of the objects of divine omniscience, must assuredly be reflected in the Hypostatic Concep-

26 Cfr. Pohle-Preuss, *God: His Knowability, Essence, and Attributes*, pp. 329 sqq.

27 Cfr. Pohle-Preuss, *op. cit.*, pp. 338 sq.

tion or Logos, as object of the "*scientia libera*"; but in such manner that the adequacy and perfection of the Logos would suffer no impairment even if the created universe did not exist. Indeed it is through the eternally pre-existing Logos that all existing things were made.[28]

Scotus, on principle, excludes from the paternal act of Generation all creatural being, even the purely possible. Puteanus holds that Paternity, Vasquez that Paternity and Filiation, and Turrianus that, besides these, passive Spiration is comprised as a supplementary object in that notional act by which the Father utters Himself adequately in His "Word." The Thomists extend the scope of God's notional understanding to the whole realm of His essential knowledge. St. Augustine taught that the essence of the Logos comprises precisely the same wisdom that is comprehended within the essential knowledge of the Triune God,[29] and St. Thomas expressly declares: "The Father, by understanding Himself, the Son, and the Holy Ghost, and all other things contained within His knowledge, conceives the Word, and thus the entire Trinity and every created being are uttered in the Word."[30] The Angelic Doctor, as Billuart[31] points out, in this passage does not refer to the actually existing creatures, but only to the purely possibles (as objects of the *scientia simplicis intelligentiae*), in as much as they are reflected in the world of divine ideas as necessary, not as free objects of divine knowledge. As free objects of divine knowledge they are, *de facto,* also contained

28 Cfr. John I, 3, 10.

29 *Supra*, p. 203.

30 "*Pater enim intelligendo se et Filium et Spiritum Sanctum et omnia alia, quae eius scientia continentur, concipit Verbum, ut sic tota Trinitas Verbo 'dicatur,' et etiam omnis creatura.*" *S. Theol.*, 1a, qu. 34, art. 1, ad 3.

31 *De SS. Trinitatis Mysterio,* diss. 5, art. 3.

in the "Word of God," but only *concomitanter et per accidens.* "*Quia Pater principaliter dicit se,*" observes St. Thomas, "*generando Verbum suum, et ex consequenti dicit creaturas* [*existentes*], *ideo principaliter et quasi per se Verbum refertur ad Patrem, sed ex consequenti et quasi per accidens refertur ad creaturam; accidit enim Verbo, ut per ipsum creatura dicatur* — Since the Father, in begetting His Word, utters Himself principally, and the [existing] creatures incidentally, the Word is principally, and as it were *per se,* referred to the Father, and only consequently, and as it were by accident, to the creature; for it is only by accident that the creature is uttered through the Word." [32]

St. Augustine says: "The Father spake nothing that He spake not in the Son. For by speaking in the Son what He was about to do through the Son, He begat the Son Himself by whom He should make all things." [33] This passage does not contradict what we have asserted, because the archetype and exemplar of the universe about to be created was eternally present in the Logos as the living concept of creation.[34]

Another difficulty has been formulated thus: The Logos owes His existence to the generative knowledge of the Father; consequently He cannot be conceived as existing prior to the act of paternal Generation. Similarly, the Person of the Holy Ghost does not exist logically without the Father and the Son, and consequently

32 S. Thom., *De Veritate,* qu. 4, art. 4.

33 "*Nihil dixit Deus, quod non dixit in Filio. Dicendo enim in Filio, quod facturus erat per Filium, ipsum Filium genuit, per quem faceret omnia.*" *Tract. in Ioa.,* 21, n. 4. Browne's translation, *Homilies on the Gospel according to St. John,* Vol. I, p. 327.

34 For a more detailed development of this thought we must refer the reader to the dogmatic treatise on *God the Author of Nature and the Supernatural,* which forms the third volume of the present series of dogmatic text-books.

the Holy Ghost cannot contribute to the production of the Logos.

This difficulty, which is considered unsolvable by some divines, arises from confusing temporal succession with succession as to origin. The Three Divine Persons are absolutely coeternal. Hence the Logos and the Holy Ghost, despite their "*posterioritas originis,*" can form essential ingredients of the Father's intellectual act of Generation from everlasting. For the rest, as Suarez justly remarks, "*Potest esse prior existentia visionis, quam rei visae; nam si Deus potest intueri futuras creaturas prius duratione, immo aeternitate, quam ipsae existant, cur non poterit Deus ut sic videre personas prius ratione vel origine, quam producantur?* — A vision may exist prior to the object seen; for if God is able to envisage future creatures temporally and even eternally before they exist, why should He not also be able to see the Persons in [their] relation or origin before they are produced?" [35]

b) Following out the analogy, it may be asked: Which are the objects embraced by the love of Father and Son that produces the Holy Ghost? According to Billuart,[36] the Holy Ghost proceeds from the notional love of all that is *necessario et formaliter* lovable in the Godhead; that is, first of all, from the love which the Spirator bears for His own essence, *i. e.,* the Supreme Good; secondly, from the love He has for His attributes, which are really identical with the Divine Essence, and, lastly, from His love for the individual Divine Persons themselves. Although the real principle of the production of the Holy Ghost is the mutual love of the Father and the Son, we are not free to reject the love of the

35 *De Trinitate,* IX, 5, 3.

36 *De SS. Trinitatis Mysterio,* diss. 5, art. 8, qu. 3.

Spirator for the Person Spirated (the Holy Ghost), as an essentially co-operative factor on the ground that the Holy Ghost cannot possibly furnish the subject-matter of an act of which He is the result or product. Some theologians exaggerate this difficulty, but it is as easily solved as the one we have considered a little farther up. The Spirator's love for creatures (irrespective of whether they are already created, or, as mere possibles, remain to be created in the future), can add its quota in the production of the Holy Ghost only *concomitanter et per accidens,* because the notional love which produces the Holy Ghost is an essential and necessary love, whereas God's love for His creatures is entirely free, quite as free as His determination to give them being.[37] As regards God's love for merely possible creatures (*i. e.,* such as will never come into being), many divines hold that their essential goodness co-incides with the Divine Essence, which is their exemplary cause; and that, consequently, since they seem to lack a proper, independent goodness and amiability of their own, these possible creatures do not contribute towards the production of the Holy Ghost.[38] We can not share this view. Having previously espoused the opinion that the goodness proper to creatures is not identical with God's own goodness,[39] consistency compels us to adhere to the view that love for the purely possible also enters into that notional act by which the Father and the Son breathe the Holy Ghost.

READINGS: — St. Thomas, *S. Theol.,* 1a, qu. 27 sqq., and the commentators; IDEM, *Contr. Gent.,* IV, 11 (Rickaby in his Eng-

37 Cfr. S. Thom., *S. Theol.,* 1a, qu. 37, art. 2, ad 3.

38 Cfr. Oswald, *Gottes Dasein, Wesen und Eigenschaften,* p. 213. Paderborn 1887.

39 Cfr. Pohle-Preuss, *God: His Knowability, Essence, and Attributes,* pp. 440 sq.

lish version of the *Summa contr. Gent.* omits this chapter); *Franzelin, *De Deo Trino,* thes. 26–31; Kleutgen, *De Ipso Deo,* l. II, qu. 4, art. 2–3, Ratisbonae 1881; Oswald, *Trinitätslehre,* § 12, Paderborn 1888; *Scheeben, *Handbuch der kath. Dogmatik,* Vol. I, §§ 116–127, Freiburg 1873 (contains a wealth of speculative thoughts).—Jos. Slipyj, *De Principio Spirationis in SS. Trinitate, Hist.-Dogm. Inquisitio,* Leopoli 1926.

SECTION 3

THE DIVINE RELATIONS—DIVINE PERSONALITY

1. Definition of the Terms "Hypostasis" and "Person."—As the Divine Persons consist in, and are constituted by, "subsistent relations," we shall have to introduce this division of our treatise with a scientific exposition of the terms *hypostasis* and *person,* as distinguished from, and opposed to, *nature.*

a) Though they differ formally, and, when predicated of creatures, even really, the terms "essence," "substance," and "nature" are applied synonymously to God. *"Tres quidem personae,"* says the Fourth Lateran Council, *"sed una essentia, substantia seu natura simplex omnino* — Three Persons, it is true, but only one absolutely simple Essence, or Substance, or Nature."[1] The physical essence of a thing—its metaphysical essence does not concern us here—is the sum total of all those notes by which the thing is what it is. By substance we understand *"ens in se,"* or, in the words of St. Thomas, "Being, inasmuch as this Being is by itself," in con-

[1] Denzinger-Bannwart, *Enchiridion,* n. 428.

tradistinction to accident, which is "that whose being is to be in something else." [2] "Nature" is the principle of activity of a substance, or its physical essence. We know from Divine Revelation that there is in the Blessed Trinity only one Nature in three Hypostases, or Persons, while in Christ, on the contrary, there are two complete natures in but one Hypostasis, or Person. It follows that, commonly speaking, there is both a logical and a real distinction between Nature and Person. Since Person is generally defined as *hypostasis rationalis,* we have first to examine the notion of Hypostasis.

b) In order to arrive at a correct idea of Hypostasis, it will be advisable to institute a process of logical differentiation, by proceeding from the universal to the particular, and constantly adding new marks, until we attain to a complete definition.

An Hypostasis, to begin with, must be an "*ens*" or being. Every "*ens*" is either an "*ens in se*" (substance) or an "*ens in alio*" (accident). An Hypostasis is manifestly not an accident; therefore it must be a substance. Now, with Aristotle, we distinguish between *substantia prima* (οὐσία πρώτη) and *substantia secunda* (οὐσία δευτέρα). *Substantia prima* is individual, *substan-*

2 *De Potentia,* art. 7; on the notion of "substance" as opposed to "accident" cfr. Pohle-Preuss, *God: His Knowability, Essence, and Attributes,* pp. 276 sq.

tia secunda abstract substance. Common sense tells us that an Hypostasis must be an individual substance. But the term *substantia prima* is applied not only to complete but also to incomplete substances, such as body and soul, or the human hand or foot, which are individual substances, but clearly not Hypostases. Consequently, the concept of Hypostasis, besides *inseitas,* must have another essential note, *viz.:* integrity or completeness of substance. *"Hypostasis est substantia prima et integra."* Since, however, Christ's humanity is a *substantia prima et integra,* that is, a complete human nature, yet no Hypostasis, it is plain that *inseitas* and *integritas* do not suffice to constitute the notion of Hypostasis. There is required a further determinant, namely, that it is not a part, and cannot be regarded as a part of any other thing. Hence the famous definition evolved by Tiphanus: *"Hypostasis est substantia prima, integra, tota in se."* In plain English: An Hypostasis is an individual substance, separate and distinct from all other substances of the same kind, possessing itself and all the parts, attributes, and energies which are in it.[3]

3 Tiphanus, *De Hypostasi et Persona,* c. 10. Claudius Tiphanus was an illustrious Jesuit theologian of the seventeenth century. Cfr. Hurter, *Nomenclator Literarius Theologiae Catholicae,* Vol. III, ed. 3a, col. 951, Oeniponte 1907.

Of these three *momenta* the first two form the proximate genus, while the third and last constitutes the specific difference. As the proper essence of Hypostasis lies in its specific difference, Christian philosophers have been at great pains to discuss and circumscribe the notion of *totietas in se.* They emphasize that it excludes every species of composition or union with other beings, and that it consequently signifies incommunicability and independent being (*esse per se seu perseitas*).[4] It is, therefore, merely a different way of expressing the definition we have given above, when we say that *inseitas, integritas,* and *perseitas* are the essential notes of an Hypostasis. Any substance that has ceased to be *tota in se* can no longer perform the functions of an Hypostasis. Conversely, as soon as a substance acquires independence or *perseitas,* it becomes an Hypostasis. As a substance which forms part of another substance becomes an Hypostasis immediately upon being detached from that substance (for example, an amputated limb of the body separated from its soul), so a substance which is *tota in se* loses its character as an Hypostasis as soon as it becomes a part or quasi-part of something else (as, for instance, the human body in the resurrection of the dead, or the humanity of Christ in the Hypostatic Union).

c) If we compare Hypostasis with nature and consider their mutual relations, we find that the Hypostasis possesses the nature, while the nature is possessed by the Hypostasis; in

4 Cfr. Alexander Halensis., *In Arist. Metaph.,* V, 18: "*Per se esse idem est, quod solum et separatum esse, ita quod 'per se' sonat privationem associationis.*"

other words, "the Hypostasis *has* the nature."[5] Hence the axiom: *"Hypostasis habet, natura habetur."* An Hypostasis operates through the nature of which it is the bearer and controller, and all attributes and operations of that nature are referred back to the Hypostasis as its subject. Hypostasis, therefore, as *subiectum attributionis,* in the language of the Schoolmen, is the *principium quod,* while nature is the *principium quo.*

Thus we say of man, who is an Hypostasis, that he eats and drinks, sees and hears, thinks and feels, digests and sleeps; that is, he operates by and in his nature and natural faculties, though the *principium quo proximum* of all these operations are the five senses, the organs of digestion, reason and will. If we take *suppositum* as synonymous with Hypostasis, we shall also understand that other Scholastic axiom: "*Actiones et passiones sunt suppositorum* — Actions belong to their respective *supposita.*"[6]

d) A Person (*persona,* πρόσωπον, also ὑπόστασις) is an Hypostasis plus the note "intellectual" or "rational." *"Persona est hypostasis rationalis."* Person and Hypostasis, therefore, differ materially, but not formally. A crystal is just as truly an Hypostasis as a human being, because it is *"substantia tota in se."* But the possession of reason exalts an Hypostasis *in ipsa ratione*

5 Cfr. Wilhelm-Scannell, *Manual,* I, 309.

6 Cfr. John Rickaby, *General Metaphysics,* pp. 280 sq.

hypostaseos, in so far as independence is increased by self-consciousness and the Ego not only is an individualized and incommunicable substance, but is also *conscious* of this fact. A person, moreover, is *sui iuris,* and hence both the responsible possessor of his natural faculties and the subject of personal rights that are entitled to respect and protection. It is for this reason that the Schoolmen define an angel as "*hypostasis cum dignitate.*"

Boëthius's famous definition: "*Persona est rationalis naturae individua* [*i. e., prima et completa*] *substantia* — A person is the individual subject, self, or ego of a rational nature,"[7] can easily be reduced to the shorter one which we gave above, *viz.*: "*Persona est hypostasis rationalis* — A person is an Hypostasis endowed with reason." For by *individua substantia* the ancients understood precisely the same thing that we mean when we speak of *substantia prima, integra et tota in se.* The Greek Fathers were adverse to the use of the word πρόσωπον for *persona,* because Sabellius had put it to heretical uses. They preferred the generic term ὑπόστασις. Thus St. John Damascene teaches: "Neither the soul alone nor the body is an Hypostasis, but they are called ἐνυπόστατα; that which is perfected and made of both, is the Hypostasis of both. For ὑπόστασις properly is and means that which exists by itself, having its own independent being (καθ' ἑαυτὸ ἰδιοσυστάτως)." (*Dialect.,* c. 44.)

[7] *De Duab. Nat.,* I. The English translation we give is rather a paraphrase in modern terms. On the theological history of the term, see Newman, *Arians,* ch. V, § i, 3.

e) If this definition of Person is correct, that invented by Locke and introduced into Catholic theology by Günther, must be false. Locke holds that personality is constituted by continued consciousness. But if consciousness were the only essential and formal note of personality, it would follow that where there is but one consciousness, there is but one person, whereas a double consciousness would constitute two persons, and so forth. Inasmuch as the Triune God has but one (absolute) consciousness, while Christ the Godman has two, Locke's theory would destroy both the Trinity and the uni-personality of Christ, which latter is based upon the Hypostatic Union. In other words, this theory entails grave Trinitarian and Christological heresies, and must therefore be false. It is also opposed to experience and the common sense of mankind, which treats a child as yet unconscious of self, or an idiot devoid of consciousness, as persons in the true sense of the word.[8]

8 For a more detailed refutation of Locke's error, see Rickaby, *General Metaphysics*, pp. 284 sqq. Fr. Rickaby says, after trying to "follow some of the meanderings of his [Locke's] famous twenty-seventh chapter" [of the *Essay on the Human Understanding*]: "The most we can grant to Locke is that continued consciousness is one test of personality; we cannot grant that it is personality. If because of the intimate connexion of thought with personality we permitted Locke to turn thought into personality, how should we resist Cousin, who because personality is asserted specially in the will, says: *La volonté c'est la personne;* and again, *Qu'est ce que le moi? L'activité volontaire et libre.* A long way the best plan is to keep to the theory that the person of man is the composite nature, body and soul, left in its completeness and *sui iuris;* the soul being substantially un-

The terminology which we have explained above is definitively fixed by ecclesiastical and theological usage. It is the product of a historical development which involved harsh and weary struggles extending over the first four or five centuries of the Christian era,[9] and it must not be changed. It took a long time to determine which were the best terms to be employed for designating Nature, Hypostasis, and Person. The Greeks said that there were in the Divine Trinity μία οὐσία καὶ τρεῖς ὑποστάσεις; the Latins, "*una natura* (*substantia, essentia*) *et tres personae.*" Both formulas mean precisely the same thing. St. Athanasius did much towards introducing a uniform terminology when, at the irenic council of Alexandria, A. D. 362, he reconciled the contending factions by showing that while one party took ὑπόστασις to mean "Substance," and the other used it in the sense of

changeable, though variable in its accidental states, the body being constantly changed as to its constituent particles, yet preserving a certain identity, describable only by reciting what are the facts of waste and repair in an organism." (Cfr. also Uhlmann, *Die Persönlichkeit Gottes*, pp. 8 sqq., Freiburg 1906.)

9 "The difficulties of forming a theological phraseology for the whole of Christendom were obviously so great that we need not wonder at the reluctance which the first age of Catholic divines showed in attempting it, even apart from the obstacles caused by the distraction and isolation of the churches in times of persecution. Not only had the words to be adjusted and explained which were peculiar to different schools or traditional in different places, but there was the formidable necessity of creating a common measure between two, or rather three languages — Latin, Greek, and Syriac. The intellect had to be satisfied, error had to be successfully excluded, parties the most contrary to each other, and the most obstinate, had to be convinced."— Newman, *Tracts Theological and Ecclesiastical*, p. 336, new ed., London 1895.

"Person," both were really agreed as to the underlying doctrine.[10]

2. THE FOUR RELATIONS IN GOD.—The origin of the Divine Persons from one another forms the basis of a double set of Relations: one between active and passive Generation, and another between active and passive Spiration. Both classes of Relations are real and mutual. This gives us four real Relations (*relationes, σχέσεις*) in the Godhead: active and passive Generation (*generare, generari*), and active and passive Spiration (*spirare, spirari*). By passive Generation and Spiration we do not, however, understand *passio* in the sense of the Aristotelian category of πάσχειν. Properly speaking, there can be no πάσχειν in God, because He is purest actuality (*actus purissimus*) in being and life, Essence and Persons. Passive Generation means that the Son, by virtue of active Generation on the part of the Father, (not so much comes into being as) exists from all eternity. Passive Spiration signifies that the Holy Ghost possesses His subsistence and personality solely in virtue of a joint act of Spiration performed by the Father and the Son, of which act He is the

10 For the meaning of ὑπόστασις and οὐσία in the writings of the early Fathers, see Newman's *Tracts, Theological and Ecclesiastical*, "On St. Cyril's Formula μία φύσις σεσαρκωμένη," pp. 331 sqq., new ed., London 1895. On the conflicts and misunderstandings regarding these terms, cfr. *Kuhn, Christliche Lehre von der hl. Dreieinigkeit*, §29, Tübingen 1857; Petavius, *De Trinit.*, IV, 4.

immanent terminus. It is an article of faith that these Relations,—*i. e.*, of the Father to the Son (*generare*), of the Son to the Father (*generari*), of the Father and the Son to the Holy Ghost (*spirare*), and of the Holy Ghost to the Father and the Son (*spirari*), are not purely logical or imaginary. Thus we read in the *Decretum pro Iacobitis,* promulgated by the Council of Florence, A. D. 1439: "*Hinc damnat ecclesia Sabellium personas confundentem et ipsarum distinctionem realem penitus auferentem* — Hence the Church condemns Sabellius, who confounds the [Three Divine] Persons and denies that there is any real distinction between them."[11] The Church has not, however, formally defined that these relations are four in number.

It is easy to see that the dogma of the Trinity stands and falls with the reality of the Four Relations just described.[12] Since the Father is a different Person from the Son, and the Son a different Person from the Holy Ghost, the relation of the Father to the Son (and *vice versa*), and the relation of both to the Holy Ghost (and *vice versa*), must evidently be quite as real as are the three Divine Persons themselves. If these Relations were merely logical (either *rationis ratiocinantis* or *rationis ratiocinatae*), the distinction of Persons in the Godhead would evaporate into a purely logical, or at most a modal trinity, as taught by the Monarchians and

11 Denzinger-Bannwart, *Enchiridion,* n. 705.

12 Cfr. St. Thomas, *S. Theol.*, 1a, qu. 28, art. 1.

the Sabellians.[13] To say that the divine Relations are real, therefore, is but a different way of formulating the Trinitarian dogma itself.

3. THE FUNDAMENTAL LAW OF THE TRINITY. —The most important corollary that flows from the doctrine of the divine Relations is the so-called fundamental law of the Trinity. This law was formulated by St. Anselm[14] and solemnly approved by the Council of Florence, A. D. 1439. It is as follows: *"In Deo omnia sunt unum, ubi non obviat relationis oppositio* — In God all things are one except where there is opposition of relation."[15] The Father differs from the Son only because there is a perfect opposition of Relation between active and passive Generation. Where no such perfect relative opposition intervenes, everything in God is one and indistinct. Consequently, all the divine attributes in general are really identical with the divine Essence and with one another, and this is true in a special manner of those attributes which, like justice and mercy, are in logical opposition to one another. This opposition is purely logical. How sharply the *oppositio relationis* in the Holy Trinity must be defined, appears from the fact that since *generare* and *spirare* do not imply a relative but only a dis-

13 *Supra*, Ch. II, Sect. 1.

14 *De Process. Spiritus S.*, c. 2 (Migne, *P. L.*, CLVIII, 288).

15 *Decretum pro Iacobitis*, in Denzinger-Bannwart, *Enchiridion*, n. 705.

parate opposition, both functions are simultaneously performed by the same Person (*i. e.*, the Father), without His thereby becoming two Hypostases. Though at the same time *generator* and *spirator,* He is but one Hypostasis. For the same reason the Son must not be excluded from the act of Spiration, because *generari* and *spirare* do not involve a complete relative opposition, such as exists between *generare* and *generari, spirare* and *spirari.* Guided by this important rule, the Latin theologians, with the exception of the Scotists, have always contended against the Greek schismatics, that if the Son were excluded from the function of active Spiration, there would remain no basis for a Hypostatic distinction between the Second Person and the Holy Ghost. For it is only in virtue of the *relationis oppositio,* or relative opposition between *spirare* and *spirari,* that the Son is a different Person from the Holy Ghost.[16] It follows that the Logos differs from the Holy Ghost not because He is begotten by the Father, but because He breathes the Holy Ghost, and the Holy Ghost is breathed by Him.

The councils of Lyons and Florence defined it as an article of faith that active Spiration must be attributed

16 Cfr. *Symbol. Tolet.* XI, a. 675: "*Quando Pater est, non ad se, sed ad Filium est; et quod Filius est, non ad se, sed ad Patrem est: similiter et Spiritus non ad se, sed ad Patrem et Filium relative refertur.*" Denzinger-Bannwart, *Enchiridion*, n. 278.

to the Father and the Son *per modum unius,* that is, as *one* really identical act. This definition is ultimately based upon the axiom of the *relationis oppositio.* Whatever does not include relative opposition in the Godhead, appertains to the indistinct identity of the Divine Being and Essence. Hence active Spiration must be identical with Paternity and Filiation, or, in other words, Father and Son are necessarily one Spirator, even as the product of their Spiration, the Holy Ghost, is one. This *unica spiratio* was interpreted by the rule of St. Anselm, which we have called the fundamental law of the Trinity, in the *Decretum pro Iacobitis,* which emphatically declares that the Father and the Son are *one* principle of the Holy Ghost in the same sense in which the Blessed Trinity, as the Creator of the physical universe, is the one sole principle of the creature.[17]

4. THE THREE "RELATIONES PERSONIFICAE." —If, as we have said, the Divine Nature subsists in three Hypostases or Persons, only three of the four real Relations existing in the Godhead can be *"relationes personificae,"* that is to say, only three constitute Persons. These three are: Paternity (*paternitas,* πατρότης), Filiation (*filiatio,* υἱότης), and Passive Spiration (*processio,* ἐκπόρευσις).

17 *Decretum pro Iacobitis: "Hae tres personae sunt unus Deus, et non tres dii, quia trium est una substantia, una essentia, una divinitas . . . omniaque sunt unum, ubi non obviat relationis oppositio. . . . Spiritus Sanctus, quidquid est aut habet, habet a Patre simul et Filio. Sed Pater et Filius non duo principia Spiritus Sancti, sed unum principium, sicut Pater et Filius et Spiritus Sanctus non tria principia creaturae, sed unum principium."* (Denzinger-Bannwart, *Enchiridion,* n. 703 sq.)

a) It is easy to perceive that, concretely, these three Relations are the three Divine Persons themselves: Father, Son, and Holy Ghost. It follows,—and this is a most important truth,—that the three Divine Persons, as such, are Subsistent Relations; and since there are no accidents in God, they must be conceived as Substantial Relations. Hence the Scholastic axiom: *"Personae divinae sunt relationes subsistentes et substantiales."* The concept of Hypostasis or Person is most perfectly realized in Paternity, Filiation, and Passive Spiration, because it is to these *"relationes personificae,"* in virtue of their exclusive opposition, that the distinctive note of *"totietas in se"* appertains. The mystery of the Divine Trinity consists in this, that the one concrete Nature of the Godhead culminates in three distinct Hypostases, who, as three perfect Persons, possess one and the same Nature in common.

Some theologians teach that the Divine Persons are constituted by their origins rather than by their Relations. This opinion does not differ substantially from the one set forth above. For as the origin of the Son by Generation and of the Holy Ghost by Spiration forms the fundamental basis of the divine Relations, there is no objective difference between origins and Relations. They differ only to our imperfect mode of thinking, which conceives the Processions as expressing primarily the "*fieri*" (*via ad personas*), and the Relations as denoting the complete state (*in facto esse, forma permanens*). Since, however, in our human conception of the Divine Persons, the point of prime importance is not their genesis, but their permanence, theologians are wont to say that the Divine Persons are constituted by their Relations rather than by their origins.[18]

b) We have still to answer the important question, why, despite the fact of its being a real Relation, the *spiratio activa* does not produce a separate Divine Hypostasis. If Paternity, Filiation, and passive Spiration are the only *"relationes personificae,"* active Spiration must manifestly be cancelled from the list of "subsistent" relations; because else we should have a quaternity instead of a trinity. Consequently, the Spirator, as such, must be impersonal.

The objective theological reason for the impersonal character of the Spirator is the fact that active Spiration is a function common to both Father and Son. In other words, the "*unus Spirator*" presupposes two complete Hypostases, constituted by the relations of Paternity and Filiation. Consequently there is no room left for a fourth person.

It follows from what we have said that Spiration in its active sense (*spiratio activa*) constitutes an essential note of the definition of Paternity and Filiation. In other words, the Father cannot be conceived adequately,

18 On the question whether and how far we may speak of an "absolute subsistence," but not of an "absolute personality," in God, see Kleutgen, *Theologie der Vorzeit*, Vol. I, pp. 363 sqq. Cfr. also Pesch, *Praelect. Dogmat.*, t. II (3rd ed.), pp. 323 sqq., Friburgi 1906; Billuart, *De SS. Trinit. Myst.*, diss. 4, art. 3.

unless He is conceived as Spirator; and the same holds true of the Son. The complete concept of both Father and Son contains *spirare* as a logical ingredient. There is this difference, however. With the Father *spirare* takes the form of giving, while with the Son it takes the form of being received: because the Father has the power of Spiration from Himself, whereas the Son possesses it only in virtue of His Generation by the Father. In defining as an article of faith the *unica spiratio* by which the Father and the Son produce the Holy Ghost, the Church has therefore erected a strong rampart around the dogma of the Blessed Trinity, effectively preventing its transformation into a quaternity.

It is easy to see how the Greek schism, "the greatest and most enduring of all the schisms that have rent the Church," affects the dogma of the Blessed Trinity. (*a*) It denies the immediate and direct union of the Holy Ghost with the Son, which can consist only in a relation of origin. At the same time it deprives the Holy Ghost of His attribute of "own Spirit of the Son." (*b*) It denies the perfect unity of Father and Son, in virtue of which the Son possesses everything except Paternity (and therefore also the *virtus et actus spirandi*) in common with the Father. (*c*) It denies the indivisible unity of the Father, since the character of Spirator no longer appears as contained in and founded on Paternity, but standing independently alongside of it, must, like Paternity, constitute a Person, and so give the Father a double personality.

READINGS: — B. J. Otten, S. J., *History of Dogmas,* Vol. II, pp. 84 sqq.— A. Sartori, *Il Concetto di Ipostasi e l'Enosi Dogmatica al Concilii di Efeso e di Calcedonia,* Turin 1927.

SECTION 4

THE TRINITARIAN PROPERTIES AND NOTIONS

1. THE TRINITARIAN PROPERTIES.—By a "Property" theologians here understand any distinctive peculiarity by which one Divine Person differs from another.

a) Properties are divided into two classes: personal properties (*proprietates personales*, ἰδιώματα ὑποστατικά), and properties of persons (*proprietates personarum*, ἰδιώματα τῶν ὑποστάσεων). The first class comprises the three subsistent Relations, each of which appertains to but one Divine Person, and thus forms a truly distinctive peculiarity of that Person. They are: Paternity, Filiation, and passive Spiration. The second class, besides these properties of the first class—for every *proprietas personalis* is *eo ipso* also a *proprietas personae*—comprises two or three others respectively. For besides Paternity there is also peculiar to the Father, as a distinctive personal note, innascibility (*innascibilitas*, ἀγεννησία); and He furthermore shares with the Son the property of active Spiration (*spiratio activa*, πνεῖν). The different Personal Properties may consequently be grouped together as follows: Three—*paternitas, spiratio activa,* and *innascibilitas*—as peculiar to the Father; two—*filiatio* and *spiratio activa*—to the Son; and one—*spiratio passiva*—to the Holy Ghost. Hence there are six properties in all. If, as would seem preferable, *spiratio activa* is dropped,[1] there remain only four.

The only one of these Properties to require an explanation is the innascibility (ἀγεννησία) of the Father. Is not the Holy Ghost, too, unbegotten?[2] And if He is, how can innascibility be said to be a Property peculiar to the Father? Yet the Fathers and theologians insist that the First Person of the Divine Trinity alone is *innascibilis,* taking *innascibilitas* strictly in the sense of a personal Property. By calling Him ἀγέννητος, they mean to say not only that He is unbegotten, but that He is the First Person, the original source (ἀρχὴ ἄνευ ἀρχῆς, ἄναρχος), because He alone is *persona a se,* who springs from none other, and in whom the other Divine Persons have their principle, source, and root (ἀρχὴ τῆς ἀρχῆς, πηγὴ καὶ ῥίζα τῶν ἄλλων). Hence ἀγεννησία, as predicated of the Father, is more than a mere negation of *generari.* It is synonymous with Unoriginate-

[1] S. Thom., *S. Theol.,* 1a, qu. 32, art. 3. "*Communis spiratio non est proprietas, quia convenit duabus personis.*"

[2] "*Pater a nullo est factus nec creatus nec genitus* (ἀγέννητος)," says the Athanasian Creed; "*Filius a Patre solo est, non factus nec creatus* (ἀγένητος), *sed genitus* (γεννητός), *Spiritus Sanctus a Patre et Filio, non factus nec creatus nec genitus* (ἀγέννητος), *sed procedens* — The Father is made of none, neither created, nor begotten; the Son is of the Father alone; not made, nor created, but begotten; the Holy Ghost is of the Father and of the Son: neither made, nor created, nor begotten, but proceeding." (Denzinger-Bannwart, *Enchiridion,* n. 39.)

ness. The Father had no beginning, He is the First Principle. This is the patristic teaching. St. Basil, *e. g.*, says: "But that which is derived from none other, has no principle; and what has no principle, is ingenerate (ἀγέννητον)."[3] This teaching is confirmed by several councils. Thus we read in the creed drawn up by the Eleventh Synod of Toledo, A. D. 675: *"Et Patrem quidem non genitum, non creatum, sed ingenitum profitemur; ipse enim a nullo originem ducit, ex quo et Filius nativitatem et Spiritus Sanctus processionem accepit: fons ergo ipse et origo est totius divinitatis* — We profess that the Father is not begotten, nor created, but ingenerate; for He derives His origin from no one, while from Him the Son receives His nativity, and the Holy Ghost His procession; therefore He [the Father] is the fountain-head and source of the whole Godhead."[4] Though the Holy Ghost, as the last Person, terminates the evolution of the Blessed Trinity, He has no claim to a distinctive personal note, since "inspirability" is not a perfection.[5]

b) There is another difficulty. If the Trinitarian Properties are distinctive prerogatives of the Divine Persons separately, how can the Three be called co-equal? *"In hac Trinitate nihil prius aut posterius, nihil maius aut minus, sed totae tres personae coaeternae et coaequales,"* says the

3 *Contra Eunom.*, I, 15 (Migne, *P. G.*, XXIX, 547). On the term ἀγέννητον, cfr. Newman, *Select Treatises of St. Athanasius*, Vol. II, pp. 347 sqq.

4 Denzinger-Bannwart, *Enchiridion*, n. 275.

5 Cfr. St. Thomas, *S. Theol.*, 1a, qu. 32, art. 3, ad 4: *"Cum persona importet dignitatem, non potest accipi notio [= proprietas] Spiritus Sancti ex hoc, quod nulla persona est ab ipso; hoc enim non pertinet ad dignitatem ipsius, sicut pertinet ad auctoritatem Patris, quod sit a nullo."*

Athanasian Creed; that is, "In this Trinity none is afore or after other, none is greater or less than another, but the whole Three Persons are coeternal together, and coequal."[6] How can this be, if any one Person enjoys a prerogative which the other two lack?

To escape this difficulty, many theologians — among them Scotus, Cajetan, Billuart, Molina — blandly deny that the divine Properties are "perfections" in the strict sense of the term. Most others, however, agree with St. Thomas, that these Properties, though not absolute, are at least relative perfections, and as such must not be confused. The perfection of Paternity, for instance, is not identical with the perfection of Filiation.[7] But how can the possession of relative perfections by any one Divine Person, exclusive of the other two, be harmonized with the Church's teaching that the Three Persons are absolutely coequal? Let us remember, in the first place, that in essence each of the Three Divine Persons is absolutely and really identical with the Divine Nature. This absolute identity cannot but extend to the relative perfections possessed by each. Hence, whatever of true perfection there is in the Divine Essence, is participated in by all Three Divine Persons severally and in consort. While it is true that no one Person can, without sacrificing His identity, surrender His peculiar prerogative to the others, it is also certain that each Person, besides His own, also possesses, equiva-

6 Denzinger-Bannwart, *Enchiridion*, n. 39.

7 This is the teaching of the Jesuit theologians Suarez, De Lugo, Ruiz, Vasquez, Tanner, Franzelin, and of the Thomists Gotti, Sylvius, Contenson, etc. Cfr. St. Thomas's *Opus. contr. Errores Graecorum*, c. 7: *"Patet quod non posset esse Pater perfectus, nisi Filium haberet, quia nec Pater sine Filio esset."*

lently, though not formally, the relative perfections of the other two. Paternity as a perfection is surely not inferior in value or dignity to Filiation, and Spiration is of equal importance with either. Hence the Son loses nothing by not being the Father, and so forth. The Father, *per contra,* could not be Father if the Son were not the Son, and the Son could not be the Son if the Father were not the Father. To this must be added another important consideration. By virtue of their mutual immanence or inexistence (περιχώρησις),[8] the Three Divine Persons communicate to one another *quasi-formaliter* even their relative prerogatives or Properties. The Father bears within Himself the Son and the Holy Ghost as the intrinsic terminus of His notional understanding and love; while, conversely, the Son and the Holy Ghost share in the relative perfection of Paternity by virtue of their immanence in the Father,—that is, so far as the Hypostatic differences between the Divine Persons allow.[9]

2. THE DIVINE NOTIONS.—As the term itself indicates, a Notion[10] is that by which one Person is distinguishable from another. St. Thomas defines it as *"id quod est propria ratio cognoscendi divinam personam."*[11] Inasmuch as we distinguish each Divine Person by His Properties, there must be as many Notions as there are Properties. Those theologians, however, who, by eliminating active Spiration, have reduced the

8 *Infra,* pp. 281 sqq.

9 For a more detailed discussion of this question, see Tepe, *Instit. Theol.,* Vol. II, p. 383-392, Paris 1895.

10 From *nosco.* The Greek technical term is γνώρισμα.

11 *S. Theol.,* 1a, qu. 32, art. 3.

number of Properties to four, posit *five* divine Notions, as we shall proceed to explain.

a) St. Thomas, in treating of this matter,[12] starts from the axiom: "*A quo alius et qui ab alio.*" Applying this principle to the Three Persons of the Godhead, he distinguishes the Father (1) by the fact that He is a *nullo alio,* that is to say, *innascibilis,* unoriginate; (2) by the further fact that He is the *principium a quo alius per generationem* (= *paternitas*); and (3) that He is the *principium a quo alius per spirationem* (= *spiratio activa*). Similarly the Notions of the Son are Filiation (*filiatio*) and active Spiration (*spiratio activa*), whereas the one distinctive Notion of the Holy Ghost is passive Spiration (*spiratio passiva*). The subjoined scheme will make our meaning clearer:

PATER	FILIUS	SPIRITUS S.
a) *innascibilitas*	a) *generatio passiva*	a) *spiratio passiva*
b) *generatio activa*	b) *spiratio activa*	
c) *spiratio activa*		

Hence there can be no more than six Notions. Since, however, *spiratio activa* is common to both Father and Son, theologians usually reduce the number to five.

In drawing up a list of divine Notions we must observe the same rule which guided us in distinguishing the

12 *Ibid.*

divine Properties, *viz.:* Negative marks of distinction cannot be counted as Notions; else the list of divine Notions would contain twelve, to-wit:

PATER	FILIUS	SPIRITUS S.
a) *non generatur*	a) *non generat*	a) *non generatur*
b) *sed generat*	b) *sed generatur*	b) *non generat*
c) *non spiratur*	c) *non spiratur*	c) *non spirat*
d) *sed spirat*	d) *sed spirat*	d) *sed spiratur*

b) Only such negative marks are really and properly Notions as signify a positive prerogative (*dignitas, ἀξίωμα*), *e. g.*, ἀγεννησία, or *non generatur,* on the part of the Father. The "infecundity" of the Holy Ghost in particular (*non generat* and *non spirat*) cannot be reckoned among the Notions that distinguish Him from the two other Divine Persons, because He "terminates and crowns the fecundity of the Divine Nature and seals the unity of the other two Persons," and His infecundity is "therefore no complement of the *notio spirationis passivae.*" [13] From the same point of view it is easy to perceive the falsity of the Scotist contention that *ἀπνευστία, inspirabilitas* (from *non spiratur*), is a distinctive Notion of the Son. The dignity of the Second Person is sufficiently determined by *generatio passiva,* while His *inspirabilitas* is virtually included in the prerogative, which He shares with the Father, of breathing the Holy Ghost. In the case of the Father *ἀπνευστία* or *inspirabilitas* is excluded for this further and special reason, that the First Person of the Divine Trinity is the First Principle, or *principium sine principio.* A doubt remains as to whether *non generatur* should be attributed as a special Notion to the Holy

13 Scheeben, *Dogmatik,* Vol. I, p. 837.

Ghost, seeing that He is called *ingenitus* (ἀγέννητος) in the Creeds. But the Third Person derives His origin not from Generation but from Spiration, and hence the *non generatur* is virtually contained in the *spiratur,* that is, passive Spiration. The case is different with regard to the negative Notion *non generatur* on the part of the Father, for *agennesia,* as predicated of the Father, and of the Father alone, means precisely that He stands unoriginate at the head of the other two Persons, and that these derive their origin from Him, not He from them.

Thus, according to the common teaching of theologians, there are in God,

1. One Nature (or Substance);
2. Two Processions;
3. Three Hypostases;
4. Four Relations; and
5. Five Properties and Notions.

READINGS: — On the subjects treated in §§ 3 and 4, cfr. Nottebaum, *De Personae vel Hypostasis apud Patres Theologosque Notione et Usu,* Susati 1852; *C. Braun, *Der Begriff Person in seiner Anwendung auf die Lehre von der Trinität und Inkarnation,* Mainz 1876; Heinrich, *Dogmatische Theologie,* Vol. IV, §§ 245–249; J. Uhlmann, *Die Persönlichkeit Gottes und ihre modernen Gegner,* Freiburg 1906; *Billuart, *Summa S. Thomae: De SS. Trinitatis Mysterio,* diss. 2–6; St. Thomas, *S. Theol.,* 1a, qu. 28 sqq.; IDEM, *Contr. Gent.,* IV, 11 sqq.; Wilhelm-Scannell, *A Manual of Catholic Theology,* Vol. I, pp. 312 sqq.; F. J. Hall, *The Trinity,* pp. 221 sqq.— P. Stiegele, *Der Agennesiebegriff in der griechischen Theologie des vierten Jahrhunderts,* Freiburg 1913.

SECTION 5

THE DIVINE APPROPRIATIONS AND MISSIONS

1. The Divine Appropriations.—The Divine Appropriations differ essentially from the Divine Properties. The latter appertain exclusively to this or that Divine Person, while the former attribute to one Person something which is common to all Three. Both are closely related, in so far as the *appropriata* are apt to lead to a knowledge of the *propria*. Appropriation (*appropriatio*) may therefore be defined as a process, based on Scripture and Tradition, by which certain absolute divine attributes and operations, which are essentially common to the entire Trinity, are ascribed to one of the Divine Persons in particular, with the purpose of revealing the Hypostatic character of that Person.[1] From this definition it is manifest: (1) That it would be heretical to make the *appropriatum* a *proprium* (*i. e.*, the exclusive property or prerogative of one Person),[2] for, in the words of the Angelic Doctor, "*appropriare nihil est aliud,*

1 Cfr. St. Thomas, *S. Theol.*, 1a, qu. 39, art. 7.

2 Abélard and Günther were guilty of this error.

quam commune trahere ad proprium."[3] (2) That the appropriations are not to be made arbitrarily, but according to a strict law. This law may be formulated thus: Between the Hypostatic character of the Divine Person to whom an attribute is appropriated, and that attribute itself, there must exist some special intrinsic relationship. This law, though strict in itself, admits of a wide latitude in application, because the Personal character of the Divine Hypostases is manifold, and various attributes and operations may be intrinsically appropriated to each.

The Appropriations most commonly employed may be divided into four categories.[4]

a) The first category comprises the substantive names of God. They are distributed among the Three Divine Persons, according to the rule laid down above, in this wise: To the Father, as the principle of the Godhead, is appropriated the name "God" (*Deus,* ὁ Θεός). The Son, because of the dominion He has received from the Father over all creation, is commonly called "Lord" (*Dominus,* ὁ κύριος).[5] The law of appropriations is, however, sometimes set aside in Holy Scripture, as when St. Paul applies to Christ the proper name יְהוָה and expressly calls Him "God."[6] In 2 Cor. III, 17, the Apostle appropriates the name "Lord" to the Holy Ghost, to whom the Creed also refers as "*Dominum et vivificantem.*"

3 *De Verit.*, qu. 7, art. 3.

4 We follow Scheeben, *Dogmatik*, Vol. I, pp. 887 sqq. (Cfr. Wilhelm-Scannell's *Manual*, Vol. I, pp. 341 sqq.)

5 Cfr. 1 Cor. XII, 4 sqq.

6 *Supra*, pp. 79 sq.

b) Of the absolute attributes which form the second class, omnipotence is appropriated to the Father, all-wisdom to the Son, and all-goodness and sanctity to the Holy Ghost. This is in perfect keeping with the Personal character of the Three Divine Persons, since the Father is ἀρχὴ τῆς ἀρχῆς, the Son, *sapientia genita,* and the Holy Ghost, Personal Love and Hypostatic Sanctity.[7] Similarly St. Augustine, starting from the fundamental notion of unity, appropriates *unitas* to the Father, *aequalitas* to the Son, and *connexio* to the Holy Ghost.[8] The Father, as the "First" Person of the Blessed Trinity, suggests *unity* pure and simple; the Son, as the Logos and intellectual image of the Father, *equality;* the Holy Ghost, as the connecting link between the Father and the Son, the *harmony of unity and equality.* A kindred though not identical appropriation is found in the writings of St. Hilary[9] and quoted by St. Augustine,[10] *viz.:* "*Aeternitas in Patre, species in imagine, usus in munere* — Eternity is in the Father, form [*i. e.,* beauty] in the Image [*i. e.,* the Logos], use [*i. e.,* fruition] in the Gift [*i. e.,* the Holy Ghost]."[11] For the Father is ἀρχὴ ἄναρχος, the Son, εἰκὼν Θεοῦ, and the Holy Ghost δωρεὰ Θεοῦ. Many divines also find an Appropriation indicated in Rom. XI, 36: "*Ex ipso et per ipsum et in ipso sunt omnia* — Of him [*i. e.,* the Father], and by him [*i. e.,* the Son], and in him [*i. e.,* the Holy Ghost] are all things." The preposition *ex,* they hold, signifies the primal power and the source of all things, the preposition *per,* the exemplary cause, and the preposition *in,* the conservative force which sustains the universe.[12]

7 Cfr. Richard of St. Victor, *De Tribus Appropriatis,* 2 (Migne, *P. L.,* CXCVI, 993 sqq.).

8 *De Doctr. Christ.,* I, 5.

9 *De Trinit.,* II, 1.

10 *De Trinit.,* VI, 10, 11.

11 St. Augustine explains this mode of appropriation, *l. c.*

12 Cfr. St. Thomas, *S. Theol.,* 1a, qu. 39, art. 8.

c) With regard to the outward manifestations of the Blessed Trinity, which form the third class of Appropriations, Catholic theologians, following St. Paul's hint in Rom. XI, 36, have laid down the general formula, that "all things have been created by the Father through the Son in the Holy Ghost." To the Father they attribute the decree or resolution to operate (*imperium, βούλημα*), to the Son, the execution (*executio, δημιουργία*), and to the Holy Ghost, the perfecting of the work (*perfectio, τελείωσις*). This is in line with the popular belief appropriating the Creation to the Father, the Redemption to the Son, and Sanctification to the Holy Spirit.[13]

d) The Appropriations of the fourth and last class are based upon the general relations of the creature to its Creator. The worship and sacrificial cult offered to the Blessed Trinity is divided among the Three Divine Persons in such manner that the Father is the object of it, while the Son and the Holy Ghost, besides being its object, are "at the same time mediators of the worship offered to the Father, from whom they originate and whose glory they reveal, and with whom they receive the same worship, because they are one with Him."[14] As the Church in her liturgical prayers is wont to appeal to "God the Father through Jesus Christ in the unity of the Holy Ghost," but never to "Jesus Christ through the Father," so Christ Himself, as man, prayed to His Heavenly Father,[15] even as He still "maketh intercession for us at the right hand of God,"[16] and generally acts as the "natural Mediator" between God and man, though, of course, the proper object of our

13 Cfr. St. Basil, *De Spiritu Sancto*, 16 (Migne, *P. G.*, XXXII, 134).

14 Cfr. Wilhelm-Scannell, *Manual*, Vol. I, 343.

15 Cfr. John XVII, 1 sqq.

16 Rom. VIII, 34. Cfr. Heb. VII, 25.

worship is not the Father alone, but the whole Divine Trinity.[17]

2. THE DIVINE MISSIONS.—The Divine Missions, so called, throw into relief the hypostatic differences of the Divine Persons, and also their Properties,[18] and hence are of no inconsiderable assistance in elucidating the dogma of the Blessed Trinity. They are related to the Divine Appropriations in so far as an operation common to the whole Trinity is not infrequently appropriated to that particular Person who is said to be "sent" for a definite purpose by another. Cfr. Gal. IV, 6: *"Misit Deus [i. e., Pater] Spiritum Filii sui in corda vestra clamantem: Abba, Pater*—God [the Father] hath sent the Spirit of His Son into your hearts, crying: Abba, Father."[19]

a) A divine Mission (*missio divina*) is defined as "the eternal procession of a Person sent from a Person sending, in its relation to a creatural terminus in time."[20] It is important to emphasize this twofold aspect of divine Mission, *viz.*: the fundamental relation of one Person to another as its *terminus a quo* and its effect in the creature as *terminus ad quem.* The *missio*

17 It remains for Soteriology to develop this point. On the special Appropriations of the Holy Ghost, cfr. St. Thomas, *Contr. Gent.*, IV, 20-22 (Rickaby, *Of God and His Creatures*, pp. 351 sqq., London 1905).

18 *Supra*, pp. 236 sq.

19 On the concept of "Mission," *vide supra*, p. 175.

20 Cfr. St. Thomas, *S. Theol.*, 1a, qu. 43, art. 3, ad 3: *"Missio includit processionem aeternam et aliquid addit, scil. temporalem effectum."*

ad intra (*i. e., processio*) is eternal, but the *missio ad extra* takes place in time. It follows: (1) that an Eternal Mission must be intrinsically as necessary and unchangeable as Generation and Spiration; while a Temporal Mission, on the other hand (*i. e.,* a proceeding to exterior effects) is subject to the free will of the Triune God. (2) There can be no Eternal Mission except from Person to Person, strictly according to the ἀκολουθία κατὰ τὴν τάξιν;[21] while Temporal Mission, being an outward manifestation, is a function common to the whole Trinity.[22] From this we may deduce a law, which is confirmed by Holy Scripture, *viz.*: that the Temporal Missions are strictly regulated by the divine sequence of origin. Consequently, the Father alone can *send,* and He can *send* both the Son and the Holy Ghost. The Son can *be sent,* but only by the Father; He can also *send,* but He can *send* only the Holy Ghost. The Holy Ghost, in His turn, cannot *send,* but can *be sent* by either the Father or the Son. The Person who proceeds (*missus*) stands as it were midway between the eternal *terminus a quo* and the temporal *terminus ad quem,* because, on the one hand, owing to the sequence of origin, He depends on the Person from whom He proceeds, while, on the other, He produces in the (rational) creature a new effect, which is again, in its turn, appropriated to Him.[23]

21 Cfr. *supra,* p. 111.

22 Cfr. St. August., *De Trinit.,* IV, 20, 28: "*Mittit, qui genuit; mittitur, quod genitum est. . . . Sed Pater non dicitur missus; . . . non enim habet, de quo sit aut ex quo procedat. . . . De Spiritu Sancto dicitur: 'a Patre procedit,' Pater vero a nullo* — He sends who begot, That is sent which is begotten. . . . But the Father is not said to be sent . . . for He has no one of whom to be, or from whom to proceed. . . . It is said of the Holy Ghost: 'He proceedeth from the Father,' but the Father is from no one."

23 No one has explained this more clearly than St. Thomas, when he says: "*In ratione missionis duo importantur: quorum unum est habitudo missi ad eum, a quo mit-*

b) A Mission is visible or invisible (*missio visibilis — invisibilis*), according as its temporal effect in the creature is sensible or insensible. A visible Mission cannot be conceived without an invisible one, but an invisible does not necessarily suppose a visible Mission. We have an example of a visible Mission in the descent of the Holy Ghost on Pentecost Day. He descends invisibly, *secundum gratiam,* whenever confirmation is administered or Holy Orders are conferred.

There are two classes of visible Missions, according as the Divine Person who is sent (*missus*) becomes visible to men by entering into Hypostatic Union with a human nature (the Word made flesh), or merely manifests Himself to men by means of a visible symbol (as the Holy Ghost descending in the form of a dove). The Incarnation is unique as a pre-eminent Mission, of which the Old Testament theophanies,[24] so far as they can be considered "Missions" at all, were merely a preparation and preamble. For this reason Suarez calls the Incarnation a *missio visibilis substantialis* in opposition to all other missions, which are merely *representativae.*[25]

Aside from the Mission of the Incarnate Logos, an invisible Mission as such invariably ranks higher than

titur; aliud est habitudo missi ad terminum, ad quem mittitur. Per hoc autem, quod aliquis mittitur, ostenditur processio quaedam missi a mittente vel secundum imperium, sicut dominus mittit servum, vel secundum consilium, ut si consiliarius mittere dicatur regem ad bellandum, vel secundum originem, ut si dicatur quod flos emittitur ab arbore. Ostenditur etiam habitudo ad terminum, ad quem mittitur, ut aliquo modo ibi esse incipiat, vel quia prius ibi omnino non erat quo mittitur, vel quia incipit aliquo modo esse, quo prius non erat. Missio igitur divinae personae convenire potest, secundum quod importat ex una parte processionem originis a mittente, et secundum quod importat ex alia parte novum modum existendi in alio." S. Theol., 1a, qu. 43, art. 1.

24 *Supra,* pp. 12 sqq.

25 *De Trinit.,* XII, 4, 17.

a visible Mission, because it aims at the supernatural sanctification of the creature. "*Nec enim Spiritus Sanctus de Patre procedit in Filium,*" says the Eleventh Council of Toledo (A. D. 675), "*vel de Filio procedit* AD SANCTIFICANDAM CREATURAM, *sed simul ab utrisque processisse monstratur, quia caritas sive sanctitas amborum agnoscitur. Hic igitur Spiritus Sanctus missus ab utrisque creditur.*" [26] The creation and conservation of the cosmos, and God's co-operation with His creatures can no more be attributed to a divine Mission than His omnipresence *per essentiam, potentiam et praesentiam,*[27] and hence all divine missions, properly so called, are confined to the production of supernatural effects, culminating in the infusion and augmentation of sanctifying grace, and in the personal indwelling of the Holy Ghost. "*Est unus* [*modus*] *specialis, qui convenit naturae rationali, in qua Deus dicitur esse sicut cognitum in cognoscente et amatum in amante. Et quia cognoscendo et amando creatura rationalis sua operatione attingit ad ipsum Deum, secundum istum specialem modum Deus non solum dicitur esse in creatura rationali, sed etiam habitare in ea sicut in templo,*" etc.[28] Consequently, sanctification is a divine Mission κατ' ἐξοχήν. This also gives us the reason why a person can be sent only to rational creatures. The supernatural communication of the so-called *gratiae gratis datae,* and of the theological virtues faith and hope, is not to be conceived as a divine Mission in the strict sense of the term, because it does not essentially — *ex vi notionis* — include sanctifying grace nor

26 Denzinger-Bannwart, *Enchiridion,* n. 277.

27 Cfr. St. Thomas, *S. Theol.,* 1a, qu. 43, art. 3.

28 *S. Theol.,* 1a, qu. 43, art. 3. Cfr. John XIV, 17, 23; 1 Cor. III, 16, VI, 19; Gal. IV, 6, and so forth. For a more thorough explanation, see the dogmatic treatise on Grace.

theological charity and the indwelling of the Holy Spirit, which are invariably connected with this grace.[29]

c) Let us remark, in conclusion, that the concept of divine Mission must be carefully distinguished from the cognate notions of Indwelling (*inhabitatio*) and Apparition (*apparitio*). Though every invisible Mission has for its ultimate object the "indwelling" of God in the soul, and the beginning of that indwelling is signalized after the manner of a "coming" or "descent,"[30] yet Mission and Indwelling are not identical,— for this reason, among others, that Mission takes place only in conformity with immanent Procession from Person to Person, while Indwelling, though appropriated in a special manner to the Holy Ghost, is common to the entire Trinity.[31] The concept of "Apparition" also is more extensive than that of Mission. For though the Father and the Blessed Trinity as such cannot be sent, because they do not proceed, there is no reason why they should not appear visibly. We have a classical example of such a Trinitarian theophany in the account of our Lord's Baptism in the Jordan.[32]

READINGS: — Besides St. Thomas, *S. Theol.*, 1a, qu. 43, and his commentators, cfr. St. Augustine, *De Trinitate*, l. II–IV; Petavius, *De Trinit.*, l. VIII; *Suarez, *De Trinit.*, l. XII; Ruiz, *De Trinit.*, disp. 82, 108 sq.; Franzelin, *De Deo Trino*, thes. 42–48; K. v. Schäzler, *Natur und Übernatur*, pp. 42 sqq., Mainz 1865; Pesch, *Praelect. Dogmat.*, Vol. II (3rd ed.), pp. 340 sqq.; De Régnon, *Études de Théologie Positive sur la S. Trinité*, Études XVII and XXV, Paris 1898.

29 Cfr. Card. Manning, *The Internal Mission of the Holy Ghost*, 5th ed., New York (*s. a.*); De Bellevue, *L'Œuvre du Saint-Esprit ou la Sanctification des Ames*, Paris 1901. Froget-Raemers, *The Indwelling of the Holy Spirit in the Souls of the Just*, N. Y. 1922.

30 Cfr. Pohle-Preuss, *God: His Knowability, Essence, and Attributes*, pp. 325 sq.

31 Cfr. John XIV, 23.

32 *Supra*, pp. 24 sq.

PART II

UNITY IN TRINITY, OR THE TRIUNITY OF GOD

Monotheism is the foundation of all true religion, and therefore we must not dismiss the subject of this volume without demonstrating that the dogma of the Divine Trinity neither destroys nor endangers the unity and simplicity of God. The Blessed Trinity must be essentially conceived not only as Trinity in Unity, but likewise as Unity in Trinity. It is impossible to separate the one from the other.[1]

We shall begin this second part of our treatise with a consideration of Tritheism, which is the heretical antithesis of the dogma of the Blessed Trinity. Tritheism is no less destructive of the dogma of the Trinity than Monarchianism (Unitarianism) in its diverse forms.[2] It is against Tritheism that the Athanasian Creed teaches: "*Sicut singillatim unamquamque personam Deum ac Dominum confiteri christiana religione compellimur, ita tres Deos aut Dominos dicere catholica religione prohibemur* — For like as we are compelled by the Christian verity to acknowledge every Person by Himself to be God and Lord, so are we forbidden by the Catholic religion to say, there be Three Gods or Three Lords."[3]

1 Cfr. *Symbol. Athanas.*: "*Ut per omnia et unitas in Trinitate et Trinitas in unitate veneranda sit* — So that in all things the Unity in Trinity, and the Trinity in Unity is to be worshipped." (Denzinger-Bannwart, *Enchiridion*, n. 39.)

2 *Supra*, pp. 115 sqq.

3 Cfr. Denzinger-Bannwart, *Enchiridion*, n. 39.

The *unitas in Trinitate* or *triunitas* (= *trinitas*) may be regarded from a threefold point of view: (1) As unity of nature;[4] (2) as unity of external operation;[5] and (3) as unity of circumincession or mutual inexistence.[6] Tritheism is the heretical contradictory of all three of these, but it is most directly opposed to unity of nature, and for this reason we proceed to consider it in the first Section of the following Chapter, which is devoted to the Consubstantiality of the Three Divine Persons.

4 *Unitas naturae s. substantiae s. essentiae.*

5 *Unitas operationis ad extra.*

6 *Unitas circumincessionis*, περιχώρησις.

CHAPTER I

ONENESS OF NATURE, OR THE CONSUBSTANTIALITY OF THE THREE DIVINE PERSONS

SECTION 1

TRITHEISM AND THE CHURCH

1. THE HERESY OF TRITHEISM.—This heresy did not assume definite proportions until after the dogma of the Trinity had been formally defined. The Arians and Semi-Arians escaped the formal charge of Tritheism, because they represented the Logos as a creature of the Father, and the Holy Ghost as a creature of the Logos. But as they held these two Persons to be divine at least by grace and merit, they were frequently accused by the Fathers of fostering the Tritheistic heresy.

a) John Philoponus, a famous expounder of Aristotle and a votary of Monophysitism,[1] is reputed to be the real founder of Tritheism, which he pressed into the service of his Christological heresy. When it was

[1] Philoponus flourished about A. D. 550. His chief theological work is entitled Διαιτητὴς ἢ περὶ ἑνώσεως. Cfr. Hurter, *Nomenclator Literarius Theologiae Catholicae*, Vol. I, 3rd ed., coll. 466–7, Oeniponte 1903.

urged against his Monophysitic position, that to confuse Nature and Person in Christ would surely lead to a similar confusion in the Divine Trinity, and therefore ultimately to Tritheism, Philoponus answered: Father, Son, and Holy Ghost are three distinct individuals of the species "God," in precisely the same way that Peter, Paul, and John are three different individuals of the species "man," and they must therefore be looked upon as "three part-substances in one common, abstract substance." [2]

b) In the Middle Ages, according to the authentic testimony of the Fourth Lateran Council (A. D. 1215), Abbot Joachim of Flora in Calabria [3] conceived the oneness of the Three Divine Persons as a mere collective and generic unity.[4] It is difficult to see under the circumstances how this rather hotblooded and ill-advised monk could dare to accuse Peter Lombard of having heretically represented the Blessed Trinity as a quaternity. We must add, however, that Joachim de Floris died penitently, professing absolute submission to the authority of the infallible Church.[5]

c) About the middle of the nineteenth century a German theologian, Anton Günther (+ 1863), gave grievous scandal by teaching that the Three Divine Persons constitute a purely formal unity, which is neither specific nor numerical. The Absolute — such in brief was his

[2] Τρεῖς μερικαὶ οὐσίαι ἐν οὐσίᾳ κοινῇ.

[3] + 1202. Cfr. Gardner in the *Catholic Encyclopedia*, Vol. VIII, pp. 406 sq.

[4] "*Quamvis concedat quod Pater et Filius et Spiritus Sanctus sunt una essentia, una substantia unaque natura: verum unitatem huiusmodi non veram et propriam, sed quasi collectivam et similitudinariam esse fatetur, quemadmodum dicuntur multi homines 'unus populus' et multi fideles 'una ecclesia.'*" *Conc. Lateran. IV*, cap. "*Damnamus*" (Denzinger-Bannwart, *Enchiridion*, n. 431).

[5] *Conc. Later. IV*, cap. "*Damnamus*," *ibid.*; H. Grundmann, *Studien über Joachim von Floris*, Leipsic 1927.

theory — in virtue of "a theogonic process of self-realization," posits itself three times in succession, first as thesis, secondly as antithesis, and thirdly as synthesis, whereby the Divine Substance becomes triplicated, that is, develops into three relative substances or Persons, who formally coalesce into an "Absolute Substance" or Absolute Personality.[6]

2. The Condemnation of Tritheism.—The Church has at all times strenuously rejected Tritheism in every guise.

a) As early as A. D. 262, Pope Dionysius, in a dogmatic epistle which Scheeben rightly calls epoch-making,[7] sharply censured certain Tritheistic expressions of Bishop Denis of Alexandria.[8] "*Neque igitur admirabilis et divina unitas,*" he declared, "*in tres divinitates est separanda neque factionis* [= *facturae*] *vocabulo dignitas ac summa magnitudo Domini* [= *Christi*] *est diminuenda* — Neither then may we divide into three Godheads the wonderful and divine Monad; nor disparage with the name of 'creature' the dignity and exceeding majesty of the Lord."[9] St. Sophronius of Jerusalem (+ 638) wrote a refutation of Monotheletism, in which the "*novi Tritheitae*" are castigated unmercifully. This treatise was declared to be orthodox and was bodily incorporated into the canons of the Sixth Ecumenical Council, A. D. 680. "*Numeratur igitur SS. Trinitas,*" we read there, "*non essentiis aut naturis et*

6 Cfr. Kleutgen, *Theologie der Vorzeit*, Vol. I, 2nd ed., pp. 379 sqq., Münster 1867. For a good account of Günther and his philosophico-theological system see Lauchert in the *Catholic Encyclopedia*, Vol. VII, pp. 85 sqq.

7 *Dogmatik*, Vol. I, p. 746.

8 *Supra*, p. 121 sq.

9 Denzinger-Bannwart, *Enchiridion*, n. 51. Newman's translation (*Select Treatises of St. Athanasius*, Vol. I, p. 47).

diversis deitatibus vel tribus dominationibus, sicut insaniunt Ariani et sicut novi Tritheitae[10] *furiunt, vanissime dicentes, essentias tres et naturas tres et tres dominationes et tres deitates. . . . Eum, qui ista recipit aut sapit aut novit, anathematibus percellimus.*"[11]

b) More important and more definite than these and in fact all other medieval decisions, is the "*Caput Damnamus*" hurled by the Fourth Council of the Lateran against Abbot Joachim de Floris (A. D. 1215). Oswald calls it "the last solemn, and also the most effective and most definite decision ever uttered by the ecclesiastical magisterium in regard to this mystery."[12]

α) The salient point of this decision is that the "one *summa res*"[13] is at the same time "truly Father, Son, and Holy Ghost," in such wise that, excluding all semblance of "quaternity," the "Three Persons together and each Person separately" actually coincide and are numerically identical with that "*summa res.*"[14] Inasmuch as no distinction attaches to the Divine Nature, which is absolute, but only to the Divine

10 The reference is probably to Philoponus and his adherents.

11 Cfr. Hardouin, *Concil.*, t. III, 1263.

12 *Trinitätslehre*, p. 112, Paderborn 1888.

13 Cfr. John X, 29: "*maius omnibus.*"

14 "*Nos autem, sacro approbante Concilio, credimus et confitemur cum Petro Lombardo, quod una quaedam summa res est, . . . quae veraciter est Pater et Filius et Spiritus Sanctus; tres simul personae, ac singillatim quaelibet earundem: et ideo in Deo solummodo Trinitas est, non quaternitas; quia quaelibet trium personarum est illa res, videlicet substantia, essentia seu natura divina.*" (Denzinger-Bannwart, *Enchiridion*, n. 432.)

Persons, who are relative, the same Council says: *"Et illa [summa] res non est generans neque genita nec procedens, sed est Pater qui generat, et Filius qui gignitur, et Spiritus Sanctus qui procedit, ut distinctiones sint in personis et unitas in natura."* [15] That is to say, it is not the Divine Nature which generates, or is begotten, or proceeds, but it is the Father who begets, the Son who is begotten, and the Holy Ghost who proceeds.

The Council elucidates this point by continuing, in more popular language: *"Licet igitur alius sit Pater, alius Filius, alius Spiritus Sanctus, non tamen aliud; sed id quod est Pater, est Filius et Spiritus Sanctus idem omnino, ut secundum orthodoxam et catholicam fidem consubstantiales credantur."* [16] From these premises flows a conclusion which is of prime importance for the consideration of the Divine ὁμοουσία = ταὐτουσία, or Consubstantiality, *viz.*: that one and the same "*summa res*" simultaneously exercises two separate and distinct functions,— the functions of one Absolute and three Relatives. Under the first-mentioned aspect of the Blessed Trinity it would be heretical to say: "The Divine Nature (*summa res*) generates, or is begotten, or proceeds"; while under the aspect mentioned in the second place, this same "*summa res*" is the Father who generates, the Son who is begotten, and the Holy Ghost who is breathed. It is this twofold functioning of the one "*summa res*" that enables

15 *Conc. Lat. IV, cap.* "*Damnamus.*" (Denzinger-Bannwart, *Enchiridion*, n. 432.)
16 *Ibid.*

us to give opposite replies to the queries "What?" and "Who?" To the query: "*What* is the Father?" the answer is: "*Id quod Filius et Spiritus Sanctus, idem omnino,*" while if it be asked: "*Who* is the Father?" the reply will be: "*Alius Pater, alius Filius, alius Spiritus Sanctus.*"

β) In order still more accurately to define this identity of nature, which underlies the distinction of Persons, the Council enters upon a somewhat detailed exposition, from which we shall quote a salient passage: "*Pater enim ab aeterno Filium generando suam substantiam ei dedit, iuxta quod ipse testatur: 'Pater quod dedit mihi maius omnibus est.' Ac dici non potest, quod partem substantiae suae illi dederit et partem ipse sibi retinuerit, cum substantia Patris indivisibilis sit, utpote simplex omnino. Sed nec dici potest, quod Pater in Filium transtulerit suam substantiam generando, quasi sic dederit eam Filio, quod non retinuerit ipsam sibi: alioquin desiisset esse substantia. Patet ergo, quod sine ulla diminutione Filius nascendo substantiam Patris accepit: et ita Pater et Filius habent eandem substantiam, et sic eadem res et Pater et Filius necnon Spiritus Sanctus ab utroque procedens.*" It would be impossible to give a clearer explanation than this of the Consubstantiality of the Three Divine Persons in the sense of absolute ταὐτουσία.

γ) On the basis of this pregnant conciliar definition theologians have attempted to answer the difficult question: Of what kind is the distinction between Nature and Person, or between *summa res absolute* and *summa res relative?* It is evident from the explanation of the Fourth Lateran Council, which we have just quoted, that the distinction in question cannot be a real distinction. For if the Three Divine Persons were really distinct from their common Nature, the Godhead would contain four separate entities, *viz.:* Nature, Father, Son, and Holy Ghost. On the other hand, it is not sufficient to posit a purely logical distinction (*distinctio rationis ratiocinantis*); else the Three Persons would coalesce with the Divine Substance — they would cease to be realities and sink to the level of mere modes of manifestation, as was alleged by the Sabellians. The truth must lie somewhere between these heretical extremes. Precisely where, is not so easy to determine.

There are three Scholastic distinctions which can be applied here without trenching on revealed dogma. They are: the *modal* distinction of Durandus, the *formal* distinction of Duns Scotus, and the *virtual* distinction of St. Thomas Aquinas. In applying these distinctions, however, we find that the modal and the formal, if pressed to their ultimate logical conclusions, entail a species of composition altogether inadmissible in the Godhead, and also a real composition in each separate Divine Person. According to Durandus, this composition is one of essence and "mode"; according to Scotus, its elements are essence and "formality." These incongruities have led the great majority of Catholic theologians to adopt the virtual distinction of the Thomists.[17]

17 Cfr. Pohle-Preuss, *God: His Knowability, Essence, and Attributes*, pp. 151 sqq.

According to this theory, the one "*summa res*" is both absolute and relative in such wise that, in the simultaneous discharge of an absolute and a relative function, it is *formaliter unum et virtualiter multiplex.* Hence the Divine Nature differs from each Divine Person by the so-called *distinctio rationis ratiocinatae sive virtualis sive cum fundamento in re,* of which Cardinal Cajetan says: "*Absolutum et relativum ita ibi sunt, ac si essent distincta, et rursus ita [una summa res] exercet munus utriusque, ac si essent distincta.*"[18] This distinction is based on the same principle as the current one between the "essential" knowledge which belongs to the whole Trinity, *qua* absolute Spirit, and the "notional" understanding which is proper to the Father alone, *qua* Begettor of His consubstantial Word. (Cfr. also the distinction between "essential" and "notional" volition or love).

c) Among the more recent pronouncements of the ecclesiastical teaching office regarding the dogma of the Blessed Trinity, special mention must be made of the dogmatic Bull "*Auctorem fidei,*" issued by Pope Pius VI against the Council of Pistoia, A.D. 1786. This Bull rejects the formula "*Deus in tribus personis distinctus*" (instead of *distinctis*) as suspicious. Günther's Tritheistic teaching was censured by the S. Congregation of the Index on January 8, 1857, and formally condemned by Pope Pius IX in a lengthy letter, addressed June 15, 1857, to Cardinal Geissel, Archbishop of Cologne. A provincial council held with the approval of Pius IX at Cologne, in 1860, cited all the Trinitarian definitions which we have adduced in this volume as an

18 *In S. Theol.*, 1am, qu. 39, art. 1. This subtle problem is treated exhaustively by Franzelin, *De Deo Trino*, thes. 21; more briefly by Pesch, *Praelect. Dogmat.*, Vol. II, 3rd ed., pp. 327 sqq., Friburgi 1906.

inexpugnable bulwark of the orthodox faith against the vagaries of Günther. And the *schema* which the Commission on Dogma had prepared for the Vatican Council shows that the Holy See intended to brand Günther's errors as formally heretical.[19]

READINGS: — P. Fournier, *Études sur Joachim de Flore et ses Doctrines,* Paris 1909.— Dom J. Chapman, O. S. B., art. "Tritheists," in the *Catholic Encyclopedia,* Vol. XV.

19 Cfr. Conrad Martin, *Collect. Documentorum Vatic.,* pp. 21 sqq., Paderb. 1873; Katschthaler, *Zwei Thesen für das allgemeine Concil,* I: "*Die numerische Wesenseinheit der drei göttlichen Personen,*" Ratisbon 1868.

SECTION 2

THE TEACHING OF REVELATION

1. SACRED SCRIPTURE.—Though we have repeatedly spoken of the Consubstantiality of the Three Divine Persons, it remains for us to prove from Scripture that this Consubstantiality is not to be conceived after the manner of the harmony of thought and sentiment that sometimes unites intimate friends, nor yet in a merely generic way, as if there were "one Godhead in three Gods," but strictly as identity of nature or ταὐτουσία. Taken in this sense the unity of the Divine Nature forms a special chapter of the revealed teaching on the Trinity.

a) Monotheism is the fundamental dogma of the Old Testament, and it has not been abrogated, but re-affirmed and re-inculcated in the New.[1] In such passages as 1 Cor. VIII, 6,[2] and Deut. XXXII, 39,[3] Holy Scripture denies the possibility of Tritheism or any other species of polytheism. There is but one alternative: Either the Father, the Son, and the Holy Ghost subsist in three separate and distinct natures, or in one nature

1 Cfr. Pohle-Preuss, *God: His Knowability, Essence, and Attributes*, pp. 212 sqq.

2 "*Videte quod ego sim solus et non sit alius Deus praeter me*— See ye that I alone am, and there is no other God besides me."

3 "*Nullus est Deus nisi unus*— There is but one God."

only. If they subsisted in three separate and distinct natures, there would be three Gods,—a belief which the Bible unmistakably condemns. If they subsist in one Divine Nature, we have the Christian Trinity as unequivocally taught throughout the New Testament. Consequently Tritheism is unscriptural. Let no one object that the term "*unus Deus*" admits of being interpreted in a specific or a generic sense. For wherever several individuals of the same species or genus coexist, none of them can truthfully assert: I alone am and there is none other besides me.

b) A special argument for our thesis can be derived from Christ's sermon "in Solomon's porch," which culminates in the words: "*Ego et Pater unum sumus*—I and the Father are one."[4] This was a favorite quotation with the Fathers. Thus St. Augustine says in the thirty-sixth of his Homilies on the Gospel of St. John: "*Quod dixit 'unum,' liberat te ab Ario; quod dixit 'sumus,' liberat te a Sabellio*—The word 'one' in this passage excludes Arianism; the word 'are' excludes Sabellianism."[5] In order to understand what kind of unity Christ means when He says, "I and the Father are one," we must examine the context.

a) The outstanding thought of the preceding verses is that Christ gives life everlasting to His sheep by virtue of His own personal dominion and power, and

4 John X, 30.

5 *Tract. in Ioa.*, 36, n. 9. (Migne, *P. L.*, XXXV, 1668.)

that "no one shall pluck them out of [His] hand." To justify this claim He affirms: "That which my Father hath given me, is greater than all," and He proceeds to explain by first stating a truth which the Jews were quite ready to admit—*viz.:* that "no one can snatch" His sheep "out of the hand of [His] Father." Then, after the manner of a minor premiss in a syllogism, follows the verse: "I and the Father are one," by which Christ evidently means to say: I and the Father have the same nature, and consequently possess the same power. The conclusion, which figures as a sort of thesis at the head of the argument, is evident, *viz.:* Therefore, "I give [my sheep] life everlasting; . . . and no man shall pluck them out of my hand."

It is worth while to con this important text somewhat more minutely. The preceding portion of the context reads: *"Et ego vitam aeternam do eis [scil. ovibus meis], et non peribunt in aeternum, et non rapiet eas quisquam de manu mea. Pater meus quod dedit mihi, maius omnibus est: et nemo potest rapere de manu Patris mei. Ego et Pater unum sumus*—And I give them [*i. e.,* my sheep] life everlasting; and they shall not perish for ever, and no man shall pluck them out of my hand. That which my Father hath given me is greater than all: and no one can snatch them out of the hand of my Father. I and the Father are one."[6] "That which my Father hath given me is greater than all," is here alleged as the reason why Christ can give life everlasting to His sheep and prevent any one from plucking them out of His hand. Now, we know from numerous parallel passages,[7] that the predicate expressed in the phrase "*maius omnibus*" can mean nothing else

[6] John X, 28-30.

[7] Cfr., *e. g.,* John XVI, 5; XVII, 10, etc.

than the Divine Nature (*summa res infinite perfecta*), in so far as it is communicated, immediately and undiminished, by the begetting Father to His begotten Son. "*Dedit mihi*" is therefore synonymous with "*gignendo mihi communicavit.*" Consequently, the Son, by this communication to Him of the Divine Essence on the part of the Father, has precisely the same power as the Father, with this sole difference, that the Father has the Divine Nature and power of Himself, while the Son derives it from the Father. Taking this truth for the antecedent of an enthymeme, the conclusion: "I and the Father are one," can only mean that the Father and the Son, as possessing the same Nature and the same power, are absolutely consubstantial, *i. e.*, identical in essence. St. Athanasius called particular attention to this when he said: ". . . *ut scilicet eandem amborum divinitatem* (ταυτότητα τῆς θεότητος) *unamque naturam* (ἑνότητα τῆς οὐσίας) *esse doceret* — In order to show the identity of Godhead in both, and the unity of Nature." [8]

This argument is not weakened by the circumstance that the *textus receptus* has: Ὁ πατήρ μου, ὃς δέδωκέ μοι, πάντων μείζων ἐστί. For, as the explanation given by St. Chrysostom [9] shows, this variant affects merely the form, and not the substance of the argument based upon John X, 29.

β) The verses which follow (John X, 34 sqq.) positively confirm the argument. The Jews obviously understood Christ's dictum, "I and the Father are one," to mean perfect consubstantiality; for they "took up stones to stone him for blasphemy." "For a good work we stone thee not," they explained, "but for blasphemy;

8 *Or. Contr. Arian.*, 3, 3 (Migne, *P. G.*, XXVI, 327).

9 *Hom. in Ioa.*, 61, 2 (Migne, *P. G.*, LIX, 338 sqq.).

and because that thou, being a man, makest thyself God."[10] How did Jesus meet this accusation? Did He retract what He had said? Did He tell the Jews that they misunderstood Him? No; He repeated His previous statement and confirmed it by an *argumentum a minori ad maius.* "Is it not written in your law," He asks, "I said 'you are gods'? If he called them gods, to whom the word of God was spoken, and the Scripture cannot be broken; do you say of him whom the Father hath sanctified and sent into the world: 'Thou blasphemest,' because I said, 'I am the Son of God'?"[11] In corroboration of His claim, Christ points to His miracles: "If I do not the works of my Father, believe me not. But if I do, though you will not believe me, believe the works: that you may know and believe that the Father is in me, and I in the Father."[12] By thus accentuating His immanence in the Father (*Perichoresis*), He merely repeats in other words what He had said before: "I and the Father are one." It is because He clearly asserted His consubstantiality with God the Father, that the Jews became convinced that He blasphemed; and to emphasize His consubstantiality with the Father He repeated His assertion in the words: "I am the Son of God." This also explains why His adversaries "sought to take him," so that He found it advisable to

10 John X, 33: "*De bono opere non lapidamus te, sed de blasphemia: et quia tu, homo cum sis, facis teipsum Deum* (ποιεῖς σεαυτὸν Θεόν)."

11 John X, 34 sqq.: "*Respondit eis Iesus: Nonne scriptum est in lege vestra: Quia ego dixi, dii estis?* [Ps. LXXXI, 6]. *Si illos dixit deos, ad quos sermo Dei factus est, et non potest solvi scriptura, quem Pater sanctificavit et misit in mundum, vos dicitis: quia blasphemas, quia dixi: Filius Dei sum?*"

12 John X, 37 sqq.: "*Si non facio opera Patris mei, nolite credere mihi; si autem facio, et si mihi non vultis credere, operibus credite, ut cognoscatis et credatis, quia Pater in me est, et ego in Patre.*"

"escape out of their hands." [13] This interpretation has ample support in the writings of the Fathers. "Had they [the Father and the Son] been two," says St. Athanasius, "He [Christ] would not have said: 'I and the Father are one,' but 'I am the Father,' or 'I and the Father am'; . . . the word 'I' declares the Person of the Son, and the word 'Father' as evidently expresses him who begat the Son, and the word 'One' the one Godhead and His consubstantiality." [14]

2. TRADITION.—Faydit, Cudworth, Placidus Stürmer, O.S.B., and others, have accused the Nicene Fathers of Tritheism, because, as they claimed, these Fathers in their naïve ignorance had understood the term ὁμοούσιον as denoting a merely generic unity. Following the example of Sabinus of Heraclea, who was a Macedonian heretic,[15] Adolph Harnack boldly charged the Bishops assembled at Nicaea with intellectual incapacity. He says there were no really able theologians among them, and adds: "The unanimous adoption of the synodal decree can be explained only on the assumption that the question at issue exceeded the mental capacity of most of the Bishops present." [16] This utterance is not surprising in the mouth of a writer who is

13 John X, 39: "*Quaerebant ergo* (οὖν πάλιν) *eum apprehendere, et exivit de manibus eorum.*"

14 *Orat., Contr. Arian.,* 4, n. 9. (*The Orations of S. Athanasius Against the Arians* in the *Ancient and Modern Library of Theological Literature,* p. 271, London [*s. a.*]. Cfr. on this topic especially Franzelin, *De Verbo Incarnato,* thes. 7, ed. 4, Romae 1893.

15 Cfr. Socrat., *Hist. Eccl.,* I, 8.

16 *Dogmengeschichte,* Vol. II, p. 222.

satisfied that "the Logos-ὁμοούσιος formula simply leads to absurdity," and that "Athanasius tolerated this absurdity, and the Council of Nicaea formally sanctioned it."[17] According to the theory of this school it was St. Augustine who invented the strictly monotheistic conception of the unity of the Godhead, and introduced it into what is properly called ecclesiastical Tradition. How unwarranted this theory is will appear from the following considerations.

a) The very method which the Nicene Fathers chose to defend the ὁμοούσιον against the attacks of Arianism, proves that they conceived the Consubstantiality of Son and Father as absolute identity of essence (ταὐτουσία). The Arian and Eunomian objections may be summarized thus: "Either God is one, or Father and Son are separate and distinct Persons. If God is one, then Sabellius is right in denying a distinction of Persons. If the Father and the Son are separate and distinct Persons, then the Godhead is divided by the act of Divine Generation, and we have Ditheism. Consequently the Son is not ὁμοούσιος with the Father." Eunomius in particular insisted that θεότης γέγονεν εἰς δυάδα. Had the Nicene Fathers been Tritheists, they would manifestly have accepted the Arian conclusion, instead of combating it so energetically. For no one who took ὁμοουσία to mean mere unity of species or genus, could consistently refuse to accept the logical inference that Generation and Spiration effect in the Divine Nature an intrinsic scission by which the Father

17 Ad. Harnack, *Dogmengeschichte*, Vol. II, p. 221.

is "God" other than the Son. The Nicene Fathers endeavor to show, on the contrary, that the act of Generation in no wise involves a multiplication of the Divine Nature, and therefore does not impair the absolute simplicity of essence proper to the Godhead. As a representative utterance, we may cite the subjoined passage from the writings of St. Athanasius: "The Fathers of the Council . . . were compelled . . . to resay and rewrite more distinctly still, what they had said before, that the Son is consubstantial (ὁμοούσιον) with the Father; by way of signifying that the Son is from the Father, and not merely like (ὅμοιον), but is the same by likeness (ταὐτὸν τῇ ὁμοιώσει). . . . For since the Generation of the Son from the Father is not according to the nature of men, but in a manner worthy of God, when we hear the word ὁμοούσιος, we must not follow the human senses, nor invent divisions and scissions, but, as when we conceive what is incorporeal, we will not rend asunder the unity of Nature and the identity of the light (τὴν ἑνότητα τῆς φύσεως καὶ τὴν ταὐτότητα τοῦ φωτός)."[18]

b) The orthodoxy of the post-Nicene Bishops manifested itself in a manner that might almost be called dramatic at a council held in Alexandria (A. D. 362) for the express purpose of restoring peace. At this council, when the assembled Fathers had got into a wrangle over the use of the terms οὐσία and ὑπόστασις, because some of them thought that the formula τρεῖς ὑποστάσεις savored of the heretical teaching embodied in the Latin phrase "*tres substantiae,*"[19] St. Athanasius

18 *De Decr. Nic. Syn.*, n. 20 sqq. On the more conciliatory position taken by St. Cyril of Jerusalem, see Schwane, *Dogmengeschichte*, Vol. II, 2nd ed., pp. 124 sqq., § 14, Freiburg 1895.

19 *Supra*, p. 227.

by a clever cross-examination brought out the fact that all really held the same faith. This led St. Gregory Nazianzen to observe: "It was indeed a ludicrous, or rather a regrettable incident; there appeared to be divergency of faith where there was merely a dispute about words."[20] The Council finally permitted the use of both locutions (*viz.*: One Hypostasis and Three Hypostases), on condition that in employing the former phrase there be no imputation of Sabellianism, and in enunciating the latter, the Arian heresy of three separate and distinct Gods be expressly disavowed. But it soon became necessary to define the dogma still more clearly. St. Basil was the first who endeavored formally to justify the phrase "Three Hypostases," and to give it universal currency.[21]

c) It is easy, in addition, to quote express Patristic texts showing that the Fathers understood ὁμοουσία to mean ταὐτουσία. St. Basil, for example, in rejecting Ditheism and Tritheism, writes: "Only one God the Father, only one God the Son, not two Gods, because the Son is identical with the Father (ἐπειδὴ ταὐτότητα ἔχει ὁ υἱὸς πρὸς τὸν πατέρα). For I do not behold one Deity in the Father, and another in the Son, nor one Nature here, and another there."[22] St. Gregory of Nazianzus anticipates the scientific terminology of a later age when he says: "*Neque enim Filius est Pater, nam unus Pater: tamen Filius est id, quod Pater. Nec Spiritus est Filius, quia ex Deo est, nam unus unigenitus; tamen Spiritus est id, quod Filius. Tres sunt unum deitate* (ἓν τὰ τρία τῇ θεότητι), *unum est tres proprietati-*

20 *Or.* 21, 35 (Migne, *P. G.*, XXXV, 1126).

21 Cfr. Jos. Schwane, *Dogmengeschichte*, Vol. II, 2nd ed., p. 151.

22 *Hom.*, 24, 3 (Migne, *P. G.*, XXXI, 604 sq.).

bus (τὸ ἓν τρία ταῖς ἰδιότησι = ὑποστάσεσιν) — The Son is not the Father, for there is but one Father: yet the Son is that which the Father is. Nor is the Holy Ghost the Son, for the reason that He is from God, because there is but one Only-begotten; yet the Holy Ghost is that which the Son is. The Three are one Godhead, and the One Godhead is threefold with regard to its Properties [*i. e.*, the Hypostases]."[23] The unknown author of the *Libri XII de Trinitate* (believed by some to be Vigilius of Tapsus, by others St. Athanasius), cries out in holy anger: "*Maledictus, qui propter tria nomina personarum tres deos confitetur* — Cursed be he who, because there are Three Personal Names, professes three Gods."[24] A conclusive and definitive testimony, which expressly echoes the faith of the preceding ages, is this of St. Augustine: "*Omnes, quos legere potui, qui ante me scripserunt de Trinitate, quae Deus est . . . hoc intenderunt secundum Scripturas docere, quod Pater et Filius et Spiritus Sanctus unius eiusdemque substantiae inseparabili aequalitate divinam insinuent unitatem, ideoque non sint tres dii, sed unus Deus* — All those whom I have been able to read, who have written before me concerning the Trinity, who is God, have purposed to teach, according to the Scriptures, this doctrine, that the Father and the Son and the Holy Spirit intimate a divine unity of one and the same substance in an indivisible equality; and therefore that they are not three Gods, but one God."[25] This declaration of the great Bishop of Hippo embodies one of the most telling arguments against Tritheism.

d) There seems to be one weak link in the Patristic chain of evidence, and that is the teaching of St. Gregory

23 *Or.*, 31, 9.

24 In Migne, *P. L.*, LXII, 278.

25 *De Trinit.*, I, 4, 7. Haddan's translation, p. 7.

of Nyssa, who puts the essential unity of the Three Divine Persons on a level with the essential unity proper to three human beings. But if we consider that, as a philosopher, Gregory advocated Platonic ultra-realism and conceived the specific unity of human individuals as a genuine ταὐτουσία, we shall be inclined to consider the remarkable parallel this Saint has drawn between divine and human unity as a confirmation rather than an indictment of his orthodoxy. If it were true, as he held, that human nature is numerically the same in all men,[26] and that "*many men* is said by an abuse of the term, not in its strict sense,"[27] that, therefore, "Peter and Paul and Barnabas are but one man,"[28] it would be perfectly orthodox to say that "*Igitur unus nobis confitendus est Deus iuxta Scripturae testimonium: Audi Israel, Dominus Deus tuus Dominus unus est,*[29] *etiamsi vox deitatis permeat sanctam Trinitatem.*"[30]

READINGS: — Hefele, *Conciliengeschichte,* Vols. III and V, 2nd ed., Freiburg 1877 and 1886.— Oswald, *Trinitätslehre,* §10, Paderborn 1888.— Albert a Bulsano, *Instit. Theologiae Dogmat. Specialis,* ed. Gfr. a Graun, tom. I, pp. 174–200, Oeniponte 1893. — Kleutgen, *De Ipso Deo,* l. II, qu. 2, cap. 1–5, Ratisbonae 1881. — Hurter, *Compendium,* t. II, ed. 9a, thes. 114–116, Oeniponte 1896.— Scheeben, *Dogmatik,* Vol. I, §112, Freiburg 1873.— H. P. Liddon, *The Divinity of Our Lord and Saviour Jesus Christ,* pp. 528 sqq., London 1867.

26 εἷς δὲ ἐν πᾶσι ὁ ἄνθρωπος.

27 λέγονται δὲ πολλοὶ ἄνθρωποι καταχρηστικῶς καὶ οὐ κυρίως.

28 These quotations will be found in Migne, *P. G.,* XLV, 180.

29 Deut. VI, 4.

30 Gregory of Nyssa, *Ad Ablabium* (Migne, *P. G.,* XLV, 119.) Cfr. Bardenhewer-Shahan, *Patrology,* pp. 300 sqq., Freiburg and St. Louis 1908.

CHAPTER II

ONENESS OF EXTERNAL OPERATION OF THE THREE DIVINE PERSONS

Oneness of external operation in the Blessed Trinity follows as a corollary from the unity of the Divine Nature, and therefore scarcely needs separate proof. For the sake of completeness, however, we shall elaborate (1) a Scriptural, (2) a traditional, and (3) a theological argument in support of this particular dogma.

At a Lateran Council held by Pope Martin I, in the year 649, 105 Bishops unanimously condemned Monotheletism. True, this synod lacks the authority of a general council; but by being incorporated into the proceedings of the Sixth Ecumenical Council, A. D. 680, its canons acquired whatever universal authority they may have originally lacked. This Lateran Council of 649 affirms that in the Blessed Trinity "will, power, operation, and dominion are one." [1] This unity is explained by the Fourth General Council of the Lateran (A. D. 1215) to be one by

1 Cfr. Denzinger-Bannwart, *Enchiridion*, n. 254. Hardouin, *Concil.*, t. III, pp. 922, 1078 sq.

which the Three Divine Persons are *"unum universorum principium, creator omnium visibilium et invisibilium* — The one principle of all things, the Creator of all things visible and invisible." [2] To remove every vestige of doubt in the matter, the *Decretum pro Iacobitis* (A. D. 1439) places the creative power of the Trinity on a par with the unity of the principle of Spiration that reposes in the Father and the Son, and from which the Holy Ghost proceeds *unica spiratione.*[3]

1. The Argument from Sacred Scripture. —Christ on various occasions formally identified His divine operation with that of His Father. Compare, *e. g.*, John V, 17: *"Pater meus usque modo operatur et ego operor* — My father worketh until now, and I work," with John V, 19: *"Non potest Filius a se facere quidquam, nisi quod viderit Patrem facientem* — The Son cannot do any thing of Himself, but what he seeth the Father doing." These texts, while they clearly show a distinction of Persons and origin, also intimate unity of action.

Other texts identify the operation of Father and Son even more positively. Thus John XIV, 10: *"A me ipso non loquor, Pater autem in me manens ipse facit omnia* — I speak not of myself, but the Father who abideth in me, he doth

2 Cfr. Denzinger-Bannwart, *Enchiridion*, n. 428.
3 *Supra*, pp. 230 sq.

the works." It is in the light of passages such as these that we must interpret the word "*similiter*" (ὁμοίως) in John V, 19: "*Quaecunque enim ille* [*Pater*] *fecerit, haec et Filius similiter facit* — For what things soever he [the Father] doth, these the Son also doth in like manner." "*Non ait,*" comments St. Augustine, "*quaecunque facit Pater, facit et Filius alia similia, sed: Quæcunque Pater facit, haec eadem et Filius facit similiter. Quae ille, haec et ipse: mundum Pater, mundum Filius, mundum Spiritus Sanctus*—[The Catholic faith] does not say that the Father made something, and the Son made some other similar thing; but what the Father made, that also the Son made in like manner. What the One made, that the Other also. The Father [made] the world, the Son [made] the world, the Holy Ghost [made] the world."[4]

This argument is corroborated by the manner in which Sacred Scripture appropriates one and the same operation now to the Father, now to the Son, now to the Holy Ghost, and then again to the Godhead as such. This procedure is intelligible only on the supposition that the Three Divine Persons are absolutely identical in essence and operation.[5] St. Augustine convincingly argues: "*Si enim alia per Patrem, alia per Filium, iam non omnia per Patrem nec omnia per Filium. Si autem omnia per Patrem et omnia per Filium,* [*ergo*] *eadem per Patrem, quae per Filium. Aequalis est ergo Patri*

[4] *Tract. in Ioan.*, 20, 3 sqq.

[5] *Supra*, pp. 29 sq.

Filius et inseparabilis est operatio Patris et Filii— For if some things were made by the Father, and some by the Son, then all things were not made by the Father, nor all things by the Son; but if all things were made by the Father, and all things by the Son, then the same things were made by the Father and by the Son. The Son, therefore, is equal with the Father, and the working of the Father and the Son is indivisible." [6]

2. THE ARGUMENT FROM TRADITION.—The procedure of deducing the unity of the Divine Nature from the unity of the divine operations, and *vice versa*, was well known to the Fathers.

Thus St. Cyril of Alexandria tersely observes, that "to attribute individual operations to each separate Divine Person, is tantamount to saying that there are three separate and distinct Gods." [7] A considerable number of the Fathers condense the dogma into a single brief phrase, which, after the manner of a mathematical formula, expresses the whole teaching of the Church in the tersest possible manner, *viz.*: "*Pater per Filium in Spiritu Sancto omnia operatur.*" [8] This formula duly stresses every essential point of the dogma: the Trinity of the Divine Persons, their succession as to origin, their identity of Nature, and the unity of their operation. The Patristic argument is drawn out in detail by Petavius.[9] It is so overwhelming that we can brush aside as irrelevant and trivial the objection which some writers base on the custom of certain Fathers of representing the Three

6 St. Augustine, *De Trinitate*, I, 6, 12. Haddan's translation, p. 13.

7 *Contr. Nestor*, IV, 2.

8 Cfr. St. Athanasius, *Ep. ad Serap.*, 1, 28. (Migne, *P. G.*, XXVI, 595).

9 *De Trinit.*, IV, 15.

Divine Persons as taking counsel with one another, as agreeing upon some common resolve or decree, or as co-operating in some common cause. St. Cyril of Jerusalem "makes a distinction between the divine operations *ad extra,* appropriating them to the Three Divine Persons separately, and thus seems to posit a certain scission in the immanent life of the Godhead. But his utterances must be interpreted in accord with the law of Appropriations, especially since he does not consistently carry out the distinction." [10]

3. THE THEOLOGICAL ARGUMENT.—The unity of operation in the Blessed Trinity is really but a simple inference from the dogma that the Three Divine Persons are absolutely identical in essence.

Philosophy teaches that "*Operari sequitur esse, i. e., naturam.*" If the nature of a thing is its "principle of operation," it follows that the number of principles of operation, and their specific manifestations (*e. g.,* intellect and freewill in spiritual natures), depend on the number of active essences or natures. "*Tot operationes, quot naturae.*" As we must distinguish in Christ, the Godman, a twofold operation, the one divine, the other human, corresponding to His double nature, so, conversely, if the Father, the Son, and the Holy Ghost are not three natures, but one, they can have but one common *operatio ad extra.* To assert that the divine operation is not one, is to teach Tritheism. Had they not harbored Tritheistic conceptions of the Godhead, Raymund Lully and Günther could never have taught that each Divine Person operates separately *ad extra.* Though from unity of Nature to unity of

10 Jos. Schwane, *Dogmengeschichte,* Vol. II, 2nd ed., p. 126.

operation in the Blessed Trinity is just as easy a step as from a duality of nature to Dyotheletism in Christ, (because a multiplication of natures always entails a multiplication of operations), the Church did not content herself with laying down the general principle, but by an express definition condemned in advance Günther's error that "When God reveals Himself to His creatures, He must reveal Himself hypostatically, *i. e.*, each separate divine operation must be attributed as *opus operatum* to a separate Divine Person, to the exclusion of the other two." [11] Günther's lapse into Tritheism convincingly shows how false was the view he took of the relation of the divine operations to the different Persons of the Blessed Trinity. Any attempt to go beyond mere Appropriation is sure to result in a scission of the Divine Essence.

READINGS: — *Franzelin, *De Deo Trino,* thes. 12.— Kleutgen, *De Ipso Deo,* l. II, qu. 5, cap. 2, art. 3.— Hurter, *Compendium Theol. Dogmat.,* t. II, thes. 117.— Kleutgen, *Theologie der Vorzeit,* Vol. I, 2nd ed., pp. 379 sqq., Münster 1867.— H. Schell, *Das Wirken des dreieinigen Gottes,* Mainz 1885.— Petavius, *De Trinit.,* IV, 15.

11 Günther, *Vorschule zur spekulativen Theologie,* 2nd ed., Vol. II, p. 369, Wien 1848.

CHAPTER III

THE UNITY OF MUTUAL INEXISTENCE, OR PERICHORESIS

1. DEFINITION OF PERICHORESIS.—By the Perichoresis of the Three Divine Persons we mean their mutual Interpenetration and Inexistence by virtue of their Consubstantiality, their immanent Processions, and the divine Relations.

In Greek the technical term for this mutual Inexistence is *περιχώρησις*, or, still more emphatically, *συμπεριχώρησις*. The Latins call it *circumincessio*, or, as the later Scholastics wrote it, *circuminsessio*. Both the Greek and the Latin terms designate exactly the same thing, but they reflect somewhat different conceptions thereof. "While the Greeks conceived the [Divine] Processions more after the manner of a temporal succession along a straight line," says Oswald,[1] "the [later] Latins pictured it to themselves after the manner of juxtaposition in space, as extension in a plain. . . . This is why the Latins derived their technical term from *circuminsidere*, *i. e.*, to sit or dwell in one another, while the Greeks got theirs from *περιχωρεῖν*, which means to go or move within one another." We have already called attention to a similar divergency in the formulas expressing the Procession of the Holy Ghost, with regard to which the

1 *Trinitätslehre*, p. 191, Paderborn 1888.

Latins commonly say, *ex Patre Filioque,* while the Greeks prefer *ex Patre per Filium.* Petavius was probably mistaken when he preferred the Greek and the early Scholastic modes of expression to that of the later Schoolmen. The Greek Fathers, besides περιχωρεῖν εἰς ἀλλήλους, also employed the locution ἐν ἀλλήλαις αἱ ὑποστάσεις εἰσίν.[2]

Suarez[3] and Ruiz[4] preferred to base Perichoresis on the attribute of immensity rather than upon the unity of the Divine Nature. Each of the Three Divine Persons, argued these eminent theologians, must be where the other Two are. It is true that the Three Divine Persons together indwell in creatures not only by virtue of Perichoresis, but likewise by omnipresence. But omnipresence is so far from constituting the formal essence of Perichoresis, that even a Tritheist could without inconsistency teach the simultaneous presence and indwelling of three Gods in a creature. Christ clearly affirms the divine Perichoresis when He says: "I am in the Father, and the Father is in me."[5] On the other hand, St. Paul's famous dictum: "In him we live, and move, and are,"[6] merely asserts the immensity of God, not the Trinitarian Perichoresis. For, as Petavius rightly observes,[7] "though the mind abstract entirely from the notion of place and location in space, and regard solely the Divine Hypostases considered in themselves and absolutely, Perichoresis and the mutual inexistence of Person in Person will still be there; be-

2 Cfr. Ioannes Damasc., *De Fide Orth.*, I, 8.

3 *De Trinit.*, IV, 16, *sub finem.*

4 *De Trinit.*, disp. 107, sect. 7.

5 John XIV, 11.

6 Acts XVII, 28.

7 *De Trinit.*, IV, n. 5: "*Nam etsi loci et 'ubi' notio omnis excludatur animo, ac solae per se absoluteque spectentur hypostases divinae, nihilominus tamen περιχώρησις et mutua in seipsis existentia personarum illic erit; quippe et una posita poni necesse erit alteram, nec a se invicem separari poterunt, et altera intime coniuncta erit alteri in eaque inerit et existet.*"

cause if one be posited it will be necessary to posit the other; they cannot be separated from one another, but each will remain intimately united with each and all three will mutually inexist." Hence the Perichoresis of the Blessed Trinity cannot be adequately explained by the divine attribute of immensity.

If we compare Perichoresis with Consubstantiality (ὁμοουσία, or better ταὐτουσία), we find that the two notions are related to each other as effect is related to cause. The ontological reason for the mutual Inexistence or Indwelling of the Three Divine Persons is primarily their possession of one and the same Divine Nature or Essence. "Perichoresis in the Godhead originates in the unity of the Divine Essence," says Petavius, ". . . and it consists in this, that one Person cannot be divided or separated from another, but they mutually exist in one another without confusion and without detriment to the distinction between them."[8] This does not, of course, preclude the existence of other secondary sources of Perichoresis, such as the Divine Processions and Relations.

2. THE PROOF OF PERICHORESIS.—The *Decretum pro Iacobitis* (A. D. 1439) expressly bases the Perichoresis of the Three Divine Persons on identity of Essence. *"Omnia [in Deo] sunt unum, ubi non obviat relationis oppositio. Propter hanc unitatem Pater est totus in Filio, totus in Spiritu Sancto; Filius totus est in Patre,*

8 "Περιχώρησις *in divinis ex unitate essentiae oritur . . . et in eo consistit, quod dividi et separari persona una non potest ab altera, sed citra confusionem et servato discrimine insunt in se invicem." De Trinit., l. c.*

totus in Spiritu Sancto; Spiritus Sanctus totus est in Patre, totus in Filio — All things in God are one, except where there is opposition of Relation. Because of this unity, the Father is wholly in the Son, and wholly in the Holy Ghost; the Son is wholly in the Father, and wholly in the Holy Ghost; and the Holy Ghost is wholly in the Father, and wholly in the Son."[9] This doctrine undoubtedly forms part of the deposit of faith. St. Thomas demonstrates it by three arguments, of which one is based on the divine ταὐτουσία, another on the origins, and a third on the mutual Relations of the Divine Persons.

a) The first and main source of the Trinitarian Perichoresis is the Consubstantiality of the Three Persons, or their identity of Essence. Sufficient Scriptural proof for this proposition, at least in so far as it regards the First and Second Persons of the Blessed Trinity, was adduced by St. Athanasius, who from a well-known sermon of Jesus[10] argues as follows: "For whereas the countenance and Godhead of the Father is the Being of the Son, it follows that the Son is in the Father and the Father in the Son. On this account and reasonably, having said before, 'I and the Father are one,' He added, 'I in the Father and the Father in me,' by way of show-

9 Cfr. Denzinger-Bannwart, *Enchiridion*, n. 703 sq.
10 *Supra*, pp. 265 sq.

ing the identity of Godhead and the unity of substance." [11] That the Holy Ghost is included in this Divine Company we know from 1 Cor. II, 11: *"Quis enim hominum scit, quae sunt hominis, nisi spiritus hominis, qui in ipso est? Ita et quae Dei sunt, nemo cognovit, nisi Spiritus Dei* (supply: *qui in ipso est*)— For what man knoweth the things of a man, but the spirit of a man that is in him? So the things also that are of God no man knoweth but the Spirit of God [that is in Him]." St. Athanasius probably found the bracketed clause, *"qui in ipso est,"* in his Bible, for he treats it like a verbal quotation.[12]

The intrinsic connexion between Trinitarian Perichoresis and the Consubstantiality of the Three Divine Persons is perhaps most effectively brought out by those of the Fathers who employed Perichoresis as a popular and intelligible middle term to demonstrate the essential identity of Father and Son against the Arians.[13]

b) A secondary source of this mutual Immanence, according to many Fathers, is the origin of the Three Divine Persons from one another, *i. e.*, the divine Processions by mode of Generation and Spiration. For inasmuch as the Logos is begotten as the "Divine Word" of the

11 *Contr. Arian.*, Or. 3, 3 (Migne, *P. G.*, XXVI, 327). Newman's translation, *Select Treatises of St. Athanasius*, Vol. I, p. 361.

12 *Ep. ad Serap.*, 3 (Migne, *P. G.*, XXVI, 626).

13 Cfr. Petavius, *De Trinit.*, IV, 16; Ruiz, *De Trinit.*, disp. 107, sect. 5.

Father by the Father's notional understanding, He is necessarily immanent in the Father, as the internal word or concept is immanent in the human intellect. "*Ex mente enim et in mentem,*"[14] says St. Cyril of Alexandria,[15] "*verbum est semper, ideoque mens in verbo.*[16] . . . *Verbum manet in mente generante et mentem generantem habet totaliter in se . . . et oportet simul existere cum Patre Filium et vicissim Patrem cum Filio* — For the word is always of the mind and in the mind, and therefore the mind is in the word. . . . The word remains in the mind in which it is conceived, and contains that mind entirely within itself. . . . So it behooves the Son to exist simultaneously with the Father, and the Father to exist simultaneously with the Son." St. Hilary expresses this truth more concisely thus: "*Deus in Deo, quia ex Deo Deus est* — God is in God, because God is from God."[17] The Holy Ghost, too, in consequence of His Procession by way of mutual love, reposes deep down in the Principle which produces Him, as love reposes in the heart of a lover. St. Ambrose aptly observes: "*Sicut Pater in Filio et Filius in Patre, ita Dei Spiritus et Spiritus Christi et in Patre et in Filio, quia oris* [=*halitus*] *est spiritus* — As the Father is in the Son, and the Son is in the Father, so the Spirit of God and the Spirit of Christ is both in the Father and the Son, because He is the spirit [a breath] of the mouth."[18] There is Scriptural warrant for this mode of conceiving the divine Perichoresis. Cfr. John I, 18: "*Unigenitus, qui est in sinu Patris* — The only begotten Son who is in the bosom of the Father." The Greek original of

14 ἐκ νοῦ καὶ εἰς νοῦν.

15 *De Trinit.*, Dial. 2 (Migne, *P. G.*, LXXV, 769).

16 καὶ ὁ νοῦς ἐν λόγῳ.

17 *De Trinit.*, IV, 10 (Migne, *P. L.*, X, 126).

18 *De Spiritu Sancto*, III, 1.

this passage implies a movement *ad intra,* which is not fully brought out by either the Vulgate or the vernacular version: —Ὁ μονογενὴς υἱὸς ὁ ὢν (= περιχωρῶν) εἰς τὸν κόλπον τοῦ πατρός.

c) The third and last source of Perichoresis are the Divine Relations, that is, the relative opposition of the Three Divine Persons to one another. The Father cannot be conceived without His Son, nor can the Son be conceived without the Father, and the Holy Ghost is altogether unthinkable without His common Spirators, the Father and the Son. St. Basil, and especially the Eleventh Council of Toledo (A. D. 675), particularly emphasized this logical aspect of the divine Perichoresis. "*Nec enim Pater absque Filio cognoscitur,*" we read in its decrees, "*nec sine Patre Filius invenitur; relatio quippe ipsa vocabuli personalis personas separari vetat, quas etiam, dum non simul nominat, simul insinuat. Nemo autem audire potest unumquodque istorum nominum, in quo non intelligere cogatur et alterum* — For neither can the Father be known without the Son, nor the Son be found without the Father; for the relation indicated by the name of a person forbids us to separate the persons who are intimated, though not expressly named. And nobody can hear any one of these names without perceiving therein one of the others."[19] Perhaps our Lord's saying: "He that seeth me seeth the Father also. . . . Do you not believe that I am in the Father, and the Father in me?"[20] — which Sabellius so egregiously misunderstood — must be interpreted in the light of these considerations, though both the context and the construction put upon it by the Fathers make

19 Denzinger-Bannwart, *Enchiridion*, n. 281.

20 John XIV, 9 sq.: "*Philippe, qui videt me, videt et Patrem. . . . Non creditis, quia ego in Patre et Pater in me est?*"

it more advisable to base the Perichoresis here expressed by Jesus, upon the notion of *Tautousia* rather than upon the divine Relations.[21]

3. Dogmatic Importance of the Doctrine of the Perichoresis.—The doctrine of the Trinitarian Perichoresis is of considerable dogmatic importance, because it tersely and luminously expresses the two salient aspects of the dogma of the Blessed Trinity, *viz.: Trinitas in Unitate* and *Unitas in Trinitate,* thus equally discountenancing the heresy of Monarchianism on the one hand, and that of Tritheism on the other. In matter of fact Perichoresis involves two important truths: (1) that there is a real distinction between the Three Divine Persons, and (2) that the Divine Nature, or Essence, in spite of the Hypostatic distinctions, is absolutely one. Sabellius, by welding the Three Persons into One, practically denied the dogma of mutual Inexistence, while the Tritheists, who imagined the Divine Essence to consist of three Gods, found themselves unable to admit a real indwelling of the One in the Other.[22]

We shall meet with a similar phenomenon in Christology, though the order is there reversed.

21 Cfr. St. Athanasius, *Contr. Arian.*, Or. 3, 3.

22 Cfr. St. Hilary, *De Trinit.*, III, 4: "*Quod in Patre est, hoc et in Filio est; quod in ingenito, hoc et in unigenito; alter ab altero et uterque unum; non duo unus, sed alius in alio, quia non aliud in utroque.*"

The Perichoresis of the two Natures in Christ can be conceived only in virtue of the Hypostatic Union from which it springs. It postulates a perfect and unalloyed duality together with absolute oneness of Person and an indivisible unity in spite of the Saviour's twofold Nature. For this very reason the doctrine of Perichoresis furnishes a powerful weapon for the defence of the faith against such extreme Christological heresies as Nestorianism and Adoptianism on the one hand, and Monophysitism and Monotheletism on the other.

The doctrine of the Perichoresis fittingly concludes the treatise on the Trinity, because it represents the final upshot of the whole discussion and clearly and luminously brings out both aspects of the dogma, *viz.:* the *Trinitas in Unitate* and the *Unitas in Trinitate.* At the same time it forms an invincible bulwark against all Antitrinitarian heresies, guarding as it does the Trinity of the Divine Persons against the Monarchians and Unitarians, and the unity of the Divine Nature against the various Tritheistic sects.

READINGS:—St. Thomas, *S. Theol.,* 1a, qu. 42, art. 5.—St. Bonaventure, *Comment. in Sent.,* I, dist. 19, p. 1, art. un., qu. 4; III, d. 29, art. 1, qu. 1, concl., al. 3.—Duns Scotus, *Opus Oxoniense,* I, d. 19, qu. 2, *init.,* ed. Paris., 1893, X, 183 sq.—Scheeben, *Dogmatik,* Vol. I, §123, Freiburg 1925.—Oswald, *Trinitätslehre,* §14, Paderborn 1888.—*Franzelin, *De Deo Trino,* thes. 14, Romae 1881.

—J. Kleutgen, S. J., *De Ipso Deo,* pp. 694 sqq., Ratisbonae 1881.—*Chr. Pesch, *Praelect. Dogmat.,* Vol. II, ed. 3a, pp. 339–343, Friburgi 1906.—Petavius, *De Trinit.,* IV, 16.—Aug. Deneffe, S. J., "Perichoresis, Circumincessio, Circuminsessio," in the *Zeitschrift für kath. Theologie,* 1923, IV. Quartalheft, pp. 497–532.

On the practical and devotional bearing of the dogma of the Divine Trinity cfr. F. J. Hall, *The Trinity,* pp. 289 sqq.; Wilhelm-Scannell, *A Manual of Catholic Theology,* Vol. I, pp. 351 sqq.; H. P. Liddon, *The Divinity of Our Lord,* pp. 659 sqq.; S. Louismet, O. S. B., *The Mystical Life,* London 1918; pp. 37 sqq.

APPENDIX

NOTE ON THE TRINITARIAN TEACHING OF ST. IRENÆUS

(See page 141)

An ancient Armenian translation has lately been discovered of a long-lost work of St. Irenæus, mentioned by Eusebius.[1] It is a treatise addressed to "Brother Marcian." The Archimandrite Carapet has published it under the title "Proof of the Apostolic Preaching."[2] The author's aim in this treatise is "not to confute heretics, but to confirm the faithful by expounding the Christian doctrine to them, and notably by demonstrating the truth of the Gospel by means of the Old Testament prophecies."[3] In this hitherto unknown treatise[4] St. Irenæus says: "Thus is the Lord the Father and Lord the Son, and God the Father and God the Son; for He who is born of God is God. Consequently, according to His being and the power of His essence, there is known *one* God, but according to the economy of our salvation strictly and properly both Son and Father. For since the Father is above all invisible and inapproachable for creatures, those who are predestined to approach God must be won and conquered for the Father by the Son. . . .

1 *Hist. Eccles.*, V, 26.

2 In *Texte und Untersuchungen*, edited by Harnack and Schmidt, Vol. 31, No. 1, Leipzig, 1907.

3 A. Poncelet, in the *Catholic Encyclopedia*, Vol. VIII, p. 131.

4 Ch. 47.

And the ointment (Ps. xlv, 8) is the Spirit, with which He is anointed."

Harnack[5] comments upon this text as follows: "Such a characteristically 'Nicene passage' is hardly to be found in the *Adversus Haereses;* but we need not assume an interpolation. It is not in accord with the teaching of the Nicene Council that the distinction between Father and Son is based solely on the economy of the Redemption (a kind of Modalism, as in *Adv. Haer.*). This conception is ante-Nicene, ante-Origenist, and Irenæan. Neither is the 'anointment by the Spirit' a Nicene conception."

It must be admitted that St. Irenæus in the text under consideration is not as explicit as were the Nicene writers in basing the personal distinction between the Father and the Son upon the eternal generation of the Son from the Father; but neither is he wrong in basing that distinction upon the "economy of the Redemption." For the Incarnation and the Redemption are the very best *de facto* arguments for the existence of the Logos-Son as the second Person of the Most Holy Trinity. If this be a sort of Modalism, fairness compels us to point out that it is not Modalism in the Sabellian sense, because St. Irenæus in the very same passage plainly traces the distinction between the Father and the Son to the fact of the latter's "being born of God."

Hence, *pace* Professor Harnack, the publication of St. Irenæus' treatise "Proof of the Apostolic Preaching" confirms the traditional Catholic teaching on the Trinity.

[5] *Loc. cit.*, p. 61.

INDEX

J

K

L

M

U

V

W

Z